T0308750

A Cuban in Mayberry

A Cuban in Mayberry

LOOKING BACK AT AMERICA'S HOMETOWN

Gustavo Pérez Firmat

University of Texas Press   *Austin*

Copyright © 2014 by Gustavo Pérez Firmat
All rights reserved
Printed in the United States of America
First edition, 2014

Requests for permission to reproduce material from this work should be
sent to:
  Permissions
  University of Texas Press
  P.O. Box 7819
  Austin, TX 78713-7819
  http://utpress.utexas.edu/index.php/rp-form

♾ The paper used in this book meets the minimum requirements of
ANSI/NISO Z39.48-1992 (R1997) (Permanence of Paper).

LIBRARY OF CONGRESS CATALOGING-IN-PUBLICATION DATA
Pérez Firmat, Gustavo, 1949–
    A Cuban in Mayberry : looking back at America's hometown /
Gustavo Pérez Firmat. — First edition.
        pages   cm
    Includes bibliographical references and index.
    ISBN 978-0-292-73905-5 (cloth : alk. paper)
1. Andy Griffith show (Television program)   2. City and town life on
television.   I. Title.
    PN1992.77.A573P39   2014
    791.45′72 — dc23
                                                              2014007098
doi:10.7560/759251

For Jen and Chris Holloway

Tell me a story of deep delight.

ROBERT PENN WARREN

Contents

Acknowledgments

COMING AT THIS PROJECT FROM VERY DIFFERENT PER-spectives, Robert Thompson and Jorge Olivares provided valuable suggestions and invaluable encouragement. Were it not for the patience, tenacity, and optimism of Theresa May, assistant director and editor-in-chief at the University of Texas Press, this book might not have seen the light of day. The by-now durable tradition of Friday night dinners in Chapel Hill with the Holloway clan—Chris, Jen, Mary Emma, and Charlotte—contributed to the book in ways too complicated, and probably too corny, to mention. Like my other books, this is a collaborative work. My silent partner, Mary Anne Pérez Firmat, another Mayberrian of the heart, has helped me to understand many things, the most relevant of which is that home is here.

To the Fishing Hole

A YOUNGISH MAN AND A BOY STROLL ALONG A DIRT road. Barefoot, the boy is dressed in a T-shirt and rolled-up jeans. The man is wearing a law enforcement uniform — the badge is visible above the flap of the left shirt pocket — and boots. Fishing poles are slung over their shoulders. Since their figures cast only a slight shadow, it must be around midday. A simple, whistled tune plays in the background. The boy runs ahead and throws pebbles into a pond. When the man catches up, he takes the boy by the hand. From their ease with each other, it's obvious that they know each other well. The sequence ends when they reach the edge of the pond and the boy flings one last pebble into the water.

Although this scene is scarcely twenty seconds long and more than half a century old, millions of Americans still recognize it today as the title sequence of *The Andy Griffith Show* (1960–1968), one of the most popular sitcoms in the history of American television. The man is Andy Taylor, sheriff of Mayberry, and the boy is his son, Opie. The pond is Myers Lake.

This rural setting, heightened by Earle Hagen's catchy melody, begins to suggest what distinguishes TAGS (as aficionados call *The Andy Griffith Show*) from other sitcoms from the 1950s and 1960s. This is not the urban world of *I Love Lucy* and *Make Room for Daddy* or the suburban world of *Father Knows Best, Leave It to Beaver*, and *The Donna Reed Show*. One establishing shot of *Father Knows Best* shows Robert Young walking into a large and well-appointed house, where he is greeted by his wife and children. The briefcase hanging from his arm conveys that he has a white-collar job. Another shows him by the front door looking at his watch, as he waits for his wife to bring him his hat and his briefcase. The title sequence for the second season of *Leave It to Beaver* shows Wally and Beaver rushing down the stairs, at the bottom of which their mother waits, lunch bag and box in hand. The following season, the episodes begin with Ward and June Cleaver coming into the boys' room to wake them up for school. Other opening sequences show June Cleaver outside the door, ready to give the boys their lunches and jackets, or coming out of the house carrying a tray with pitcher and glasses while her husband and sons tend to the front yard. *The Donna Reed Show* opens with Donna coming down the stairs in the morning and answering the phone. She is followed by her two children and her husband. She hands the kids their lunches, and her husband his briefcase, and gets a peck on the lips as he rushes out the door.

These scenes portray a family unit composed of two or more children, a mother who is the heart of the household, and a father who brings home the bacon (in a briefcase). In the opening of TAGS, nothing suggests labor or domesticity. Even though the show is usually lumped together with other "affable family comedies,"[1] TAGS focuses on the father-son dyad, the minimal unit of community, rather than on the nuclear family. For sure, this is not the only TV show of the 1960s focused on a widower. The long-running *My Three Sons*, which debuted the same year as TAGS, did likewise, as did *The Courtship of Eddie's Father*, some years later. But TAGS is the first sitcom to feature a single father and an only son, and to suggest by the two-shot title sequence that they constitute an autonomous unit. (To make this point in a different way, Griffith insisted that the first episode of each season deal with Andy and Opie's relationship.) Like other sitcoms, TAGS will also have a domestic component, but the viewer gets no inkling of this from the initial images, which show Andy and Opie Taylor off in the woods by themselves. Absent is the wife and mother who stands by the door with lunch box and briefcase. Absent also is any suggestion that father and son are leaving for work or school. On the contrary, it seems that Andy and Opie are taking time off. The easy pace at which they are walking tells the viewer that they don't have a care in the world. And instead of briefcases and books, they carry fishing poles. It's clear that this slice of Americana has less to do with the ethic of hard work than with the enjoyment of leisure.

Another of the title sequences of *Leave It to Beaver* shows the Cleavers emerging from their house in the morning. Since Ward Cleaver is carrying a thermos jug and Mrs. Cleaver a picnic basket, we can assume that he is not going to work. And yet they all rush into their late-model sedan. Andy and Opie would not understand their hurry or the necessity to drive to their destination. The Cleaver home, as well as the shiny car sitting in the driveway, situates the show in 1950s suburban America. The opening scene of TAGS is more difficult to place. Andy's uniform is generic; Opie's T-shirt and jeans are even less datable. The vagueness of temporal reference hints that TAGS will tap into areas of cultural identification older and deeper than those evoked in other family shows. There's something of *Walden* here, as there is of *Tom Sawyer*. If not exactly an errand into the wilderness, Andy and Opie's outing to Myers Lake suggests breaking away, playing hooky. If Andy is dressed for work, why is he not working? If Opie is dressed as he would be for school (minus the sneakers), why is he not in school?

Vague about the time frame, the opening sequence is no more precise about the whereabouts. The foliage is indistinct; the pine trees in the background could be almost anywhere in America. But Andy is wearing his uniform, so we can assume that he works somewhere nearby. That somewhere is Mayberry, a fictional town in the North Carolina foothills based on Mount Airy, North Carolina, where Andy Griffith was born and raised. Mayberry is the quintessential small town, the kind of place where everyone is kith or kin and life's troubles are brief, comic, and solvable—and also the kind of place that sets TAGS apart from other rural sitcoms. Successful shows like *Petticoat Junction* and *Green Acres* also extolled the virtues and exposed the follies of small towns. If TAGS was a "rubecom," so were *The Real McCoys*—which started the genre—and *The Beverly Hillbillies*. But *The Real McCoys* and *The Beverly Hillbillies* extracted hillbillies from their natural habitat—West Virginia and Tennessee—and plopped them down in California; and neither *Green Acres* nor *Petticoat Junction* did much to make Hooterville more than a gag site: the village of hoots and hooters.

In TV land, perhaps only *Cheers*, named after the bar "where everybody knows your name," has exploited as effectively the spirit of place and sense of community. But nobody actually lives in Sam's bar, even if it sometimes seems that Cliff and Norm are glued to their stools. In TAGS we see the locals not only relaxing after work but also going about their daily business. And although *Cheers* takes place in Boston, every city has a neighborhood bar like the one in the show. Mayberry has to be in the rural South, and, more particularly, in the Piedmont. As often happens with Southern fictions, place is crucial. And not only because the speech of many of the characters would be incongruous anywhere else, but because TAGS derives meaning from location. The implicit premise is that what happens in Mayberry does not happen anywhere else. As the episodes stress repeatedly, the townsfolk's ways are unique to this Southern town, population 1,800 (coincidentally the same number as that of another fictional town, Sherwood Anderson's Winesburg).

In the course of the series, hundreds of Mayberrians appear on the screen or are spoken of, but the episodes revolve around a select group of worthies. In addition to Andy and Opie, the regulars or semiregulars include Andy's Aunt Bee, who looks after her nephew and his son; Barney Fife, the reliably unreliable deputy; Floyd Lawson, owner of the "best clip joint" (barbershop) in town; Otis Campbell, an amiable dipsomaniac who locks himself in jail every Friday and Saturday evening; Gomer Pyle, the gas jockey with the tenor voice; a couple of irksome mayors, Pike and Stoner; a preacher, Reverend Tucker of

All Souls Church; merchants like Ben Weaver of Weaver's Department Store and Orville Monroe, a mortician who doubles as TV repairman; Helen Crump, Andy's girl; Thelma Lou, Barney's girl; Skippy and Daphne, the "Fun Girls," demimondaines from nearby Mt. Pilot who compete for Andy and Barney's attention; Malcolm Merriweather, an English tourist and the only outsider who makes repeated visits to Mayberry; and a passel of farmers and hillbillies, among them Rafe Hollister, the Darling clan, and the indomitable Ernest T. Bass, rhymester and rock thrower extraordinaire.

During the show's eight seasons there was considerable turnover in the cast. After the fifth season, Don Knotts (Barney Fife) left to pursue a movie career. Gomer (Jim Nabors) and Floyd (Howard McNear) were written out. Nabors went on to star in *Gomer Pyle U.S.M.C.*, and McNear became too ill to perform. As these actors left, new characters were added: Warren Ferguson (Jack Burns), Barney's short-lived replacement; Goober Pyle (George Lindsey), Gomer's cousin and successor at Wally's Service; Howard Sprague (Jack Dodson), the nerdy county clerk; and Emmett Clark (Paul Hartman), whose Fix-It Shop takes over the locale of Floyd's barbershop. After the eighth season Andy Griffith and Ron Howard called it quits. When the show resurfaced the next season as *Mayberry R.F.D.*, another widower and his son, Sam Jones (Ken Berry) and Mike (Buddy Foster, Jodie's brother), took over from Andy and Opie. Of the original characters, only Aunt Bee was left. By the time *Mayberry R.F.D.* went off the air three years later, none of the original characters lived in Mayberry, since Aunt Bee had been written out at the end of the second season. Yet in its last season, *The Andy Griffith Show*'s offspring still ranked among the top fifteen programs on television. In contrast to almost every other sitcom then or now, the appeal of TAGS and *Mayberry R.F.D.* had more to do with the setting than with any particular character or group of characters. People came and went, but Mayberry remained.

In 1964 the show's popularity led CBS to begin rerunning TAGS on weekday mornings; to differentiate between the daily reruns and the weekly shows, the former were retitled *Andy of Mayberry*. Griffith recognized that the town was, by design, "as much a character on the show as Sheriff Andy Taylor."[2] Move Andy and Opie to the San Fernando Valley, as in *The Real McCoys*, or Los Angeles, as in *The Beverly Hillbillies*, and the show would not have survived the relocation. Embodiments of the genius of the place, the townsfolk belong to Mayberry as much as the town belongs to them. A case in point: Barney Fife, who leaves to work for the police department in Raleigh. Away from Mayberry, Barney is a fish out of water, much like Gomer Pyle in the Marines or Old Sam, the legendary silver carp from Tucker's Lake, when it is moved to an aquarium.

Early in the first season, "Stranger in Town" (episode 1.12) introduced a New Yorker who, having heard so many good things about Mayberry, intends to adopt it as his hometown.[3] The stranger, Ed Sawyer, knows as much about Mayberry as any of the natives. He can tell apart the Buntley twins. He remembers that it was in room 209 of the Mayberry Hotel where Wilbur Hennessey got drunk and fell out the window. He knows about Floyd's rheumatism, which sometimes prevents him from indulging his hobby of tossing horseshoes. He is in love with Lucy Matthews, though he has never seen her. He even knows that Sarah, the switchboard operator, takes a pinch of snuff now and then. Some of the townsfolk think he's a foreign agent; others believe that he comes from another planet.

But Ed Sawyer's intimate knowledge of the town's everyday life derives from causes less exotic. While in the armed forces, he struck up a friendship with Joe Larson, a Mayberrian who talked about his hometown all the time. By the time Ed left the service, he was so enamored of the town that he subscribed to the *Mayberry Gazette* to keep up with local doings, and as soon as he was able, he moved to Mayberry. When Andy asks him how he knows he is going to be happy in Mayberry, Sawyer replies: "Mayberry is my hometown." Ed Sawyer represents TAGS viewers, Mayberrians by choice rather than birth. The remarkable thing, however, is that "Stranger in Town" was filmed in September 1960, before a single episode of TAGS had been broadcast. By the time it aired, in December, Griffith had been proved prescient, for Mayberry was already on the way to becoming America's favorite hometown.

In the following week's episode, "Mayberry Goes Hollywood," a movie producer shows up in town. He too has been captivated by the relaxed and simple ways of Mayberry. Suspicious of outsiders, the locals initially fear that the movie will make fun of how they talk and look. Once the producer reassures them, they agree to let him proceed with his project; but the prospect of being in the movies induces the locals to act up. Barney dons a new uniform that makes him look like a member of the Canadian Mounties. The barbershop is rebranded a "Tonsorial Parlor" and the Bluebird Diner the "Cinemascope Café." Orville's mortuary starts advertising "Hollywood Funerals." Even the old geezers who sit in front of the courthouse get "gussied up" with suits and ties. The producer is dismayed: "What's gotten into you people? What have you done to the town, and to yourselves? This isn't the Mayberry I wanted to photograph. I could have built a set like this in Hollywood." Chastised, Mayberrians revert to their old ways, which were odd enough. As the episode ends, the producer reiterates his intention of making a movie about Mayberry. His movie, divided into 249 segments, is TAGS, a convincing fiction of unscripted life.

Mayberry is a far more compelling fictional locale than Hooterville or, for that matter, the Hilldale of *The Donna Reed Show*, the Springfield of *Father Knows Best*, and other similar fields and dales. Seemingly a placid backwater, the town contains (and fails to contain) undercurrents that complicate the town's way of life. The townspeople's view of the rest of the country, to the extent that they have one, is conflicted to the point of incoherence. Their hostility to outsiders belies the friendliness they advertise. Their insistence on town traditions, particularly Founder's Day, betrays worry about their continuance, worry that arises from the ever-present threat of invasion by outsiders, raids that the townsfolk are hard-pressed to rebuff. There's more to this paradise than meets the viewer's eye. The charm, simplicity, and sunny disposition of Mayberrians make it easy to overlook the occasional darkness of TAGS. Mayberry is a paradise, but an anxious one, Arcadia under siege. Floyd is right that Mayberry is "the garden city of the state," but there are serpents in the garden.

In fact, Mayberry is doomed. Several late episodes make clear that the sleepy Southern town with the oddball characters and quaint customs is undergoing a quiet revolution. Barney, the most unforgettable of the many memorable characters in the show, once said he had a clock in his stomach, a trait that he inherited from his mother. When Barney's clock strikes midnight, Mayberry will disappear, taking him with it. The new day will bring forth the town of *Mayberry R.F.D.*, a progressive, New South community that, for better and worse, bears little resemblance to the Mayberry of old. According to Griffith, TAGS was superior to other rubecoms because the humor relied less on jokes than on character, but TAGS also stands out because of the complexity of its fictional world, which sinks its roots into Southern history, and specifically into the South's legacy of loss. As we will see, old-time Mayberrians reject the New South because, to them, the New South is a Northern South, and hence no South at all. Barney also believed that "your true schizophreeniacs" are the ones who don't look it. What applies to the deranged applies to Barney's hometown: superficially placid but in distress.

THE ANDY GRIFFITH SHOW PREMIERED ON CBS ON OCTOber 3, 1960, at 9:30 in the evening, following *The Danny Thomas Show*.[4] It remained on Monday night for the rest of its run, the last show airing on April 1, 1968. For all of its eight seasons, TAGS ranked among the top seven programs on television. Every Monday night millions of viewers in all parts of America dropped in on Mayberry, among them such unlikely fans as Gipsy Rose Lee and Frank Sinatra. When Griffith called it quits as Sheriff Andy, TAGS was number one in the ratings, one of only three shows—the others being *I Love Lucy* and *Seinfeld*—to have accomplished the rare feat of going out on top. After 1968, TAGS continued its life in reruns on local stations. With the arrival of cable networks, the show found a home on TBS (Ted Turner is a lifelong TAGS fan) and later on Nickelodeon's Nick at Nite and TV Land, where it remains one of the network's most popular shows. During TAGS's last season on CBS, it had a weekly audience of about fifteen and a half million viewers. In 1998 the *Chris-*

tian Science Monitor estimated that every day about five million people watched *TAGS* reruns on more than one hundred television stations across the country.[5] More than ten years later, *TAGS* is still syndicated in almost one hundred local TV markets. In Roanoke, Virginia, *The Oprah Winfrey Show* ended its spectacular twenty-five-year run without ever beating reruns of *TAGS*.

When *TAGS* commemorated its fiftieth anniversary in 2010, the milestone was duly observed by the *TAGS* community with a telethon on TV Land, a festival in Mount Airy, and the maiden race of the "Andy Griffith" stock car at the Banking 500 in Charlotte ("Andy" finished 31st). Websites devoted to the show abound. One of them, The Andy Griffith Show Rerun Watchers Club (TAGSrwc.com), originally a fan club founded at Vanderbilt University in 1979, has grown to more than twenty thousand members and over a thousand local chapters with such names as All Us Fifes Are Sensitive; Pipe Down, Otis; Aunt Bee's Pickles; Briscoe's Jug; and Ernest T. Bass Window Removers. At the virtual franchise of Mayberry's own Weaver's Department Store, fans can purchase T-shirts, calendars, mouse pads, board games (Mayberry-opoly), greeting cards, and bumper stickers ("This Sure Ain't Mayberry"). Ever since its publication in 1991, *Aunt Bee's Mayberry Cookbook* has sold more than a million copies. Its success spawned several sequels: *Postcards from Aunt Bee's Cookbook* (1993), *Aunt Bee's Delightful Desserts* (1996), *The Best of Mayberry* (1996), and *Aunt Bee's Mealtime in Mayberry* (1999). Offering thirty-two different "fixin's," Mayberry's Finest, a line of canned foods, made its debut in stores throughout the South in 2007. The Mayberry Ice Cream Restaurants, a chain of soup and sandwich shops, have existed in North Carolina since 1969.

It's not only fixin's, but food for the soul, that Mayberry has to offer. During the last fifteen years, a small cottage industry has developed around the teachings of the show's episodes. *Life Lessons from Mayberry* (1997), by John and Len Oszustowicz, "captures the message of Mayberry and offers it in a downhome style as warm and relaxed as Andy's front porch." Religious groups and individuals have also used the homespun homilies in *TAGS* as an accessible vehicle for the dissemination of Christian doctrine. In *The Way Back to Mayberry* (2001) Joey Fann examines the show "in the light of Biblical truth." Sunday school and Bible classes have available to them several study guides based on *TAGS*: *The Andy Griffith Show: Bible Study Series* (2000), *The Mayberry Bible Study* (2002), and *Mayberry Moments* (2008). In *The Mayberry Bible Study*, the episode in which Andy lets Malcolm Merriweather work off a debt he can't pay dramatizes the biblical principle of service, as set out in the Gospels. The episode in which Barney fills the courthouse with dogs, another "primetime parable," demonstrates that in Mayberry the quality of mercy is not strained.

When *TAGS* came on the air, the highest rated show in its time slot was *Adventures in Paradise*, an ABC offering about the captain of a schooner in the

South Seas. James Michener's brainchild, *Adventures in Paradise* drew its appeal from the exotic settings and the handsome star, Gardner McKay. No sooner would Adam Troy, the dreamboat of the *Tiki III*, sail to Hong Kong to rescue a kidnapped damsel than he would be trolling the Pitcairn Islands looking for a black pearl. Inhabited by landlubbers rather than seadogs, Mayberry was an entirely different kind of paradise. Mayberrians' idea of a south sea is Myers Lake. To satisfy their taste for adventure, they dine on pounded steak at Morelli's or travel to the Chinese restaurant in Mt. Pilot. Insensible to the romance of the road, Mayberrians have little desire to go anywhere but where they have already been. Their fantasies are all déjà vu. Adam Troy and Andy Taylor may be young, good-looking, and share the same initials, but that's where the resemblance ends. Until he spends a few days in Hollywood in a couple of episodes from the sixth season, Andy has never been farther from his hometown than Fayetteville, North Carolina. When the producers ordered six scripts that took the principal characters to Rome, Paris, and London, Griffith nixed them because he felt that they didn't fit the show.[6]

The other show opposite TAGS on Monday nights was NBC's *Dante*, whose title referred to the ex-con owner of a nightclub in San Francisco called—you guessed it—Dante's Inferno. TAGS found itself in the position of competing with both paradise and inferno. No matter. In 1961 TV watchers were no more interested in one than in the other. Neither noir stories in gritty San Francisco nor romance in far-flung island settings could match the cornball charisma of Mayberry. The debut episode of TAGS easily outdrew both shows. As the weeks went on, the disparity in ratings increased. *Dante* was cancelled at the end of the season. *Adventures in Paradise* would hang on, in a different time slot, until 1962. In the following seven seasons, TAGS would continue to dominate its competition, which ran the gamut of TV genres: comedies, Westerns, crime shows, variety shows. During the 1964–1965 season, TAGS was up against a short-lived remake of *No Time for Sergeants*, the play and movie that had launched Andy Griffith's rise to stardom in the 1950s. In 1967–1968 the competition was Danny Thomas, at the time the host of a variety show on NBC, *The Danny Thomas Hour*, who years earlier had introduced Mayberry to the world in an episode of *The Danny Thomas Show* (a.k.a. *Make Room for Daddy*). Neither one had better luck than *Dante*.

From the critics TAGS received mixed reviews. Describing the first episode as "warm, human, comical, and for a change, tastefully dramatic," the *Chicago Daily Tribune* thought that the show would be a hit. The *Philadelphia Inquirer* also predicted that TAGS "would be a good bet for laughs and longevity." But other reactions, particularly from the New York press, ranged from the lukewarm to the hostile. The *New York Times* remarked that the show was "only mildly entertaining." The *New York Journal American* agreed, calling TAGS "a friendly, shaggy-comedy study in the obvious which doesn't offend, and — for Andy Griffith fans — may amuse." *Variety* chimed in that the show might hold its own provided it didn't overdo "the molasses to the detriment of the comedy." The *Newark Evening News* considered TAGS a "dull" but "acceptable" addition to the CBS lineup. According to the *New York Herald Tribune*, the show was "trite, tedious and unimaginative." Syndicated columnist Fred Danzig piled on by observing that TAGS's allure was easy to resist, since Griffith's manner was copied from Tennessee Ernie Ford, his smile from Bert Parks, and the dialogue came straight out of *Lassie*. A few years later, once TAGS was firmly entrenched, *Variety* remarked that its popularity "plain defies rational analysis, even allowing for the rube taste in TV literature." It did concede that Andy Griffith "makes a hick almost likeable."[7] During its eight-year run, TAGS was nominated twice for an Emmy, not winning either time. By contrast, *The Dick Van Dyke Show*, on the air during five of those years, won three Emmys for best comedy series.

Surprisingly, perhaps, few of TAGS's principals had any connection with the South. Sheldon Leonard, the executive producer, had made his name initially by playing heavies in 1940s movies like *Week-End in Havana* and had gone on to become a successful director and producer. Neither Aaron Ruben, the producer for the first five seasons, nor Bob Ross, who produced the last three seasons, nor the writers who contributed many of the finest scripts — Charles Stewart and Jack Elinson, Bill Idelson and Sam Bobrick, Everett Greenbaum and Jim Fritzell — were Southerners. Greenbaum, a Buffalo native, came up with the "hick" characters: Ernest T. Bass, the Darlings, and Gomer Pyle. (He and Fritzell had a knack for writing what Greenbaum called "odd ducks"; they got their start as a team working on Wally Cox's *Mister Peepers*.) Howard Morris, who portrayed Ernest T. and directed several episodes, was a native New Yorker who had appeared on Sid Caesar's *Your Show of Shows*. Some of the actors, like Griffith, did hail from the South: Don Knotts from Morgantown, West Virginia; Jim Nabors from Sylacauga, Alabama; and George Lindsey from Jasper, Alabama. Frances Bavier (Aunt Bee), a stage actor from New York, began her career playing ingenue parts on Broadway. Ron Howard was born in Oklahoma. Howard McNear was a lifelong Californian. Like her character, Helen Crump, Aneta Corsaut was a Kansan.

Andy Griffith often praised the genius of the writers for being able to capture the "feeling of North Carolina without ever being there."[8] But the lifelikeness of the portrayal derived in no small part from Griffith's attention to every aspect of the show, from the plots to the speech and names of the characters to the toponymy of Mayberry County. TAGS is not only *The Andy Griffith Show* but Andy Griffith's show. It's an auteur sitcom, to use a concept not often applied to television, and Griffith is the auteur.[9] Although the initial idea for the series — Griffith as the sheriff of a Southern town — was Leonard's, Griffith fleshed out Leonard's idea with his temperament, tastes, and memories. Even his self-avowed "difficulty" with women made it into the show, as we will see. Although Griffith didn't write any of the scripts, he suggested plots, crafted individual scenes, and meticulously edited every script for verisimilitude and consistency. In the papers he donated to the University of North Carolina at Chapel Hill, almost every script contains his handwritten changes and annotations. *TV Guide* accurately labeled Griffith the "Cornball with the Steel-Trap Mind."[10] His vision made TAGS what it is, or what it has been taken to be: an iconic portrayal of life in a small Southern town.

The enduring appeal of TAGS has generated several excellent guides to the show, beginning with Richard Kelly's groundbreaking *The Andy Griffith Show* (1981), written by a professor of English at the University of Tennessee. Equally useful are *Mayberry: My Hometown* (1987) by Stephen J. Spignesi; *Inside Mayberry* (1994) by Dan Harrison and Bill Habeeb; *The Official Andy Griffith Show Scrapbook* (1995) by Lee Pfeiffer; *The Definitive Andy Griffith Show Reference* (1996) by Dale Robinson and David Fernandes; and *Mayberry Memories* (2005) and *The Andy Griffith Show Book* (2010) by Ken Beck and Jim Clark. The hardiest of the lot, *The Andy Griffith Show Book*, has gone through several editions and updatings since its original publication in 1985. These books contain plot summaries, descriptions of the characters, information about the people involved in the making of the show, and abundant catalogs of TAGS trivia. Neal Brower's *Mayberry 101: Behind the Scenes of a TV Classic* (1998), which includes comments on selected episodes by actors, writers, and directors, derives from a continuing-education course that the author, a Methodist minister, has taught in North Carolina community colleges.

A latecomer to Mayberry, I cannot claim the length of acquaintance or depth of knowledge of the authors of these books. In "Mountain Wedding," an episode from the third season, Barney Fife takes his leave from Briscoe Darling by saying, "Adios, amigo," a Spanish-language echo of Mayberry's motto, "The Friendly Town." Briscoe turns to Andy and asks: "He one of ours?" Were this question addressed to me, of course I'd have to answer in the negative. Mayberry is as foreign to me, a Cuban professor of Spanish, as Marianao, the neighborhood in Havana where I was born, would be to most Americans. If nothing else, my "Southern" accent—from the *truly* deep South—would give me away. In the 1930s, advertising posters used to lure Americans to Cuba with the slogan, "So near and yet so foreign." Although I make my home in Chapel Hill, North Carolina, a couple of hours from Mount Airy, I could say much the same thing about Mayberry: physically close yet culturally remote, so near and yet so foreign. For someone who was raised among people who wouldn't know a dumpling from a duck, Mayberry is something of a blank, "a riddle wrapped in a mystery inside an enigma," as Winston Churchill said about Russia. Like

Cuba to Americans, Mayberry is physically close but culturally remote, so near and yet so foreign.

Some time ago, when I told a Cuban friend that I was writing a book about TAGS, his response was: "Eso es una americanada." An *americanada* is a vaguely derisive term used by Cubans for behavior regarded as typical of Anglo-Americans—and hence unbecoming to a Cuban. Until a few years ago, I shared my friend's attitude. I've lived in North Carolina for most of my of adult life, but I can't count myself among longtime fans of the show. I had never watched an entire episode until I began to spend several months of each year in those parts unknown that Mayberrians identify as "up North." Before then my only significant contact with the show had been through a cockatiel named Sunshine, my daughter's, which spent its long life endlessly whistling TAGS's familiar theme. But once I became a part-time northerner, I became homesick for North Carolina, a place that I had never considered home. At the time the show came on Nickelodeon in the early evening, and my wife and I got into the habit of watching it every weeknight after dinner. At first what struck me is what strikes most TAGS viewers: each episode is a little morality play that teaches us something about loyalty, generosity, neighborliness, parenting. But as I continued to watch, I noticed that the most interesting things in TAGS occur on the margins of the plot, in scenes where a lot is going on because nothing is happening. My fascination with the show had less to do with North Carolina than with my status as a foreigner, and more concretely, as an exile. I envied Mayberrians because, unlike me, they don't spend their lives among strangers; indeed, they do everything they can to avoid them. Following the Biblical precept, Mayberrians love their neighbors—to the exclusion of everyone else. As one of Opie's friends puts it, "You gotta keep somebody out, or it ain't a club" (3.23).

One part of me found the townspeople's mild and comical xenophobia off-putting; another part of me wished I were part of the club. Unlike other TAGS fans, I wasn't watching the show to relive the golden years of my childhood. There was no nostalgia in my attachment to Mayberry, not even the second-hand nostalgia derived from other people's memories, as happens with my nostalgia toward pre-Castro Cuba. It's not always true that the allure of reruns depends on the viewer's memory track, which the rerun jogs. It can be equally true that the allure of a rerun can reside in the fact that it's not a rerun in any personal sense, that it takes us to a time and a place where we've never been. What I liked about TAGS was Mayberry, and what I liked about Mayberrians was that they lived in their hometown, a word that has no exact translation in Spanish, since a hometown is not simply the town where one makes one's home. Someone who emigrates leaves many things, but none more strictly irreplaceable than the intimacy between person and place. Watching TAGS, I developed a sense of what it must be like to enjoy such intimacy, to feel rooted in the ground under your feet and to know that you live among people who are similarly rooted.

My interest in the show as a mitigation of exile dictates the structure of this book. In the first part I look at the Mayberrian world as a whole — its geography, atmosphere, the distinction between outsider and insider, and the townsfolk's view of history. The last chapter of this section, an extended obituary, traces the decline and fall of Mayberry as it evolves from TAGS to *Mayberry R.F.D.* and subsequently to the 1986 reunion movie, *Return to Mayberry*. In the second part of the book, I draw partial portraits of many of the town's citizens to explain how they contribute to the personality of the town. Rather than discussing the characters in descending order of prominence, as guidebooks to the show usually do, I have opted for a sequence that brings out the dynamic relationship among them. And so, for example, I discuss Opie and Floyd together in "Growing Up, Growing Old," for what I intend to bring out is the pathos created by the contrast between Floyd's aging and Opie's growing up as the series unfolds. For the same reason, the portrait of Mr. McBeevee follows the discussion of Andy Taylor, since Mr. McBeevee, the protagonist of one of the best-liked episodes, represents an alternative father figure. Given the large number of characters in the show, I have not tried to be exhaustive, but I have included all of the principal characters and several secondary ones.

If in part 1 the discussion of the Mayberrian sense of place is motivated by my own displacement, the portraits in part 2 are underwritten by an exile's search for community. Throughout, my aim has been to understand, on the one hand, the conditions that make possible the intimacy of person and place, and on the other, the sequence of events that leads to the erosion of this intimacy. The interlude and the epilogue explain in greater detail the reasons for my effort to put myself in the place of people who have never lost their place.

As a naturalized Mayberrian, I'm aware that, unlike Groucho Marx, I belong to a club that may not welcome me as a member. Mayberrian soil — red clay — is not receptive to transplants. Imagine someone walking into the Bluebird Diner and ordering arroz con pollo. The outlandishness of this request lies at the root of my investment in TAGS. My hope is that this admittedly subjective perspective — my *americanada* — promotes a more comprehensive appreciation of this exemplar of "pure Americana."[11]

When Andy Griffith passed away on July 3, 2012, all of North Carolina seemed to go into mourning. In addition to the normal reruns (here in Chapel Hill two episodes of TAGS are shown back to back on weekends), local stations launched weeklong TAGS marathons, and thousands of North Carolinians sent in testimonials to the stations of the impact that the program had had on their lives. Some said that they had learned from Sheriff Andy how to raise their children; others talked about the joy that the program had brought into their lives.

Someone from Greenville wrote: "Andy is my hero. He has been for most of my 49 years. Andy represented the very best of what makes North Carolina so special. My family will never forget him." Many others echoed this sentiment; Andy—the actor as well as the persona—was a "true Tarheel." At the time I was working on a draft of this book. By then I had spent the better part of two years watching and thinking about the 249 episodes of TAGS. My home office in Chapel Hill, where I watched the show on a computer, had become an outpost of Mayberry. On the shelf nearest me, the handful of books about the show and its stars. On the wall, still shots of some of my favorite scenes. Like other fans, I had begun to feel that I was a Mayberrian. I had become as familiar with the characters on the show as with my own kin. I knew their secrets: I knew that Barney subscribed to men's magazines, that Andy's true love was not Helen Crump but Sharon DeSpain, and that old Emma, busybody par excellence, bleached her hair with peroxide.

I was tempted to add my own testimonial about what TAGS has meant to me, but I was embarrassed to do so. As a less-than-true Tarheel and, moreover, a relative newcomer to Mayberry, I did not share the experiences of the authors of the testimonials. I didn't grow up watching TAGS and I felt no special connection to Andy Griffith. Had I submitted a testimonial, I would have been like the stranger who shows up at a funeral and no one knows what he is doing there. The Spanish word for someone who sticks his nose into other people's business is *metido*, literally, inserted. I didn't think it was right to insert myself into Carolinians' sorrow.

Nonetheless, whatever its limitations, this is a fan's book. Although my comments about TAGS will not be uncritical, I have no desire to deconstruct, disparage, or otherwise knock the show. If our work should be the praise of what we love, as John Ruskin believed, this book tells the story of a late-blooming love affair with Mayberry.

I suspect that mine will seem a strange passion—a Mayberry-December romance—even if I were not excluded from Briscoe's band of brothers. In universities and their environs, *The Andy Griffith Show* is not highly thought of or, in fact, much thought of at all. Gerard Jones, the author of a superb history of sitcoms, recognizes TAGS's production values but dislikes Mayberrians, a "population of idiots and provincials" who represent "the traps and limitations of old southern ways." Gomer is "cretinous"; Floyd, "an old gossip quick to think evil of others"; Emma, "an aging hypochondriac with a paranoic streak"; and Barney, "a wired-up pop-eyed lunatic." Another influential scholar of sitcoms, David Marc, dismisses TAGS as "surrealist small-town fantasia." Harry Castleman and Walter Podrazik label Mayberrians "a handful of citizens who had long ago lost the fight for mental stability."[12] In response to these criticisms, I am reminded of Flannery O'Connor's remark that for Northern readers any fiction coming out of the South is going to be called grotesque unless it is really grotesque, in which case it is going to be called realistic.[13]

Because of this antirural (perhaps anti-Southern) sentiment, discussions of sitcoms from the 1960s and 1970s give pride of place to the "smart" shows, "litcoms" as Marc calls them: *The Dick Van Dyke Show, That Girl, The Mary Tyler Moore Show, All in the Family*. Rubecoms, which merit no more than passing mention, are exiled to the boonies of TV-land: scorn for corn. Dandy for Andy and his neighbors, I take a different view. Barney is Mayberry's Everyman, no more or less lunatic than the rest of us. Floyd wouldn't know evil even if the devil himself plopped down in his barber chair; his gossiping, like that of the other gadflies in town, performs a crucial function, that of perpetuating local history. As for Gomer, I'd call him flouncy rather than cretinous: he is Mayberry's queen. And if old Emma is paranoid, it's only because Barney keeps arresting her for jaywalking.

For *TAGS* fans, Mayberry exists not only for the twenty-five minutes of each episode. Our access to Mayberry is intermittent, but the town's life doesn't stop, *Truman Show*–like, when the camera is turned off. What takes place in Mayberry during each episode is important, but so is what happens when we're not looking. One example: since Aunt Bee's last name is Taylor, she must be Andy's father's sister, though this relationship is never mentioned. We are told that she's from West Virginia and that, along with her best friend, Clara Edwards, she attended Sweet Briar Normal School. We also know that she's never been married, apparently not for lack of opportunity. Since Aunt Bee raised Andy after his parents died, she must have lived in Mayberry while Andy was growing up. But apparently it's been so long that in the first episode of the series, "The New Housekeeper," she is treated like a newcomer. By the next episode, however, she has become a town fixture, known and respected by all. Her reacclimation occurs between the first and the second episodes — one week in real time, an indeterminate span in Mayberrian time. *TAGS* offers small slices of larger life, scattered pearls from a longer string.

A different kind of viewer would dismiss these comments as silly. Hardheaded, he would point out that Aunt Bee only exists while she is on the screen. She is born the moment we see her come through the door of Andy's house and dies after her last scene in *Mayberry R.F.D.* In between the scenes and episodes in which she appears, she slumbers like a dowdy zombie in a 1940s updo. To believe otherwise is to confound flimsy fiction with hard fact. Soft-minded viewers, people like me, concede that the hardheaded critic is right, yet we also know that the pot simmering on Aunt Bee's stove contains lamb stew. We know it because lamb stew is Andy's favorite dish.

My point is that the number and distinctiveness of episodes in which the principal characters appear engenders a continuity of contact whose analogue, as viewers have pointed out many times, is kinship. With characters who show up less frequently—the Fun Girls, the Darlings, Ernest T. Bass—the ruckus they create compensates for the rarity of their appearances. They too are kin, like the uncle you see only two or three times in your life but who leaves an indelible impression.

In an influential analysis of early twentieth-century aesthetic movements, the Spanish philosopher José Ortega y Gasset likened the appreciation of a modern painting to looking at a garden through a windowpane and only attending to the glass.[14] Since the observer's vision is focused on the medium—the geometrical shapes and pigments of color—rather than on the representation, he called the type of art that encourages this point of view "intranscendent" (today we might call it "self-referential"). But in fiction, and particularly in the classical novel, intranscendence takes a very different form, for it is the represented world that monopolizes our attention. A great novel, according to Ortega, tricks us into thinking that there is no windowpane. As a result, our access to the world of the characters seems unmediated. And so in the novels of Stendhal or Trollope intranscendence appears as hermeticism, the power of these books to lure their readers into imaginary gardens and block the exit.[15] I can think of no better description of the effect of watching TAGS, which also transports its viewers, novel-like, to the closed world of Mayberry. Other sitcoms don't do this, or do it to a lesser extent, not because they are self-referential (though some are: witness *The Adventures of Ozzie and Harriet* or *It's Garry Shandling's Show*), but because they are permeable to contemporaneity. Their imaginary gardens can't help reminding us of real toads. But TAGS makes a point of insulating Mayberry from the amphibian here and now, frog gigging notwithstanding. Mayberry is less a microcosm than a heterocosm, a world apart. The episodes of TAGS do not literally unfold in another era, like those of *The Waltons* or *Happy Days*, but they might as well have. According to Harvey Bullock, the scriptwriters "never really designated the period we were writing about, but we were always thinking earlier, back in the amorphous middle age of innocence, if you will."[16] Ortega also points out that the finest novels turn their readers into provincials, temporary inhabitants of narrow, confined realms. TAGS has turned millions of Americans and at least one Cuban into Mayberrians, whether or not Briscoe Darling consents.

Something else that TAGS has in common with the classical novel is what Ortega calls *morosidad* (slowness, long-windedness). This may seem paradoxical, given how quickly the half-hour episodes fly by. But if one regards them as installments in a serial narrative—"The Mayberry Chronicles"—then it takes much longer to watch the 249 episodes of TAGS than to read *War and Peace*. What the viewer retains from all those hours of exposure are not only specific scenes—Barney dressed up like a mannequin, Charlene Darling singing "Salty

Dog," Goober dismantling a car inside the courthouse—but also an abiding sense of what it's like to live in Mayberry. Remarking on the novel's subordination of event to experience, Ortega adds that recalling the title of a novel that we've read is tantamount to naming a place where we have lived. What we remember most distinctly is not the plot but the climate, the faces on the street, the pace of life. In sum, "la hora simple y sin leyenda" ("the simple, unremarkable hour")—that is, uneventful duration.[17] One of the keys to the success of TAGS is its ability to render uneventful duration, a notion whose material correlate is whittling, a favorite activity of the townsfolk. Crazy things go on in Mayberry, but they are temporary disturbances, like the pebbles Opie throws into Myers Lake at the beginning of each episode.

During its original run, Mayberry barely registered a tremor of the social and political upheavals that were sweeping the country. Never mind that in February 1960, a few months before TAGS premiered, African American college students staged a sit-in at a segregated lunch counter in Greensboro, a stone's throw away from the fictional location of Mayberry, an event that set off similar protests in other segregated facilities in North Carolina. Like other denizens of sixties sitcoms, the inhabitants of this almost lily-white town lived in blissful ignorance of the turmoil around them. Even so, if the show was escapist in the 1960s, today, in the second decade of the twenty-first century, it must seem like the jawbone of a dinosaur, especially to younger viewers, most of whom have never used a typewriter, much less a candlestick phone.

When TAGS went on the air, one-third of Americans still lived in rural areas. By 2010, that number had dropped to 15 percent. To mark the show's thirtieth anniversary in 1990, Mount Airy celebrated its first Mayberry Days. At the time, most of the actors who had appeared on the show were still alive, and many of the attendees had seen it on Monday nights. But those people are now at least in their sixties. (Before his death Andy Griffith usually topped the list of celebrities that AARP members were most interested in.) As I write, the median age in the United States is thirty-eight, which means that most Americans are not old enough to have seen the show except in reruns or on DVD. And yet the show retains its appeal. A Google search for "Mayberry" will yield over five million hits.

For the last couple of years, I've been performing an unscientific survey in my classes at Columbia University. I bring to class a still shot from the episode of TAGS in which a young Barbara Eden (later of *I Dream of Jeannie* fame) arrives in Mayberry and installs herself as a manicurist in Floyd's barbershop, much to his bewilderment. The shot shows the "boys" (Andy, Barney, Floyd, Mayor Pike, and a couple of other Mayberrians—a barbershop sextet) staring wide-eyed at Barbara, "a calendar come to life," as she gets off the Nashville bus. I pass the photo around, tell my students that it's from an old TV program that their parents or grandparents might have watched, and ask whether they know

The "boys" check out the new manicurist.

the name of the show or of any of the characters. Typically, in a class of twenty, at least half will be able to identify the show. Many of them will also be able to name Barney and Andy. On one occasion a student not only knew the name of the program and all of the main characters, but was able to recall that particular episode. It turned out that she was born in Montgomery, Alabama, and grew up watching TAGS every afternoon on a local station.

I marvel at the fact that these young people, a generation of texters and tweeters, are still drawn to Mayberry. But maybe I shouldn't. The *Mayberry Gazette*'s gossip column was called "Mayberry after Midnight," a funny name because the town's night owl, Barney Fife, hits the sack at the late hour of 10:45 p.m. The reason for watching TAGS was never its timeliness. From the outset, the show was framed in the past tense. In this respect, the more that time passes, the more irrelevantly seductive Mayberry becomes, like the image of a man and his son, poles over their shoulders, heading for a fishin' hole.

Part One

THE PLACE

Mayberry — wherever that is, that's where I am.

EDDIE BLAKE, "THE TAPE RECORDER" (8.8)

CHAPTER ONE

A World unto Itself

IN "THE EDUCATION OF ERNEST T. BASS" (5.4), ANDY DE-
cides to teach Ernest T. Bass, the hick from the sticks, the basics of
American geography. He shows Ernest T. a map and asks him what the United
States is bounded by in the west. Ernest T.'s answer: Old Man Kelsey's Woods.
Andy tells him that it's a body of water. Ernest T. tries again: Old Man Kelsey's
Creek. Andy tells him that it's an ocean. Ernest T. tries yet again: Old Man
Kelsey's Ocean. By the end of the lesson, Ernest T. can enumerate the places
that border America: "Mexico, Canada, Atlantic Ocean, Pacific Ocean, Kelsey's
Woods, Kelsey's Creek, Kelsey's Ocean."

The most backward of all Mayberrians, Ernest T. lives in a cave, has never
been to school, and his idea of a gourmet meal is possum steak. But the view
of the world from Ernest T.'s cave is not so different from that of his better-
educated and better-housed neighbors, for whom Mayberry is also the whole
of their universe. The town and its environs, what in Spanish is called *la patria
chica*, the small homeland, is as far as the Mayberrian eye can see. Even Andy
suffers from this chronic nearsightedness. The episode in which he meets Helen
Crump, his eventual fiancée, is titled "Andy Discovers America" (3.23). Like
Dorothy in *The Wizard of Oz*, Helen hails from Kansas, the heart of the heart of
the country; but for Andy, getting to know Helen amounts to discovering a new
world, which makes it appropriate that Helen is Opie's history teacher. History
is a subject that, Andy says, he was never much good at.

The title of this episode, written by John Whedon, echoes a couplet from
John Donne's raunchy "To His Mistress Going to Bed": "O, my America, my
Newfoundland, / My Kingdom, safest when with one man manned." Far be it
from Andy to "man" Miss Crump or anyone else, but the episode's title does
suggest that Mayberry is apart from America, or rather—what amounts to the
same thing—that Mayberry is all of America. This notion underlies Goober's

Andy discovers America.

adaptation of a sentence from John F. Kennedy's inaugural address: "It ain't what Mayberry can give to you, it's what you can give to Mayberry" (8.27). The episode about a Hollywood producer's plans to film a movie includes a shot of the front page of the *Mayberry Gazette*. Under "News of the World," these are the headlines: "New Library Dedicated," "Board Head to Speak," "Political Placards Removal Is Asked by Zoning Director," "Engineer Is Killed as Limited Crashes," "Thousands See Industry Fair," "Grand Jury Probe of County Flood Control Dams Due." For Mayberrians, "the world" is no larger than their own backyard. Only one rather strange story, in small headlines, relates events outside Mayberry: "130,000 Chinese living in trees as a result of flood" (1.13). What happens outside Mayberry differs so starkly from the residents' daily lives—compare the local probe into flood control with the catastrophic Chinese flood—that it might as well be taking place on another planet. Hence the titles of the science fiction movies at the local theater: "The Beast That Ate Minnesota," "The Monster from Mars," "The Monster from Out of Town." From the townsfolk's perspective, China, Minneapolis, Mars, and "Out of Town" are different names for the same thing: the monster-filled terra incognita beyond Old Man Kelsey's Woods.

This narrowness of outlook is what others—the monsters from out of town—would label a "small-town mentality." As such, it is not specific to Mayberry. At the beginning of Thornton Wilder's *Our Town*, Dr. Gibbs asks the newspaper boy whether there's "anything serious goin' on in the world." The boy replies that his teacher, Miss Foster, is getting married. Rather than smiling at the boy's naïveté, Dr. Gibbs endorses it: "I declare." Dr. Gibbs's horizons are no more expansive than Ernest T.'s. What sets Mayberry apart from Grover's Corners, as from other fictional towns in theater and television, is the density of local reference. Griffith and the writers made a habit of filling in Mayberry's human and physical environment with references to people, businesses, features of the landscape. Hardly an episode goes by that does not contribute a detail insignificant in itself, but that enhances what Roland Barthes called the "reality effect," TAGS's simulacrum of real life. Someone mentions the name of another farmer or another store or another hill or holler, and the Mayberrian world acquires a little more heft.

Most of the town's business is conducted on Main Street, anchored on one end by the courthouse, a plain two-story building whose second floor houses the mayor's office. On the bottom floor, one large room contains the sheriff's office and two jail cells. Behind the courthouse is the Feed and Grain Store. Next to the courthouse is Floyd's barbershop, with its wide front window and barber pole. The rest of the street is occupied by Orville's Mortuary, Foley's Market (which goes through other owners), Weaver's Department Store, Walker's Drugstore (which also changes hands), Bigg's Furniture Store, the Bluebird (or Mayberry) Diner, the bank, and Boysinger's Bakery, a late addition. At the far end of Main Street sit the Mayberry Hotel and the Grand (or Mayberry) Theater. Nearby is Wally's Service, where Gomer and Goober pump gas, as well as Reverend Tucker's All Souls Church, apparently the only house of worship. The town's landmarks include the David Mendlebright Memorial Horse Trough, the Civil War cannon (probably a fake), and an ancient oak tree that Andy used to climb as a child.

Of the private homes, the only one we see regularly is Andy's, on Maple (or Elm) Road, a tree-lined street of frame houses built close together. His is a thirty-five-year-old bungalow with a wide front porch furnished with a wicker rocker and settee. The driveway ends in a garage used for storage, since the Taylors do not own a car until well into the seventh season. In the backyard Opie has a clubhouse and Aunt Bee grows roses. The screen door on the porch opens into a well-appointed living room centered by a sofa and two wing chairs. A stone fireplace with a mantelpiece spans one wall. Up against another wall is the upright piano where Aunt Bee and Clara compose their hit song, "My Hometown."

Adjacent to the living room is the dining room, with a swinging door that connects to a small kitchen where Aunt Bee putters around and the Taylors have breakfast, sometimes joined by Barney. Of the four bedrooms upstairs, Opie's is the only one that appears often on screen, its main feature a window that looks out onto the front yard (and that allows us to look into the room). As one would expect, the room is cluttered with toys, sports paraphernalia, and occasional pets. This is an important space, for the only "bedroom scenes" in TAGS, all of which show a father and son in intimate conversation, occur in Opie's room.

Aunt Bee and Clara compose "My Hometown."

The roads leading out of town, most of them unpaved, take Mayberrians to such popular destinations as Morelli's, an Italian restaurant known for its pounded steak; Tucker's Lake, home to the legendary silver carp; and Duck Pond, where Barney goes "parking" with his dates. Other locations, like Old Man Kelsey's Woods, the viewer never sees: Eagle Rock, Finnegan Flats, Snake Skin Creek, Hansen's Hill, Franklin Holler, Hawk's Point, DeQueen Junction, Fancy Gap, Lover's Leap, and many more. Twelve miles away is Mt. Pilot, a larger and somewhat corrupted version of Mayberry that is frequently mentioned and occasionally visited. It too has its jail, restaurants, banks, movie theaters, and shops.

Beyond the immediate vicinity of Mayberry are other towns, most of them real communities in North Carolina, among them: Triplett, Bannertown, Toast, Siler City, Elm City, Macon, Yancey (in *TAGS* the location of the disreputable Gigolo Club), and Manteo (where Andy Griffith lived for many years). Further out are cities and towns in other Southern states, foreign but still familiar. Helen's niece lives in Wheeling, West Virginia. Aunt Bee grew up in Morgantown. The town choir performs in Roanoke. Barney has a sports coat "imported" from Richmond. Outside of Dixie, on the far side of the Mayberrian universe, lie New York, Cleveland, Chicago, Los Angeles, and other lands unknown whose precise location is never specified and whose customs are as enigmatic to Mayberrians as the news of 130,000 Chinese living in trees.

As in the Book of Genesis, once the world has been created, it needs to be peopled. Ken Beck and Jim Clark, among the world's foremost *TAGS*ophiles, have compiled a "Mayberry Town Directory" with over six hundred names. Add to these their "Mt. Pilot Directory," and the count swells by at least another hundred.[1] Many of these names correspond to characters who appear in one or several episodes, but more belong to phantom characters, people who are mentioned and never appear on-screen. (Two phantoms in particular play important roles: Sarah, the nosy phone operator, and Juanita, the waitress at the diner whom Barney lusts after.) The deliberate and constant name-dropping creates the impression that there's more to Mayberry than meets the viewers' eyes. In an episode from the next-to-last season, "Opie's Piano Lesson" (7.26), a piano tuner named Mr. Higby is mentioned several times, although he doesn't appear in the episode, is never heard from again, and has not been heard from before. For the purposes of the plot, which revolves around the conflict between Opie's piano lessons and football practice, Aunt Bee only needs to establish that the piano needs tuning; instead she talks about Mr. Higby as if she knew him well. The evocation of characters like Higby engrosses the tiny but crowded world of Mayberry. In "Barney's Sidecar" (4.16), an important cog in the plot is that trucks can't make it up a certain incline unless they surpass the 35-mph speed limit. Like everything else, the incline has a name, Turner's Grade. Oddly, the larger the number of phantoms, the stronger the viewer's sense that the town is real. And when we add to the names without faces the faces with no names, the hundreds of extras that appear in crowd scenes or walking down the street, it is not difficult to believe that, as county clerk Howard Sprague says, Mayberry encompasses "a whole throbbing rural area" (8.27).

Once again Ortega's ideas about the novel are helpful. According to Ortega, classical novels include far more detail than the reader can remember. Anticipating Barthes, he points out that these novels are tightly packed, "stuffed" (*tupido*) with trivialities that convince the reader that the world of the novel is as rich and variegated as reality itself.[2] No sitcom of the 1960s makes a point of giving such human and physical density to its setting. Whatever the name of the town, all these shows unfold in some version of "Centerville," the mythical middle-American town of *The Aldrich Family* (1948–1953), which set the pattern for family-centered shows. (*TAGS* also has a Centerville, but it's a real town a few counties to the east of Mount Airy.) Gerard Jones describes the locale of these shows as "the suburban Neverland of family sitcoms, in which details of locale and occupation are intentionally evaded and a homogenous, threatless world is shown as being already in place, waiting to welcome the new exurbanite."[3] This characterization does not apply to Mayberry, not because the town is not a Neverland, but because of the wealth of knowledge we acquire about the town and its citizens.

Contrast Mayberry with another of its antecedents, Mayfield, the suburb in *Leave It to Beaver*, which came into existence in 1957. The echoing names underscore the differences. A platonic suburb, Mayfield hovers vaguely above middle America. Since in one episode Wally and Beaver plan to buy a surfboard, they may be living in California; but at other times, Mayfield seems located in the Midwest, perhaps near Chicago or in Wisconsin, for the Cleavers consider moving to the neighboring town of Madison, which in the real world is not far from Mayfield, Wisconsin. The location of the Cleaver home is left up in the air because *Leave It to Beaver* is not a show about a place but about a social class — the upwardly mobile, post–World War II American family. The same could be said of Springfield, the town of the Andersons in *Father Knows Best*. There are several Springfields in America, but none corresponds to the one in the show, whose location remains unspecified, as does that of the Springfield of *The Simpsons*.

The pilot for TAGS was an episode from the 1959–1960 season of *The Danny Thomas Show*, "Danny Meets Andy Griffith." In the opening scene, the viewer sees the town's name three times: on the courthouse door ("Mayberry Jail and Courthouse"); on the squad car ("Mayberry Sheriff"); and on the newspaper's masthead (*The Mayberry Gazette*). Six months later, the inaugural TAGS episode also opens with a shot of the courthouse door. Halfway into the episode, the town's name is repeated when Barney fears that if old Emma is allowed to jaywalk, Mayberry will turn into a "sin town." The second episode of the series, "The Manhunt," will establish that Mayberry is an out-of-the-way community, "a hick town where nothing ever happens," but it's not until the middle of the first season that the location of the town is pinned down to rural North Carolina. From then on, the characters will often mention the nearby state capital, Raleigh, or Mayberry's sister city, Mt. Pilot (based on Pilot Mountain). We will also find out that the Taylors have kin in Asheville and Jacksonville (North Carolina, not Florida), and that Andy plans for Opie to attend the University of North Carolina at Chapel Hill (Griffith's alma mater). Confounding art and life, Aunt Bee reads the *Mount Airy News* rather than *The Mayberry Gazette* (5.27).[4]

As Mayberry's physical location gains definition, so does its cultural landscape. In this town the sheriff doesn't carry a gun; his deputy has only one bullet, tucked away in his shirt pocket; the town drunk checks himself in and out of jail every week; and old ladies are allowed to jaywalk because it is believed that jaywalking prolongs their lives. Many of the early episodes will stress the contrast between the Mayberry methods and customary law-enforcement techniques. In "The Manhunt" the state police set up a complicated series of checkpoints to catch a dangerous escaped criminal. They ask Andy and Barney to stay out of the way, but Andy has a hunch that the criminal may have been lured by the aroma of freshly baked pies wafting from Emma Brand's kitchen. Andy tricks him into fleeing in a leaky rowboat. When the boat capsizes in the middle of Myers Lake, the criminal swims to shore, where the state police await, not having had to fire a shot. Early in the episode, the state troopers take over the courthouse and replace Andy's map of the county with one of their own, which is newer and more detailed. The two maps illustrate contrasting views of the Mayberrian universe: the insider's and the outsider's. The capture of the criminal demonstrates the superiority of the insider's view, a recurring theme in *TAGS*.

The superiority of the Mayberry method is conveyed in a social rather than professional setting when Ellie Walker, the college-educated niece of the owner of Walker's drugstore, comes to town (1.4). A stickler for the rules, the "new lady druggist" does not issue pills without a prescription. Once again old Emma appears, this time looking for the little blue pills that relieve her multiple, mostly imaginary, ailments. When Ellie refuses, Emma sneaks into the drugstore to take them anyway. Ellie catches her and demands that Andy arrest her for stealing. After learning that the pills are only sugar pills, Ellie gives in and gladly supplies Emma with as many as she wants. Andy is pleased: "dag-burned technicalities" should not get in the way of "the human equation."

Like other episodes, "Ellie Comes to Town" has a secondary plotline that parallels the main action. Barney is attempting to memorize the "sheriff's rules," but even if he were able to accomplish this, the knowledge thus acquired would be useless because "technicalities," whether requiring a prescription or enforcing laws about jaywalking, matter less than the "human equation." Barney keeps filling up citation pads because he insists on enforcing laws that don't apply, or apply differently, in Mayberry. Although he loves to cite the "code," Mayberry has its own unwritten code whose interpreter is Andy, the justice of the peace in more than the formal sense. When his methods clash with the code, the former will always prevail. And it's a good thing too, even for Barney, who keeps his job when Andy, the sheriff ex machina, comes up with a way to circumvent the height and weight requirements for police officers. Andy doesn't carry a gun not only because the residents are law-abiding, but because in Mayberry the authority of the law does not carry any more weight than Barney. This is the reason the Town Council, headed by the mayor, has no substantive role in governance. (By contrast, in *Mayberry R.F.D.*, the life of the town will revolve around the Town Council.)

Although Mayberry is surrounded by farms, it is not an agrarian village but a town. Farmers are much in evidence, though none of the principal characters owns a farm. Even if Mayberry is the county seat of Mayberry County, with an area of 267 square miles, a lot of it farmland, the show revolves around town life. What novelist Josephine Humphries has said about Southern fiction applies equally to *TAGS*: "The natural setting of Southern fiction is not wilderness, nor farm nor city. It is town. For the most part, that is where our fictional vision has been focused; that is the place that has seemed most fitting for the kinds of stories we have wanted to tell—narratives of the human community."[5] These kinds of stories are also *TAGS*'s essential subject. What characterizes Mayberrians are not their ties to the soil—these are largely symbolic—but

their ties to the town and, hence, to one other. This is why the founding of Mayberry, incongruously, dates from the middle of the nineteenth century rather
than from the period of British colonization. In "The Pageant" (5.11), the celebration of Mayberry's centennial involves a reenactment of the founding of
the town, which occurred when Indian Chief Noogatuck (Barney) and James
Merriweather (Andy) smoked a peace pipe in the settlement that would become Mayberry. Oddly, this event took place in 1864, in the midst of the Civil
War. As a result of the conflation of historical periods, Mayberry was already
a mature community on the day of its founding. No sooner had James Merriweather led the settlers into the "Happy Valley" than the settlers had turned
into townsfolk—tradesmen, shopkeepers, civil servants.[6]

Contrary to logic perhaps, our hometown is not the town where our home
is, nor is it necessarily the place where we were born. Everyone was born someplace, but not everybody has a hometown. Size matters, inversely. Millions call
New York City their hometown without a trace of quaintness. That they do so is
a compensatory fantasy that allows them to imagine a degree of intimacy with
their birthplace that one can truly have only with a town. By calling New York
City a hometown, we imagine it to possess the exhaustiveness of social connection characteristic of small towns, an impossibility acknowledged by the rarity
of the expression "home city." A city is too large to be a home, and to refer to
a city's "downtown" is simply to archaize. In a real town you can't go uptown
or downtown because you are already there. Mayberrians never spoke about
"downtown" Mayberry. The town was all one, indivisible and whole.

The South's "tribal ethics," as Jack Temple Kirby calls it, has been much dis-
cussed and criticized.[7] But if one is a member of a tribe, one enjoys a security
that nontribalists like me envy. Since the term "hometown" extends to a community the virtues of a home—closeness, security, familiarity—the perimeter
of acquaintance that encircles townsfolk needs to be circumscribed. The proverb that a man's home is his castle supposes that a man needs to shield himself
and his family from danger. For the TAGS tribe, Mayberry is the castle. A metaphorical moat rings the town. In *Poor White* (1920), an elegy to the small-town
life of fictional Bidwell, Ohio, Sherwood Anderson likens the bonds among
residents to those that knit a family: "The people who lived in the towns were
to each other like members of a great family . . . A kind of invisible roof beneath
which everyone lived spread itself over each town . . . Within the invisible circle
and under the great roof every one knew his neighbor and was known to him."[8]
What is true of Bidwell is also true of Mayberry. There is no homelessness in
Mayberry because the town itself functions as a home. There is no anonymity
in Mayberry because a town is a community without strangers. (When a town
begins to fill up with unfamiliar faces, it's on the way to becoming a city.)

Nobody in Mayberry finds it odd that a three- or four-year-old little boy

Otis at home—in jail.

named Leon wanders around town dressed in a cowboy suit with a peanut-butter-and-jelly sandwich in his hand. Is Leon an orphan? No, he's proof that a town such as Mayberry cannot have orphans. Homemakers all, the townsfolk stand in loco parentis. Barney likes to complain that Mayberry has the lowest crime rate in the state, which leaves him nothing to do. He's right: there is no need to police inside a home; thus in Mayberry police functions are largely devoted to keeping outsiders from breaking into the invisible circle that encloses the town and its environs.

It is puzzling that *TAGS*, ostensibly a family show, downplays the impact of family ties on the characters' lives. According to Barney, everyone in Mayberry is either "friend or kin," but the truth is that the former far outnumber the latter. Andy, Opie, Gomer, Goober, Howard, and Barney are only children. They are also all single, as are Aunt Bee, Helen, Thelma Lou, Clara, Howard Sprague, Ernest T. Bass, and Briscoe Darling and his four sons. Other than Emmett Clark and his wife, who appear only in the last season, the most prominent married couple in town is Otis and his wife Rita; but we see her, briefly, only on three occasions, and Otis spends most of his time sobering up at the jail. In a few episodes Floyd is given a "missus," though she is another phantom character. The barbershop is to him what the courthouse is to Otis, more of a home than his home.

When there are courtships in Mayberry, they tend not to result in marriages. In the 249 episodes of the series, three weddings occur: Rose and Wilbur Pine's (1.1), Hannah Carter and Josh Wakefield's (1.9), and Charlene Darling and Dud Wash's (3.31). Andy and Helen don't tie the knot until the first episode of *May-*

berry R.F.D. Barney has to wait even longer to wed Thelma Lou—until the reunion movie in 1986.

In Barney's first scene in TAGS—he comes out from behind Andy's garage—he mentions that Andy is his cousin, but after the second episode the relationship is dropped altogether. Their kinship is unimportant for the same reason that traditional two-parent families are nearly absent: what makes Mayberry cohere is not kin but kith. There is little in TAGS of that mythologizing of the nuclear family crucial to so many fifties and sixties sitcoms.[9] If anything, TAGS demonstrates how a collection of like-minded people can serve as surrogates for family. Rather than a domcom, a domestic comedy, it's a *comcom*—a community comedy. Of the quintessentially American "motherhood and apple pie," TAGS will furnish only the second, and even that will have a different flavor, since Andy prefers gooseberry.

For this reason the central space in TAGS is not the family's living room, as happens in countless sitcoms, but the courthouse, a different kind of venue, part juridical and part social, and, unlike a home, open to all. More plaza than casa, in the courthouse the public and the private, the civic and the domestic, coalesce, as they do in Andy's conduct as sheriff. In contrast to government offices, the courthouse never closes. When Andy and Barney arrive in the morning, the doors are unlocked. Anytime they go out, the doors stay open. The only locks are those on the two jail cells, and these do not bar ingress or egress, as Otis well knows. Many an episode begins in the courthouse with Barney or Opie engaged in domestic tasks—throwing out the trash, sweeping the floor—while Andy cleans one of the guns in the rifle rack. The jail cell where Otis sleeps is furnished like a bedroom, with a rocking chair, a reading lamp, a night table with a doily made by Aunt Bee, and a vase with flowers. Otis even has a blue terrycloth bathrobe to wear while he is in residence. Andy reads him bedtime stories or Barney sings him to sleep. If Aunt Bee doesn't bring him breakfast, Barney will fix him a boiled egg, toast, and coffee. The back room has a cot where Barney takes a nap or spends the night. Sooner or later, all Mayberrians have something to do with the courthouse. It's where the women dress up for the Halloween play, where the town band rehearses, where the Taylors celebrate Christmas, where the rummage sales take place, where Barney babysits, where a goat with a belly full of dynamite is sequestered, where Goober takes apart a car and puts it back together, where Aunt Bee hangs a clothesline to dry a female prisoner's stockings.

Every time someone other than Andy or Opie calls Beatrice Taylor "Aunt Bee," the metaphorical use of the term reveals the attenuated significance of family ties. At the beginning of "Family Visit" (5.3), Andy, Opie, and Aunt Bee are sitting on the porch, watching their fellow citizens walk to church. Seeing four generations of Beamons going to services together—a "sweet sight"—Aunt

Bee laments that the Taylors don't have more family. There's nothing she would enjoy more, she says, than cooking a big chicken dinner for a houseful of relatives. Andy replies that they do have a few kin "sprinkled around here and there." Aunt Bee thinks it's a shame that Opie hasn't met any of his relatives. In spite of Andy's reservations, she asks her sister, Norah, her husband, Ollie, and their children to spend the weekend. Remarkably, Andy hasn't seen them in fifteen years, even though they live in Lake Charles, a one-day's drive from Mayberry.

The visit doesn't turn out well. Andy can't stand Ollie; Norah bosses Aunt Bee around the kitchen; and Opie doesn't like sharing his bed with his two obnoxious cousins. When the relatives decide to stretch the visit to a week, Andy pretends that a couple of dangerous convicts are on the loose and asks Ollie to "help track down the outlaws." Panicking, Ollie rushes his family into the car and takes off. In the "tag," or epilogue, Aunt Bee and Andy once again are sitting on the front porch. Andy is whistling that paean to quietude, "Down in the Valley." Aunt Bee admits that Andy was right. It's a lot more peaceful without family around. Not coincidentally, the subject of Reverend Tucker's sermon a week earlier, on the Sunday when Aunt Bee extended the invitation to her sister, was the story of Cain and Abel, another tale of sibling relations gone awry.

TAGS pays lip service to the idea of family, but it does not practice what it preaches. The Taylors, a makeshift nuclear family, feel no need to create or cultivate family ties. Two episodes later (5.5), the Taylors will have another houseguest, Roger Hanover, Aunt Bee's old beau, with whom she is still smitten. This will not turn out well either. Roger is a con man who demands $400 from Andy in exchange for not proposing to Bee. A connoisseur of human nature, Andy calls his bluff. Roger gets on the noon train to Florida. Though she doesn't know about the blackmail attempt, Aunt Bee is relieved. She wouldn't have wanted to marry Roger anyway.

In a study of a composite midwestern town he calls Appleton, the anthropologist Hervé Varenne concludes that this community is held together by bonds of affection that he likens to the Greek *philia*, a form of nonerotic love that designates an individual's behavior as a social being.[10] The Mayberrian term for *philia* is friendship, as proclaimed in the sign at the town's limits, "Welcome to Mayberry, The Friendly Town." As we will see, the town's *philia* does not extend to non-Mayberrians, but it does embrace all of the members of the community, even fractious ones like Ernest T. Bass and the Darlings. Just as Mayberrians have a confined worldview, they have a strict definition of neighborliness. The two complement each other. When Johnny Paul Jason says, "You gotta keep somebody out, or it ain't a club" (3.23), he is articulating the central tenet of the town's ethos. Mayberry is an exclusive club, a closed society: in Ortegan terms, hermetic — not only because it draws the viewer in (we're also part of the club), but because it keeps strangers out. Tolerance, kindness, and loyalty are required toward all members of the club, those like who we are, those whose lives and values we share, but not toward the strangers whose homes lie beyond the community's invisible circle.

As *philia*-philes, Mayberrians have mastered the middle distance — in the *Nichomachean Ethics* Aristotle calls it "the intermediate state" — between intimacy and diffidence. Their sociability does not carry the intensity of connection of family ties. With the exception of some literally and figuratively touching scenes between Andy and Opie, moments of physical affection in *TAGS* are few and far between. Expressions of physical desire, whether it's Barney's horniness, Charlene Darling's randiness, or Ernest T.'s florid crushes, are uncouth, unkithlike. In all the years that Aunt Bee and Andy live together, only rarely do they exchange an embrace. But if there are few hugs and fewer kisses in Mayberry, there are also fewer disputes. Of course, as a sitcom, *TAGS* is not the appropriate venue for the portrayal of unbridled passion or bloody dissension (no room in Mayberry for Cain and Abel). The darkest side of the darkest Mayberrian is still sunny. Yet the show did not avoid serious subjects, like Opie's motherlessness or Barney's record of failure. But it did avoid eros, as it also avoided agape, love for God, since the religious fervor of Mayberrians is no less formalistic than their romancing. The most important parts of our lives, *TAGS* seems to say, are lived on the level ground of *philia*, where there are no peaks or precipices.

The community's stability is reinforced by the deliberately fostered illusion of permanence. Just as Mayberrians inhabit an enclosed space, they live in their own time. Unlike other sixties sitcoms, which varied their title sequence frequently, *TAGS* retained the same scene — Andy and Opie strolling to the fishing hole — for the duration of the show. The message is that Mayberry is impervious to change, a "backwoods Brigadoon," as Paul Harvey once called it.[11] The name of the town suggests eternal spring — the "May" in Mayberry — as well as wistfulness — the "maybe" in Mayberry. Holiday shows, a staple of TV series, track seasonal changes and yearly cycles. In *TAGS* there are no Thanksgiving episodes and, after the first season, no Christmas episodes. Instead, the one anniversary often mentioned is Founder's Day, a community-affirming celebration of the town's genesis. Every once in a while a character will refer to someone's age, but there are no birthday episodes either. Equally unchanging is Mayberry's weather. Occasionally Andy will put on a jacket or Floyd will fuss about the heat, but that is the extent of seasonal variation. It never snows in Mayberry. Rain comes rarely and mildly. Thunderstorms are as unknown as hurricanes and tornadoes (both of which do occur in North Carolina). The only seasons in *TAGS* are television seasons, which are not seasons at all. In Mayberry every day is like that of the title sequence: sunny and fair — as befits a town founded by a man named Merriweather.

Another Arcadian feature of Mayberry is the absence of deaths. The one episode that deals most explicitly with death falls outside TAGS proper, in the pilot from *The Danny Thomas Show,* during which Andy discusses the deaths of Opie's mother, Opie's turtle, Henrietta Perkins's husband, and the town drunk's father (from whom the current town drunk has inherited his position). In TAGS itself, the Grim Reaper is another of those strangers who are excluded from the invisible circle. Although the town has a funeral parlor, it is never used, which explains why Orville Monroe moonlights as a TV repairman. The one time a hearse shows up in front of his establishment, it is not carrying a corpse but repair parts. On the rare occasions when the passing of a Mayberrian is mentioned, the purpose is to set up a comedic dilemma that, in the context of the episode, is a fate worse than death. In "The Church Benefactors" (8.20), Reverend Tucker announces that ninety-three-year-old Jared Hooper has passed away and left the church a legacy of $500, which gets the parishioners fighting about how to use it. In "Aunt Bee's Medicine Man" (3.24), the passing of Aunt Bee's friend Augusta Finch explains why Aunt Bee starts worrying about growing old and buys two bottles of Colonel Harvey's Indian Elixir, which is almost pure alcohol.

Typical of the irrelevance of death is the story of Tom Silby, narrated in "Opie's Charity" (1.8). When Tom leaves Mayberry, his wife, Annabelle, lets it be known that he was run over by a taxicab in Charlottesville and proceeds to hold the fanciest funeral in memory. To everyone's surprise, Tom reappears two years later. It turns out that he left town to get away from nagging Annabelle, who was too proud to admit to being jilted. And so Tom enjoys the rare privilege of going along with Andy to visit his own grave. This too is the Mayberry method, which forbids the death of anyone we care about. After Tom returns from his grave, he and Annabelle reconcile. Even for "late" husbands, it is never too late.

The one truly significant death in the show is not that of a Mayberrian but of the "mama bird" that Opie kills with his slingshot, an accident whose emotional impact derives from the oblique evocation of Opie's orphanhood. What happens more frequently is that, like Orville Monroe, who wasn't seen after the first few episodes (probably because he had nothing to do), characters disappear without explanation. This is the fate of Miss Ellie and Miss Rosemary, Andy's and Barney's first girlfriends, and Warren Ferguson, Barney's replacement as deputy during the first part of the sixth season. TAGS may be unique among sitcoms for the number of disappeared, characters too unimportant to be written out, as Barney and Floyd were, and who instead simply vanish. Another notable example: Barney's mother. She appears in "The Manhunt" — Barney pats her down to make sure that she's not the criminal on the loose — but we do not see her again. Although we're never told that she has passed away, Barney speaks about her as if she were long dead. Like Andy, Opie, and the Darling sons, he is, in effect, motherless.

The presence in Mayberry of widows like Clara and widowers like Andy and Briscoe makes clear that death has not entirely spared Mayberry—et in Arcadia ego—but the sad events are removed to that corner of the town's life that remains unfilmed and unstoried. This unseen history, like the town's phantom characters, will sometimes have an impact on what happens on-screen, but Mayberrian decorum requires that life's tragedies, however inevitable, should be heard about rather than seen. In "Opie's Charity," the only readable tombstone in the cemetery is that of Tom Silby, "Fine Man and Dear Husband," who isn't dead after all. The three acts in Wilder's *Our Town* are "Daily Life," "Love and Marriage," "Death." The closed world of TAGS offers an abundance of the first, a little of the second, and hardly any of the third.

CHAPTER TWO

Against Change

> *Barney*: If only somebody would just commit a crime. One good
> crime. If only somebody'd just kill somebody.
> *Andy*: Barney!
> *Barney*: Oh, I don't mean anybody we know. But if a couple of
> strangers was to come to town and well, if one of them was going
> to kill the other anyway, well, he might just as well do it here.
>
> "ANDY THE MATCHMAKER" (1.7)

W HAT LENDS COHERENCE TO *TAGS* IS NOT ONLY THE setting but also the consistency of plotting and characterization. Of course, given the number of episodes, some mistakes were bound to creep in. Mayberry is a dry county, but Ben Weaver sells "spirits" in his store. Sometimes Floyd has a wife and at other times — as in "Floyd, the Gay Deceiver" (3.9), where Howard McNear delivers one of his best performances — he is single and looking. In his debut episode, his last name is Colby; afterwards, it's Lawson. Likewise, Emma Brand later became Emma Watson. Before he was a Pyle, Goober was a Beasley, sharing a last name with Juanita. Barney has three different middle names: Milton, Oliver, and P. Three different addresses are given for the Taylor home: 14 Maple, 332 Maple, and 24 Elm. The high school that Andy and Barney attended is identified as both Mayberry Union High and Mayberry Central High. Barney and Andy graduated either in 1945 or in 1948.

But these lapses are minor and inconsequential. Like some story cycles, *TAGS* tracks a group of recurring characters whose experiences in the aggregate possess an intelligibility lacking in the individual segments. As one would expect, some episodes are stronger than others. There are repetitive plot lines, clichéd resolutions, a few epilogues that fall flat. For the most part, however, weak episodes are few and far between, an achievement all the more notable given that the series lasted considerably longer than other comparably excellent sitcoms. *I Love Lucy* ran for 194 episodes; *The Dick Van Dyke Show* for 158; *All in the Family* for 208. If we add to TAGS the pilot episode, the 78 episodes of its sequel, *Mayberry R.F.D.* (1968–1970), and the 1986 reunion movie, the Mayberry Chronicles encompass no less than 329 installments, a linked series of self-contained narrative units spread out over three decades.

The quality of TAGS is partly a product of the way the show was filmed. Desi Arnaz's technical innovation in *I Love Lucy*, TAGS's precursor on Monday nights on CBS, was to film before a live audience using three cameras that recorded the action simultaneously. The multiple-camera technique, which was adopted by other sitcoms—*The Danny Thomas Show*, *The Dick Van Dyke Show*, *The Mary Tyler Moore Show*, *All in the Family*—remains a dominant shooting style for the genre. Its advocates cite the advantage of capturing an audience's spontaneous reaction rather than having to resort to canned laughter (though, truth to tell, the live audience's response is often "sweetened" or "unsweetened" mechanically). But what is gained in spontaneity is sometimes lost in precision. As fine as *I Love Lucy* is, at times the timing of the actors is a little off or someone flubs his or her lines. If significant enough, these slips can always be edited out or the scene can be reshot later. What filming before a live audience does not allow, however, is the use of more than two or three basic sets, and it all but eliminates exterior scenes. Almost everything in *I Love Lucy* takes place either in the Ricardos' apartment or in Ricky's nightclub. In *The Mary Tyler Moore Show*, the vast majority of scenes are set in the newsroom.

Preferring a more controlled and at the same time a more flexible filming environment, Griffith and Aaron Ruben decided to shoot the show the way a motion picture is filmed, with a single camera, the setup used by *The Adventures of Ozzie and Harriet* and *Leave It to Beaver*. If someone misspoke a line, the scene would be reshot. If some particular piece of business didn't work, it would be tinkered with until it did. Exteriors, crucial in creating the sense of place, posed no problem. The artful use of the "laff box," which had been invented a few years earlier, cued the viewers to the interpretation of a line or a situation, making it unnecessary for actors to play to an audience. (In the early episodes of TAGS, the laugh track is sometimes overdone, perhaps because the producers were not sure that the audience would "get" the show's downhome humor, but by the middle of the first season the canned laughter had become much less obtrusive.) It is enough to watch the pilot, filmed before a live audience for *The Danny Thomas Show*, to realize that the single-camera shooting style is more congruent with the nature of TAGS. In the pilot, when Danny blows his top and goes off on one of his insult-filled tirades, he looks to the audience for approval. When Opie delivers a funny line, Andy turns to the audience and laughs along.

I recall only one occasion, early in the series, when a TAGS character looked straight into the camera and addressed the viewer.[1] Mayberrians lead their lives oblivious to the fact that we are looking in. In other dramatic situations, as well as in other situation comedies, "breaking the fourth wall" can be used to good effect, but here it would undermine one of the defining features of Mayberry: its standing as a world apart.

Most of the episodes in TAGS fall into one of two categories: the domestic and the exotic. Domestic episodes involve an intramural disturbance caused by a dispute or misunderstanding among the town's inhabitants. The exotic episodes center on the arrival of someone the townsfolk regard as an outsider, an exotic (from the Greek *exos*, outside). The core domestic plotlines exploit Andy and Opie's relationship, but since in TAGS the *domus* is the town itself, the rubric also includes episodes about the town's life beyond the Taylor household. Sometimes these episodes set Barney against another character, as in "Hot Rod Otis" (4.19), which has Barney hounding Otis, or "Citizen's Arrest" (4.11), a very funny show during which Barney and Gomer almost come to blows. At other times, domestic plots involve difficulties between Mayberrians, as in "A Feud Is a Feud" (1.9), about an eighty-year-old feud between two families of farmers, the Carters and the Wakefields; "The Haunted House" (4.2), about "ghosts" who turn out to be Otis and a moonshiner; or "Only a Rose" (7.12), about Aunt Bee and Clara's competitiveness. Other episodes in this genre narrate the mild romantic entanglements of Andy, Barney, Gomer, Goober, and Howard. Still others grow out of the restlessness that occasionally seizes Mayberrians, and primarily Aunt Bee, who suffers from a recurrent itch that induces her to learn to drive, fly an airplane, open a restaurant, host a cooking show, vacation in Mexico, run for the Town Council, and field (or invent) offers of marriage. But she's not the only restless soul: Gomer trades Wally's Service for the Marine Corps, Howard starts a new life on a Caribbean island, and Barney takes a job in the police department in Raleigh. Even Goober aspires to own his own gas station (and eventually does), and Floyd considers buying a two-chair shop in Mt. Pilot (but backs out at the last minute).

Since TAGS teaches that it's better to stay put, Mayberrians who stray typically come to regret it. Jim Lindsey, a guitar player, joins Bobby Fleet's Band with a Beat. He comes back some months later driving a shiny red convertible. It seems that he's made it big, but in fact he quit the band and he's broke, and Andy's good offices are required for Bobby Fleet to take him back. Barney goes off to Raleigh to work in the police department. When Andy visits, Barney is on the verge of getting fired, but once again Andy saves the day. Episodes during which an ordinary citizen takes on law enforcement duties convey the same message. At one time or another, Gomer, Goober, Floyd, Otis, and Howard are all "deputized," with predictably disastrous results. When Goober fills in for a sick Andy, he gives out fourteen traffic tickets in one day. Similarly dire outcomes, all of which arise from the lack of fit between the person and the job, occur when Barney subs for Andy or when Aunt Bee runs for the Town Council. Goober is not a deputy, he's a grease monkey; Barney's not a sheriff, he's a deputy; and for all of her role restlessness, Aunt Bee is most like herself when she's in the kitchen gossiping on the phone with Clara.

In "Class Reunion" (3.19), Andy and Barney discover that only nine out of the thirty-five students in the class of 1945 still reside in the town—a surprising exodus for a community in which sedentariness is next to godliness. At the reunion Andy meets up with his high school sweetheart, Sharon DeSpain, who lives in Chicago. According to Barney, Andy and Sharon's courtship was "one of the great natural romances of all time." Andy and Sharon go for a stroll in the garden and the flame is rekindled. They embrace and kiss—the one tender kiss that Andy ever gives any woman, including Helen. But when Andy asks Sharon to come back to Mayberry, she demurs: "In a big city you have room to grow, to expand. You live a different kind of life. I like trying to be a big fish in a big pond, not a big fish in a little pond." Andy doesn't understand her reasoning because he's happy where he is. "How do you know?" she asks him. "You've never tried anything else." His reply summarizes Mayberrian philosophy: "I don't have to. Even if I did try I'd find out I already found it." Sharon knows that you can't go home again, as another resident of the North State put it. Andy knows that what you *can* do is not leave.

If domestic plotlines center on Mayberrians, exotic episodes—about a third of the total—revolve around intruders. This category includes the city slickers, hobos, crooks, con artists, and convicts who come upon Mayberry, as well as the state or federal agents who look down upon Andy's police methods—all of them people who, from the townsfolk's point of view, are also exotic in the usual sense: alien, unfamiliar, not only strangers but strange. (Of course, TAGS derives much of its humor from the fact that, for the majority of viewers, it is the townsfolk who are strange.) These newcomers, who show up in Mayberry far more often than they would in a real town in the Piedmont, are almost always unwelcome. The show's inaugural episode, "The New Housekeeper," sets the pattern. Since Opie doesn't want Rose, their housekeeper, to leave, he tries to disrupt her wedding ceremony by refusing to hold his peace. But Rose does leave, and Aunt Bee arrives. For Opie, who has never met his father's aunt, Aunt Bee is an outsider. He pointedly excludes her from his nightly prayers, which mention nearly everyone he knows: Rose; his father; Barney; his friends; and, not least, his dog, Gulliver, his lizard, Oscar, and his bird, Dickie. Opie's hostility is typical of the townsfolk's attitude toward outsiders, the basis of many subsequent episodes. What sets this episode apart is that in the end Opie accepts Aunt Bee into the *domus,* an outcome made possible only because Aunt

Bee wasn't a newcomer to begin with, since she had raised Andy in Mayberry. Thus, the title of the episode is something of a misnomer. Aunt Bee is not "the new housekeeper" but the old housekeeper who has returned to care for Opie as she had cared for his father.

With a few exceptions, like Aunt Bee and Helen, a Mayberrian is someone who was born in Mayberry. Homeplace is birthplace. Unlike "The New House-keeper," most of the episodes that begin with the arrival of a newcomer end with a scene not of community enhancement by inclusion but of community restoration by exclusion. Since the strangers typically aim to cheat the locals, they are to be feared. In Barney's parlance, they are "beasts of prey" that come out of the "wilderness" (3.7). The one time when the townspeople seek out an outsider (to serve as "guest of honor" in the Founder's Day celebrations), the guest is a pickpocket who thinks he has "stumbled into Shangri-La" and almost robs them blind (2.21). After the exotic's scheme is revealed, he (more rarely, she) is forced to get out of town. Etymologically a villain is a villager — in Spanish, a *villano*, which can mean either villain or villager; but in Mayberry the villains are not the villagers. When Barney, in the epigraph to this chapter, sets the boundary of his human concern at the edge of acquaintance, he reflects the town's deep-seated but harmless xenophobia. The fundamental message of TAGS is not that small is better than big, that slow is better than fast, that simple is better than complicated, but that like is better than unlike.

The character of Howard Sprague illustrates the extent to which Mayberry prizes sameness. It is highly improbable that Howard, the longtime county clerk, has not had regular dealings with Andy, as the mayor and the Town Council do. Yet when he first appears, at the end of the sixth season, he and Andy haven't seen each other in years, a lack of contact all the more puzzling given that they went to high school together. It would have been more credible to make Howard a newcomer who has just taken the position of county clerk, which would then explain his difficulties in being accepted into the town's inner circle. But the requirement of nativeness trumps verisimilitude. Similarly, the same thing happens with Emmett Clark, the fix-it man. The reason he hasn't been seen before the eighth season is that he has been working out of his house (and apparently never leaving it). Griffith and the producers preferred to strain credibility rather than violate the prohibition against outsiders.

Underlying this prohibition is the town's aversion to change. Outsiders are suspect not only because they are dishonest, but because they undermine the status quo. A stranger arrives, tries but fails to disturb the peace, and departs — and nothing has changed. The typical episode ends where it began: the same characters, in the same place, doing whatever they were doing before the disturbance occurred: the Taylors relaxing on their front porch, Floyd and the boys shooting the breeze in the barbershop, or Andy and Barney tidying up the courthouse. This is why the epilogues, which are often deleted in the syndication packages, are indispensable. Without these brief closing scenes, the denouements do not change—by then the trouble, whether domestic or exotic in origin, has been quelled—but their place in the show's overall vision does.[2] In "Mayberry Goes Hollywood," after the Hollywood producer has left, Barney accidentally locks himself in jail, as he is wont to do. Andy speaks the closing lines: "Yes, sir, everything's back to normal in Mayberry. Barney just locked himself in jail" (1.13).

In the first episode, Opie's bird, Dickie, which Aunt Bee inadvertently allowed to escape, mysteriously returns home. Opie runs out onto the porch screaming, "Paw! Paw! It's Dickie! He's come back. Flew into the cage all by himself." That's the way things go in Mayberry. By the end of each episode, everyone, including pets, has returned to his or her place in the Golden Cage. This circular structure expresses in narrative what Mayberry's isolation expresses in spatial terms—anxiety about the effect of incursions from the outside. It's difficult not to notice that behind the humor of these episodes, including the often hilarious tags, lurks an intuition of danger, the apprehension that one day everything will not go "back to normal." Whether by his shady dealings or by his advocacy of change, every out-of-towner represents a threat to the established order. Week after week, Mayberry is being pounded, its way of life under assault. Barney is more right than he realizes when he says: "You know, Andy, I never thought that our town would come to this. Mayberry—Gateway to Danger" (1.30).

One location in particular symbolizes the ever-present character of the danger: the bus stop, where Mayberry meets the outside world. As a crossroads, a place of passage, the bus stop is not inside Mayberry in the same sense as Floyd's barbershop or Weaver's department store. Situated in the middle of town, kitty-corner from the courthouse, it's an emblem of the fragility of Mayberrian sedentariness. Bus stop scenes, no matter how brief, always unfold in an atmosphere of uncertainty, for they remind us that Mayberry's hermeticism is perpetually on the verge of fracture. The members of Andy and Barney's senior class who chose to migrate did so by hopping on the bus. The last we see of the Taylors before they go off for a vacation in Hollywood is when they say good-bye to their friends at the bus stop. The question: will Hollywood change them as Chicago changed Sharon DeSpain? When they come back from California, three episodes later, the repetition of the same scene as they get off the bus indicates that nothing has changed.

The second of Mayberry's mayors, Mayor Stoner, wants to construct an underpass to connect Mayberry to the outside world, a plot idea probably inspired by the building of the Interstate Highway System in the 1950s. According to Stoner, the detonations to clear the way for the underpass are "the sound of progress" (3.18). But the underpass is the bus stop writ large, which is why Andy and the others object to it. In 1986 Griffith explained: "People come from small towns. They can't go home because the interstate has wrecked it. But they can come home with us. On our show, we never let the highway through."[3] Years earlier, one of the Southern Agrarians, Andrew Lytle, expressed similar sentiments: "The good-roads programs drive like a flying wedge and split the heart of this provincialism — which prefers religion to science, handcrafts to technology, the inertia of fields to the acceleration of industry, and leisure to nervous prostration."[4] Mayberrians share Griffith and Lytle's refusal of America's romance with the automobile, especially passionate in the decades following World War II. Andy doesn't own a car. Otis sells his right after he has purchased it. Barney owns a car briefly, a lemon foisted on him by a gang of swindlers. When he gets his money back and the opportunity arises to own another car, he passes it up. Cars encourage and enable mobility, as in Dinah Shore's popular jingle from the 1950s, "See the U.S.A. in Your Chevrolet." Mayberrian society tends toward immobility, horizontally as well as vertically: the townspeople don't move up, down, or away.

Sedentariness is so ingrained in their psyche that it extends to displacements within the town itself. To make extra money, Barney decides to become a realtor and negotiates a complicated sequence of transactions: the Clarks will sell their house and buy the Mortensens', who will in turn buy the Simses' house so that the Simses can buy Andy's house and Andy can purchase the Williamses' (5.16). But in the end no one buys or sells anything. Mayberrians don't like to move, whether the displacement entails a trip out of town or a switch in residences. In Spanish, to move from one house to another is *mudarse*, literally, to mutate. Barney's plan to have homeowners trade houses with one another is called *permutar*, to permutate. Mayberrians shun mutations and permutations. Even if it's true, as Barney claims, that "everybody wants to sell their house," the townsfolk are willing to sell their houses only if they don't have to move as a result.

As a reformer, a progressive, hardheaded Stoner repeatedly tries to bring change to Mayberry. His predecessor, Mayor Pike, a plump little man dressed in a jacket and Kentucky Colonel string tie, bumbled his way through two years in office without making waves. He was a traditionalist. But his successor, who takes over in the third season, intends to "change the face" of the town (3.3). He demands that Andy carry a gun. He is outraged when Andy arrives late for a meeting because he and Opie have gone fishing. He is equally incensed at the informal way Andy treats his prisoners, releasing them before they have served their sentences. He is even more shocked when he finds Barney using the jail to babysit. Worst of all, he wants to put a No Parking sign on Willow Lane near Duck Pond, where Barney takes his dates. As Stoner says apropos of his plan for the underpass: "I am trying to make something out of Mayberry. Why, with that underpass we could be a real metropolis" (3.18). If he had had his way, Mayberry would have become a suburb like those that ring North Carolina cities like Raleigh and Charlotte. An outsider within, Mayor Stoner did not last the season; after he left, he was not replaced.

The suburban world of 1960s sitcoms is not constantly under threat from outsiders. No mysterious strangers, flimflam artists, or escaped convicts move in on the residents of Springdale or Mayfield. Not so with Mayberry, a world apparently secure in its foundations, yet one whose foundations are beginning to crack. In contrast to other 1960s sitcoms, *TAGS* is not "a comedy of reassurance."[5] At the end of each episode the outsiders have been rebuffed, as we know that they will be, but we also know that in a week's time Mayberry may have to fend off another assault. It may seem odd that a little town in the foothills of North Carolina is more vulnerable to intruders than the easily accessed suburbs of Middle America. But what Mayberry has to resist—the vertically and horizontally mobile lifestyle of the suburbs—is far more powerful than crooks and con men.

A special kind of challenge to Mayberrian sedentariness occurs when the out-of-towner is not a criminal but a drifter. Often the drifters also turn out to be criminals, like the Gypsies who camp out in the woods, but sometimes the drifter is only a drifter, which means that he is all the more threatening because his life consists of continual displacement. If sedentariness is next to godliness, drifters are the devil's disciples. In other fictional contexts—think *High Plains Drifter*, think *Easy Rider*, think the 1960s TV series *The Fugitive*—itinerancy is a positive value, or at least a condition of survival, but Mayberry upholds a different ethos: not that of the simple genuine self against the whole world (as Emerson said), as embodied in the Wild West hero or the rebel with or without a cause, but that of the sociable and socially obligated individual—the deputy, the barber, the gas jockey, the town drunk. It has been said that *The Fugitive*, which ran contemporaneously with *TAGS* (from 1963 to 1968), explores "the loneliness at the core of the American heart."[6] If so, Mayberry gives us the prescription to cure, or at least alleviate, the malady: stay in your place.

In "Opie's Hobo Friend" (2.6), Buddy Ebsen (soon to star as Jed Clampett in *The Beverly Hillbillies*) plays the part of Dave Browne, a hobo who befriends Opie. Well spoken and educated, Browne is not your run-of-the-mill bum. He is not at all like the hobo who, two seasons later, uses the Robin Hood story to persuade Opie and his friends to steal from "the rich" (the citizens of Mayberry) to give to "the poor" (himself) (4.12). Browne is not above pinching a pie or stealing a chicken, but in other ways he is not that different from the townsfolk. He meets Andy and Opie on the way to Myers Lake, where he is also going to spend the day fishing. "Mr. Dave" becomes Opie's fishing buddy, taking Andy's place. According to Opie, "hoboing seems like a lot more fun than sheriffing." When his son skips school to go fishing, Andy realizes that it's time to intervene.

At the freight yard—another place of passage—Andy and Mr. Dave, the father and the false father, face off. Andy takes a seat on an empty box and tells Mr. Dave that he doesn't want him spending time with Opie. Mr. Dave counters that Andy should let Opie decide.

> *Andy*: No, I'm afraid it don't work that way. You can't let a young'un decide for himself. He'll grab at the first flashy thing with shiny ribbons on it. And when he finds out there's a hook in it, it's too late. Wrong ideas come packaged with so much glitter it's hard to convince them other things might be better in the long run. All a parent can do is say, wait, trust me. And try to keep temptation away.
>
> *Mr. Dave*: That means you're inviting me to leave.
>
> *Andy*: That's right.
>
> *Mr. Dave*: Well, you're wearing the badge, so I'll leave. That wasn't so difficult. Your problem's solved.
>
> *Andy*: That's where you're wrong. That boy thinks just about everything you do is perfect. So my problem is just beginning. You left behind an awful lot of unscrambling to be done.

From Andy's perspective, Browne is one of those glittering packages of wrong ideas, the shiny lure with the hidden hook, like the magical "gollywobbler" that Browne uses to catch fish. In the next scene, Barney arrests Mr. Dave for snatching Aunt Bee's purse. When Opie sees Mr. Dave being put in jail, he changes his mind about hoboing. Since Aunt Bee had thrown the purse in the trash days ago, Mr. Dave set himself up to be caught, as Andy realizes. Mr. Dave is a drifter who understands that drifting sets a bad example for young'uns, and so he lets Opie off the hook, even if it costs him Opie's regard. As one of several father figures that come through Mayberry, Mr. Dave initially offers an alternative to Andy, a competing role model, but in the end he becomes Andy's accomplice rather than his competitor. Since Andy is also not above bending the law now and then, he releases Mr. Dave from the jail so that he can hitch a ride on the train that stops for water in the afternoon.

The first time that Barney arrests Mr. Dave, he books him on a "vag" charge. Vagrancy, literally, is wandering, drifting. This is Browne's real crime. It's fine to spend a week at the Raleigh YMCA, as Barney does on his vacations, but it's another thing not to have a fixed address, a homeplace. Mayberrians take pride in being fixtures, to us not less than to one another. Routine rules: the same characters, in the same places, doing the same things, week after week— Floyd at the barbershop, Gomer or Goober at Wally's Service, Howard at the county clerk's office, Sarah at the switchboard, Juanita at the diner. The antithesis of the nonplaces that, according to Marc Augé, proliferate in advanced societies—the malls, the airports, the rest stops on the interstate—Mayberry scorns transients. For the town's residents, the urge to wander is dromomania, the affliction of drifters. To *dromos*, Greek for wandering, the Mayberrians oppose *domus*, Latin for house.

The other thing wrong with hobos is that they don't seem to have a past. Interested only in staying clothed and fed, Mr. Dave lives for the moment. He says nothing about where he comes from, where his travels have taken him, how he decided upon a life of hoboing. At the opening of *Silas Marner*, George Eliot's narrator explains the attitude of country folk toward "wandering men," one of whom will be the novel's protagonist: "No one knew where wandering men had their homes or their origin; and how was a man to be explained unless you at least knew somebody who knew his father and mother?" Mayberrians, like George Eliot's peasants, are people to whom "the world outside their own direct experience was a region of vagueness and mystery: to their untravelled thought a state of wandering was a conception as dim as the winter life of the swallows that came back with the spring."[7] No matter how articulate and well intentioned, wandering men like Mr. Dave must be expelled.

This is the tragedy of Malcolm Merriweather, Mayberry's Marner, who tries to make a home in the town. An Englishman on an extended biking tour of America—another form of drifting—Malcolm visits the Friendly Town three times over the span of four television seasons (3.26, 4.28, 6.3). Unlike Mr. Dave, Malcolm is the straightest of arrows, yet he's not any more compatible with the town's ways. His introduction is a harbinger of things to come: bicycling on the wrong side of the road, he crashes into Fletch Roberts's truck, causing forty dollars' worth of damage. Since Malcolm doesn't have the money for the repairs and Aunt Bee is away visiting her sister, Andy hires him as a temporary helper so that Malcolm can pay off the debt. But it is not long before Malcolm's obsequiousness—he used to be a "gentleman's gentleman" in the old country—gets on Andy's nerves. When Malcolm overhears Andy complaining to Barney, he realizes that he has to leave, though not before Andy apologizes and assures Malcolm that he is welcome any time he wants to return.

Upon his return, however, he runs afoul of Aunt Bee. Once again Andy hires him, this time to help him defray the expenses of his travels. Soon Malcolm has taken over all of Aunt Bee's duties. He cooks, cleans, accompanies Opie to birthday parties. Feeling useless, Aunt Bee takes to bed, refusing even to attend Sunday "preaching." When Malcolm realizes what he has done, he pretends to get drunk so that Andy fires him. The last time Malcolm shows up, two years later, he says that after getting to know America, he is convinced that there's no friendlier place than Mayberry, which reminds him of the small town in Derbyshire where he was born. This time, he has come to stay. But this visit is even more star-crossed than the previous ones, since he raises the ire of Ernest T. Bass, Malcolm's rival for the job of school-crossing guard, a confrontation that culminates in a boxing match. The last time we see Malcolm, he is hurrying out of the courthouse to avoid getting beat up by Ernest T., but the wild man from the mountains is not the reason Malcolm leaves. Malcolm's run-ins with Fletch, Andy, Aunt Bee, and Ernest T.—a cross section of Mayberrian society—signal an impediment less correctible than customs or driving habits. There is no path to citizenship in Mayberry. Malcolm can become an American, as tens of millions of immigrants have done, but he cannot become a Mayberrian. Unlike Lady Liberty, Lady Mayberry doesn't welcome huddled masses. She gives British settlers her blessing to live in the "Happy Valley" without anticipating that other settlers will follow (5.11). The problem with outsiders is that they bring the outside with them. Were Malcolm to shed his accent, unlearn his manners, and lose his memories of Heckmondwike, his hometown, *then* he could become a Mayberrian. But for that to happen he would have to be born again—in Mayberry. That he shares a last name with the town's founder, James Merriweather, only makes his predicament all the more poignant.

In "The Horse Trader" (1.14), the Town Council is considering replacing the rusty old cannon that sits in the town square with a plaque that Milford Phillips, a well-to-do ex-Mayberrian, is planning to donate. Barney can't understand why anyone would want to get rid of one of the town's landmarks. He's used to seeing it there.

> *Andy*: You don't like change, do you?
> *Barney*: As a matter of fact, I don't.
> *Andy*: Little bit conservative there, are you?
> *Barney*: Well, what's the matter with that?
> *Andy*: Oh, nothing. I just noticed that you like things to stay the same.
> *Barney*: Lots of people are like that. I just happen to be one of them,
> that's all. I like things to stay the way they are. And if something
> happens to change it, well, it upsets me.

Even though Barney sometimes upbraids Andy for his reluctance to get with the times, he is no Mayor Stoner. At heart he is no more an advocate of change than his neighbors. He even objects to stamp machines in the post office. Eager to acquire the plaque, the Town Council outvotes Barney and sells the cannon to an antique dealer. But the antique dealer sells it to Mr. Phillips, who thinks that the cannon makes a much better gift than the plaque. And so by a circuitous route the cannon ends up where it started, in the town square: order disrupted, order restored. As Andy might say, everything's back to normal in Mayberry.

In the seventeenth and eighteenth centuries, tradition-bound Spaniards used to ridicule reformers with the proverb, "Novedad, no verdad" (If it's new, it's not true). This idea was codified in one of the earliest dictionaries of the Spanish language, Sebastián de Covarrubias's *Tesoro de la lengua castellana* (1611), where the word "novelty" is defined as "a dangerous thing for bringing with it a change in old customs" (*novedad: cosa peligrosa por traer consigo mu-danza de uso antiguo*). Though continents and centuries apart, Mayberrians en-dorse this view, even if modern dictionaries classify it differently, as a disease: kainotophobia, the irrational fear of change. The larger point is that the town's phobias—fear of change, fear of outsiders—are the necessary complement to the town's *philia*. The ties that bind Mayberrians together require that they resemble one another. An infusion of strangers—whether immigrants, exiles, tourists, or mere out-of-towners—would change the face of the town, as Mayor Stoner intended but failed to do. The day that Floyd steps out of his barber-shop and sees unfamiliar faces milling about on Main Street, Mayberry will be no more.

CHAPTER THREE

Stopping the Story

*T*AGS IS OFTEN PRAISED FOR THE WHOLESOME MES-
sages in the plots; but it's not always the plots that make episodes memorable; it's also what happens before and after and in the middle of
them. Without intending to, Aunt Bee alludes to this aspect of the show when
she says that the barbershop, "an institution," is "the center of the town's activities" (7.22). It would be truer to say that the barbershop is an institution
because it's the center of the town's *in*activity, or that the town's main activities are forms of inactivity. A barber who turns away customers who interrupt
a conversation, Floyd is less interested in making a living than in shooting the
breeze with the "boys," who are equally addicted to, and adept at, idle chatter.
Griffith labeled these scenes where nothing happens "porch comedy," "where
you meet with neighbors and just chuckle a bit."[1] When these scenes occur at
the beginning of an episode, they ease the viewer's transition into the peculiar
Neverland that is Mayberry. At the end, they reaffirm the status quo. But wherever they occur, they capture better than any hijinks the feeling of everyday life
in Mayberry.

In the barbershop, the boys are grousing about the hustle and bustle of modern life. Spaceships are circling the earth; jets are flying from coast to coast in
a few hours. Mayor Pike, ever the traditionalist, speaks fondly of the good old
days of covered wagons, when people who crossed the country could appreci-
ate where they were going. Sam, the owner of the hardware store, sums up the
assembly's consensus when he asks, "What happened to the fine art of settin',
just settin' and starin'?" (2.16). Of course, that's exactly what the boys are doing,
settin' and starin'. Of all the regulars, perhaps only Barney would ask, like one
of Sherwood Anderson's characters, "Why doesn't something happen?"[2] And
even Barney's thirst for excitement, as we have seen, hinges on the condition
that its source has to be a stranger. In Mayberry, life is what happens when

nothing is happening. There are no black swans in Myers Lake. There are no monsters among the townsfolk. There aren't even any skeletons in the closets, as Barney finds out when he gets lost in a supposedly haunted house. The plots of the episodes don't portray town life as much as they interrupt it.

Other than fishing, which also involves a great deal of settin' and starin', the emblematic example of active inactivity is whittling, another favorite pastime of the locals. Andy whittles, as does Opie, as do old-timers like Judd and Jubal, who sit in front of the courthouse shaving sticks of wood with a penknife. Andy comes upon an old man who is whittling. After complimenting him on his craft, Andy says, "Tell you what. When you're finished tell me what it is and I'll give you fifty cents for it" (3.21). Like the conversations in the barbershop, whittling is not goal-directed; it's a way of passing time, lollygagging. What working is to other towns, whittling is to Mayberry.

In "Prisoner of Love" (4.18), one of the episodes with an exotic plotline, the out-of-towner is female. Harvey Bullock's script calls for her to be "breathtakingly beautiful." Susan Oliver, in the part of a jewel thief who spends the night in the Mayberry jail, doesn't disappoint. A stunning blonde who wears a form-fitting tailored dress and a string of pearls, she fits Bullock's description of her character as "soft, beguiling, feminine."[3] Her overnight at the courthouse sets up the only risqué moment in all of TAGS. As Andy and Barney watch, the curvy criminal begins to undress in a darkened courthouse, silhouetted behind the bedsheet that has been hung in front of her cell. Earle Hagen's underscoring, which evokes the famous torch song that the episode's title puns on, heightens the seductiveness of the scene. Reluctant voyeurs, Andy and Barney can't help watching. But unlike the speaker in the song, figuratively shackled

"Tell me what it is and I'll give you fifty cents for it."

A risqué moment in the courthouse.

by the woman he loves, the sheriff escapes the chains that bind him. At the last minute he catches the jewel thief as she is about to escape from under Barney's distracted eyes.

Before the prisoner shows up, in the opening scene, Barney and Andy are sitting on two chairs outside the courthouse. The back of each chair is tilted against the wall. Barney has his cap pulled over his eyes. After a few moments, he pulls his cap up.

> *Barney*: You know what I just might do tonight?
>
> *Andy*: What?
>
> *Barney*: Go home. Change. Drop by Thelma Lou's. Watch that George Raft movie on the TV.
>
> *Andy*: Good.
>
> *Barney*: Yes sir, that's just what I might do. Go home. Change. Drop by Thelma Lou's. Watch the George Raft movie on the TV.
>
> *Andy*: I might drop over at the choir meeting. They're voting on the new robes for next year.
>
> *Barney*: They're gonna change them, are they?
>
> *Andy*: Yeah. Sissy Noonan wants all black with white collars. Fred Henry he wants white with black collars. I reckon they'll be fighting about it all night.
>
> *Barney*: That's where you're gonna go then, choir meeting?
>
> *Andy*: I might.

Barney: Not me. You know what I'm gonna do?
Andy: Go home. Change. Over to Thelma Lou's. Watch that George Raft movie on TV.
Barney: Yeah.

At this point the phone rings. Sergeant Jacobs calls to say that he needs to "park" a jewel thief in Mayberry while the state police look for her accomplice. In the script, the scene heading for Andy and Barney's conversation is as follows: "It is seven p.m., the beginning of another highly uneventful evening in Mayberry. The town is hushed and darkened."[4] The key words are "highly uneventful," a paradoxical turn of phrase in that it names a fullness of nothing. But this is what everyday life is like in Mayberry, fertile in its lack of incident, abundantly devoid of novelty. Hagen, who did all the scoring for the show, mentions that TAGS required more music than other sitcoms because of the "long places of time" in the episodes.[5] These interludes reflect not only the relaxed pace of life, but the many occasions when the pace slows to a standstill.

In Andy and Barney's conversation, Barney's plans for the evening are stated three times, twice by him and then again by Andy—an indication that uneventfulness arises from iteration, the nemesis of change, even when the change is something as inconsequential as the color of the choir robes. Iteration is everywhere in TAGS: in the circular plots, the repetitive plot lines, the echoing subplots, the obsession with local history, the repeated tunes, the unchanging attire of the characters. It is not only Andy and Barney whose dress is "uniform." Floyd has his barber's smock, Howard his bow tie, Aunt Bee her dowdy dresses, Opie his striped T-shirts, Goober his hitched-up pants and jughead hat. On the job, Andy is always going through papers on his desk, walking over to the file cabinet to retrieve or replace a folder, or preparing mysterious "reports" for the state police. This is the simulacrum of activity, a nod toward the Puritan work ethic. But Mayberry counters the Puritan ethic with Southern comfort. The less busy they are, the more the town's residents are like themselves. In a well-known passage of "History of the Dividing Line" (1728), a history of the border between North Carolina and Virginia, William Byrd II writes: "Surely there is no place in the World where the Inhabitants live with less Labour than in North Carolina. It approaches nearer to the Description of Lubberland than any other, by the great felicity of the Climate, the easiness of raising Provisions, and the Slothfulness of the People."[6] The capital of Lubberland is Mayberry.

The conversation between Andy and Barney in "Prisoner of Love" is itself repeated, with slight variations, several times. In one of his last appearances before moving on to bigger and darker things in Raleigh, Barney and Andy are sitting on the porch dressed in their Sunday best: Andy with a coat and tie, Barney in his salt and pepper suit. Andy is reading the comics and Barney is slumped

back in a wicker chair. He catches a fly that is buzzing around and releases it—
"well, it's Sunday." After wondering what he is going to get Thelma Lou for her
birthday, he asks Andy whether he wants a bottle of pop. Andy declines.

> *Barney*: Well, I do. You know what I think I'll do?
>
> *Andy*: What?
>
> *Barney*: I think I'll go down to the filling station. Get me a bottle of pop.
> Go home. Take a nap. And go over to Thelma Lou's and watch some
> TV.
>
> (Andy nods.)
>
> *Barney*: Yeah, that's what I'm gonna do. Go down to the filling station.
> Get me a bottle of pop. Home. Take a nap. Then go over to Thelma
> Lou's and watch a little TV. You sure you don't feel like a bottle of
> pop?
>
> *Andy*: No.
>
> *Barney*: Well, I do. Yes, that's what I'm going to do. Go down to the
> filling station. Get me a bottle of pop. Home. Take a nap. Then over
> to Thelma Lou's.
>
> *Andy*: Watch a little TV?
>
> *Barney*: Yeah. (5.29)

According to Don Knotts, these scenes sprang from memories of his small-
town upbringing, when people would sit around after dinner without saying
very much.[7] As he explains, at first the producers and directors were reluctant
to include dialogue that did nothing to advance the action:

> Of course, in the beginning they didn't write that into the scripts. In
> the beginning the feeling was that, as in all television shows, the story
> should go from point A to point Z, plot all the way. During the read-
> ings I would sit in with Aaron, Bob Sweeney [the director], Andy, and
> usually Sheldon and we would pick the script apart. Andy would begin
> to tell how people talked back home. We got a little static at first be-
> cause they'd say, "We can't stop the story," but the more we did it, the
> more they liked it. Soon they began to write it into the scripts, and that
> turned out to be one of the things in the show that people identified
> with the most.[8]

These do-nothing scenes—which were written also for Andy and Floyd
or Andy and Goober—not only stop the story; they exaggerate the delay by
the glacial rhythm of the conversation. Griffith and Knotts sometimes remain
silent for several seconds between utterances, as if they had all day rather than

twenty-five minutes to transact the episode's comedic business. These utterly nonsuspenseful, nonpregnant pauses embody uneventful duration in its purest state, an effect exclusive to cinematic fiction or theater. In a novel (or a script), the author can tell the reader that nothing is happening, but the sentence that says that nothing is happening—a linguistic event—belies the assertion. Even if the text includes blank pages, as some experimental novels have done, the gap encourages readers to supply what is missing. Rather than a void, it is a blank waiting to be filled in. Not so with the silences that prolong the scenes that stop the story.

It's not surprising that viewers of *TAGS* take to these moments because, in a broader sense, stopping the story is what Mayberry is all about. In the pilot, Danny Williams (Danny Thomas) runs a stop sign as he is driving back to New York City from Florida. Andy gives him a ticket. A confrontation ensues between the drawling southerner and the fast-talking, cigar-wielding, finger-pointing northerner. Danny complains that there is no road by the stop sign. Andy says, "Well, now, the Town Council did vote to put a road in there, about six years ago I believe it was. Only trouble is, so far we've just raised enough money for the stop sign." The stop sign signals what the show as a whole intends. *TAGS* says "Stop." That the sign stands where there is no intersection is no more relevant than the end product of whittling. Like Andy and Barney's pointless conversations, stopping is an end in itself. This is why the front porch of Andy's house is such an important location. When Andy, Aunt Bee, and Opie sit on the front porch, humming a hymn or making small talk, life comes to a stop, as it does when the boys in the barbershop spend their time sitting and staring.

No episode better illustrates the whittling ideal, the injunction not to speed through the stop signs of life, than "Man in a Hurry" (3.16), a *TAGS* classic written by Everett Greenbaum and Jim Fritzell that, according to Aaron Ruben, "symbolizes what the show was about and why it endures."[9] In the opening scene, a heavy-set middle-aged man in a dark suit is sitting in his stalled late-model Lincoln Continental. He gets out of the car and walks into a deserted town. It's Sunday, and the townspeople are attending services at All Souls Church. The stranger, Malcolm Tucker, owner of Tucker Enterprises, meets Andy outside the church. He has an important business appointment in Charlotte on Monday and needs to have his car fixed. Andy drives him over to Wally's Filling Station, where Gomer is minding the store, but Gomer's not a mechanic. Andy takes Mr. Tucker over to Wally, the owner of the gas station, who is sitting on his porch reading the funny papers. Wally diagnoses the problem as a clogged fuel line and says that he'd be happy to take care of it—on Monday. Tucker gets more and more frustrated. But as Andy tells him, "It's nigh impossible to get anything done here on Sunday."

When Tucker makes a phone call, he finds that the line is busy. On Sunday afternoon the Mendelbright sisters, Maude of Mayberry and Cora of Mt. Pilot, visit by phone for several hours to talk about their various ailments. Tucker can't conceal his exasperation: "You people are living in another world! This is the twentieth century, don't you realize that? The whole world is living in a desperate space age. Men are orbiting the earth. International television has been developed. And here a whole town is standing still because two old women's feet fall asleep!" To calm him down, the Taylors invite him to sup-per—fried chicken, corn on the cob, biscuits—but Mr. Tucker, still trying to get the Mendelbright sisters to end their conversation, refuses the offer. After dinner, on the porch, Barney launches into his usual routine about his plans for the evening: "Go home, have a nap, go over to Thelma Lou's for a little TV." All the while Mr. Tucker is pacing up and down, impatiently puffing on a cigar. As Andy strums his guitar, he and Barney sing "Church in the Wildwood," a nostalgic hymn that extols the simpler life of a bygone time: "No place is so dear to my childhood than the little brown church in the vale." For a moment Mr. Tucker gets caught up in the spirit of the hymn and hums a few bars. His faraway look and faint smile suggest that he is recalling a time when *his* life was simpler. Tucked away inside Mr. Tucker is a stop sign, a longing just to sit and stare. But the moment doesn't last. Soon he's back to his old self, "all keyed-up." Annoyed by Barney's repetitiveness, he screams, "For the love of Mike, do it, do it! Just do it! Take a nap, go to Thelma Lou's for TV. Just do it!" Barney replies: "What's the hurry?"

Mr. Tucker is in a hurry because for him time is money. The businessman is a busy man, but in Mayberry only Aunt Bee is always busy, and that's because she's a busybody. For most of the townsfolk, neither time nor money matter very much, least of all on the Sabbath, the day of rest. Early in the episode, when Andy sees Opie and Johnny Paul Jason exchanging a penny for a horsehair, he warns: "No trading on Sunday." Later, Gomer refuses to charge Mr. Tucker for the work on his car, a gesture that Mr. Tucker finds incomprehensible.

This episode is *TAGS*'s version of a Biblical fable. The "man" in the title refers not to one man but to mankind. Mr. Tucker is most men in a hurry, a con-trast to the sitters and the whittlers. More interested in the art of living than in making a living, Mayberrians never have enough of church socials, county fairs, camping trips, fishing and shooting competitions, visits to neighbors, nights out at the movies, dinners at Morelli's, bowling tournaments. Not to mention all those quiet evenings on the porch, as well as the hours spent hanging out at the barbershop or drinking a bottle of pop at Wally's Service. Every time we see Andy and Opie going fishing, as we do at the beginning of every episode, we understand that the business of Mayberry is leisure.

After a delay of several hours and Mr. Tucker's funny failed attempt to drive away in a pickup truck, Gomer gets ahold of his cousin Goober, who unclogs the fuel line. As Mr. Tucker gets ready to continue on his way, Aunt Bee comes out with a brown bag containing two chicken legs and a piece of cake. For good luck, Opie gives him the lucky penny he got from Johnny Paul Jason. Mr. Tucker gets into his car and turns on the engine. According to Gomer, it is running "smooth as silk," but Mr. Tucker claims that it doesn't sound right. He thinks that it's best for him to spend the night in Mayberry and have Wally take a look at the car in the morning. It's an excuse, of course; there's nothing wrong with the engine, but the man in a hurry has undergone a conversion. The site of the conversion is not All Souls Church but an equally sacred place, the Taylors' front porch, and the inducement is not a sermon but the quiet influence of Andy, Aunt Bee, Opie, Barney, and Gomer.

In the following season, another Sunday-themed episode, "The Sermon for Today" (4.4), makes the same point in a complementary way. Another stranger arrives in town: Dr. Harrison Everett Breen, a famous preacher and author from New York City whom Reverend Tucker has invited to deliver a guest sermon at All Souls Church (no relation, or perhaps only a symbolic one, to Tucker the entrepreneur). Dr. Breen's subject: "What's your hurry?" Andy is not eager to hear the visiting celebrity. As he tells Aunt Bee, "We've been taking from Reverend Tucker for a good many years and I ain't about to change." His reluctance to "take" from an out-of-town preacher, a New Yorker no less, is proved right when Dr. Breen behaves like a pompous phony. The irony is not only that he doesn't practice what he preaches—like Malcolm Tucker, he declines a dinner invitation because he has to rush off to Mt. Pilot to deliver another sermon—but that he is preaching to the choir. When he says that in their "senseless rush" people have forgotten "the joy and serenity of just sitting," one group to whom this doesn't apply is Mayberrians, who, as one of the boys in the barbershop points out, have turned sitting into a "fine art." It's no wonder that Gomer and Barney fall asleep during the sermon.

In "Man in a Hurry," Andy invites Mr. Tucker to come back to Mayberry when he has more time: "We don't like to see folks hurrying through like this." Andy's statement is disingenuous; the truth is that, when it comes to strangers, the quicker they pass through the better. But the folks that Andy is really talking about are the townsfolk, who spend their time chatting on the phone, reading the funny papers, or peeling an apple without breaking the peel, as Andy likes to do. (Or, I might add, the people who watch TAGS episodes over and over). Mr. Tucker, a closet Mayberrian, learns the lesson that escapes Dr. Breen, who returns from his sermon in Mt. Pilot but cannot spare the time for a cup of coffee at the Taylors' before he hurries back to New York City.

"Man in a Hurry" ends with another porch scene, an iteration of the first one. After deciding to spend the night with the Taylors, Mr. Tucker is back on the porch with Andy and Barney. But this time Mr. Tucker is sitting, not pac-

Man no longer in a hurry.

ing. After Andy and Barney croon an old folk song, "Go Tell Aunt Rhody," they launch into another nonmusical villanelle about whether or not to get a bottle of pop. They turn to Mr. Tucker to ask whether he wants to come along. Up to this moment, the camera has been shooting Andy and Barney over Mr. Tucker's shoulder. Now it moves to a close-up of Mr. Tucker, who has fallen asleep in a rocking chair. As the camera pans down, we see that he's holding a half-peeled apple in his hand.

CHAPTER FOUR

Great Pages in History

Once it's gone, it's gone. You can't go back.
Of course, sometimes a man wonders . . .

BARNEY, "THE RETURN OF BARNEY FIFE" (6.17)

R ICHARD KELLY POINTS OUT THAT MAYBERRIANS ARE unusual TV characters in that they remember.[1] In particular, characters in the living-room-bound sitcoms of the sixties are not only blissfully unaware of what they did a week ago but also have no sense of the historical past. In *TAGS* the episodes are also self-contained, but the characters recall incidents from other episodes, whether it's earlier visits by the Darlings, Aunt Bee's deplorable pickles, or Opie's first dance. In addition, they remember the town's history, and since most families have lived in Mayberry for generations, the communal and the personal intertwine. Thus, the ancestors of the show's regulars were the heroes of the famed Battle of Mayberry. Andy and Aunt Bee's ancestor was Colonel Carlton Taylor; Floyd's, Colonel Caleb Lawson; Clara's, Colonel Edwards, whose sword she treasures; Goober's, Colonel Goober Pyle. Even Mayberry's lone Native American, Tom Strongbow, descends from the Cherokee chief who opposed the settlers in the battle, which Tom calls by a different name: The Battle of Tuckahoosee Creek. Emmett Clark has an old Edison gramophone that, he says, is "rich in memories" (8.4). Mayberry is like that too.

In "The Storyteller," Walter Benjamin divides storytellers into those who bring news from faraway places and those who tell the community's tales. The model for the first is the trading seaman; for the second, the tiller of the soil.[2] As befits a residually agrarian society, Mayberrians favor the narrator of local tales.

The wanderer who tells of adventures in unknown lands, New York City or the jungles of South America, holds little interest for them. Thus, the most important date in the Mayberrian calendar is not the Fourth of July or Thanksgiving or Christmas but Founder's Day, which commemorates the marriage of person and place, thereby giving continuity and coherence to the town's identity. The celebration includes pie-eating contests, street dances, white elephant sales, free watermelon, and a beauty contest. The main event, however, is a reenactment of the town's founding. In one of the celebrations, Floyd, playing John Mayberry, leads the first settlers through "savage wilderness" to the "promised land" (1.16). In another, Clara Edwards takes the role of Lady Mayberry, the symbolic figure who formalizes the pact between Indians and settlers (5.11).

Of course, these events and personages are not all that they're cracked up to be. Seth Taylor, Andy's great-great-grandfather, is widely regarded as the town's greatest benefactor. He built the sawmill, donated some of his land to the town, and even loaned the town money during the fiscal crisis of 1874. Over Floyd's objections, the Mayberry Civic Improvement Committee votes to erect a statue in Seth's honor. (Floyd believes that the honor should go to Mayberry's first Indian agent, Daniel Lawson, beloved by "the noble redman.") Using old photographs as a guide, the local stonemason sculpts the statue. On the day that the statue is going to be unveiled, the owner of a seed company in Mt. Pilot shows up with proof that his great-grandfather, Winston Simmons, and Seth Taylor were "two of the biggest swindlers that this part of the country has ever known" (7.23). It seems that they led people to believe that the railroad terminal was going to be built in Mayberry, all the while knowing that the terminal was going to be in Mt. Pilot. This deception made it possible for them to sell their land in Mayberry at a premium and buy property in Mt. Pilot on the cheap. When they sold their Mt. Pilot holdings to the railroad company, they made a fortune.

A similar deflation happens with the Battle of Mayberry, which took place in the spring of 1762. (Although Mayberry was not "founded" until 1864, it seems that the area was named—or at least settled—a century earlier.) As Opie discovers after researching the subject at the Raleigh public library, the famous battle was not the "great page in history" that Mayberrians have been taught in school. According to an eighteenth-century account, the casus belli was nothing more serious than the accidental death of Bessie Lawson, a scrawny cow. No arrows or bullets filled the air, only insults. The casualties, other than Bessie, were three deer and a mule that looked like a deer. And the differences between Indians and settlers were patched up when the contending parties got drunk together on corn liquor. Hence, "No battle, no heroes, no colonels" (6.29).

But no amount of revisionism will convince Mayberrians that their town is not "the greatest place," in the words of Aunt Bee's song. After Simmons reveals the truth about Seth Taylor, Floyd, who had opposed the project, saves the day by pointing out that thanks to Seth and Winston's swindle, Mayberry did not develop into Mt. Pilot, "with all that hustle and bustle and dirty air," becoming instead "a nice, clean community, tucked away in our peaceful valley, where all our children have good teeth—the garden city of the state." And so the statue goes up in the town square. Opie's dismantling of the myth of the Battle of Mayberry has an equally happy resolution. When his prize-winning essay, "The True Story of the Battle of Mayberry," is published in the *Mayberry Gazette*, the Taylors become the town's black sheep. The ostracism ends when the governor of the state, in his weekly radio address, commends all Mayberrians for the peaceful way in which their "wise founders" resolved their differences. Once again Floyd delivers the moral: "It's what we've all known for some time, Mayberry has always been an honest and peaceful town, and we all have a right to be proud." ·

Mayberry's investment in the past is demonstrated in a different way by the proliferation of anachronisms. As Griffith pointed out, though the look of the town is contemporary, many details create a "retro" atmosphere. Candy bars cost five cents and ice cream cones a dime. Admission to the Grand Theater is a quarter. At the hotel, the overnight room rate is $2.50. The Feed and Grain Store dates from 1890. The façade of the Mayberry Hotel indicates that it opened in 1878. Even in a small town like Mayberry, by the 1960s dial phones should have replaced switchboards. When Floyd quotes a president, it is always Calvin Coolidge; his idea of a hit tune is "Roses of Picardy." When Warren Ferguson says that he had a cousin stationed in California during the war, he means World War II, not Korea or Vietnam. In several of the first season's episodes, the magazine rack in Walker's Drugstore displays an issue of *TV Guide* with Lucille Ball on the cover. In July of 1960, a few months before these episodes were filmed, Lucille Ball did appear on the cover of *TV Guide*. But this is not the issue for sale in the drugstore; it's the cover for the October 9, 1954, issue. Apparently Mayberrians were watching the 1954 television season six years too late—which is early for them.

Unlike other sitcoms, TAGS has no cameos by celebrities. *The Donna Reed Show* included guests ranging from Lassie to Dodgers pitcher Don Drysdale. Jimmy Stewart made a cameo appearance in *My Three Sons*. John Wayne did the same in *The Beverly Hillbillies*. In *I Love Lucy*, when the Ricardos visit Hollywood, they meet movie stars like Wayne, William Holden, and Rock Hudson. But when the Taylors visit Hollywood, the closest they get to a celebrity is Cesar Romero's lawn. Since life in Mayberry is backdated, the Taylors' idea of a famous person is a minor star from the 1930s and 1940s who had yet to revive his career by playing the Joker in the *Batman* TV series.

In a critique of Arnold Toynbee's concept of "Archaists," Donald Davidson distinguishes between Archaists who strive to revive outmoded ways of thought and behavior and those who only want to keep things as they are.[3] Mayberrians belong in the latter category; they are not revivalists but survivalists. Their "now" is everybody else's "then." Customs that in the outside world have gone the way of the candlestick phone continue unchanged. Young men don't date, they go "a-courtin'"; young women don't get engaged, they're "promised." As Davidson points out, the relevant distinction is not between Archaists and Futurists, as in Toynbee, but between traditionalists and anti-traditionalists. Mayberrians do not engage in the futile effort to resurrect dead worlds, but they do what they can to value and perpetuate their own traditions.

To fans of the show, of course, TAGS is anachronistic. Its enduring popularity owes much to the superb craftsmanship, but even more to viewers' desire to visit small-town America as it used to be, or as it should have been. *We* are the Archaists in Toynbee's sense, people who insist on idealizing the past. But within Mayberry anachronisms are not perceived as such. The status quo is the status ante. Mayberry is what the outside world has been, and it refuses to be what the outside world has become.

A recurring motif throughout the series, and especially while the show was filmed in black and white, the pastness of the present is the explicit subject of "The Case of the Punch in the Nose" (5.25). Barney and Andy are sifting through old files when Barney comes upon the report of an unresolved case, dated August 1946, involving the barber and the grocer, Floyd and Charley Foley. Insisting that the case needs to be settled, he begins an investigation. He interviews Floyd, Foley, and Goober, who, as a five-year-old, witnessed the incident. It seems that when Foley refused to pay for a shave he had not asked for, Floyd punched him in the nose. To get to the bottom of the incident, Barney reenacts the event. During the reenactment old passions flare up and Floyd punches Foley again. A fracas ensues: Foley punches Goober, who punches Otis, who punches Floyd. Pretty soon all of Mayberry has become embroiled in the Battle of the Barbershop, with the townspeople taking either Floyd's or Foley's side. Even Johnny Paul Jason, Foley's nephew, gets into it with Opie.

When Opie comes into the courthouse with a black eye, Andy has had enough. He brings Floyd and Foley together and has them shake hands, which is exactly how Sheriff Poindexter, Andy's predecessor, had settled the dispute nineteen years earlier. What he says summarizes the traditionalist view: "It worked then. I don't see why it shouldn't work now." The premise of traditionalism is that "then" and "now," rather than markers of historical ruptures, are points along a continuum of changeless duration. This is the real meaning of the reenactments, whether they involve the town's founding or a silly quarrel; they stress the continuity between past and present. Floyd and Foley obviously haven't changed, and neither has the Mayberry method of conflict resolution. Barney's desire for closure notwithstanding, the case will never be closed. In Mayberry the less things change, the more they remain the same.

A related issue is the relation of TAGS to Southern history. Though Sheriff Andy has been called "The Lincoln of Mayberry," the omission most often noted is any acknowledgment of the region's history of racial strife. Barney brags that history was one of his best subjects in school, but Malcolm Merriweather, the Englishman, knows more about the Gettysburg Address than Barney, and he corrects Barney's assertion that Lincoln was the fourteenth president. In the episode that introduces Helen as Opie's history teacher, Andy asks Barney to explain the Emancipation Proclamation to Opie. Fumbling for an answer, Barney can say only that it had to do with "folks" getting emancipated: "so they got this proclamation and they called it The Emancipation Proclamation" (3.23). By the end of the episode, he still doesn't know the contents of the Emancipation Proclamation, and Andy makes no effort to educate him. (Does *he* know?)

Barney's transformation of slaves into "folks" reflects the near invisibility of blacks in TAGS. Black actors will sometimes appear as extras in exterior shots, as in "Barney Gets His Man" (1.30), in which a well-dressed black woman stands behind Andy and Barney on the sidewalk, or "Barney Comes to Mayberry" (7.19), in which the crowd greeting Barney on his return includes black faces. In "Ernest T. Bass Joins the Army" (4.3), standing in the line of recruits are several black men. But it's not until the next-to-last season, in "Opie's Piano Lesson" (7.26), that a black actor, Rockne Tarkington, has a speaking role, that of Flip Conroy, a former NFL star who returns to his hometown to work in his father's business and coach the boys' football team. The plot, however, has nothing to do with Flip's race. When Opie, the quarterback of the team, arrives late for practice, the coach is not pleased. Flip drops by the Taylors' home and finds out that the reason for Opie's tardiness is that his father insists that his son stick to his piano lessons. To show Andy that piano and pigskin are compatible, Flip sits down at the piano and plays a classical piece from memory. Like Mr. Dave, Flip is an alternative role model, but a positive one. "Opie's Piano Lesson" turns out to be a lesson for Andy as well. (Ironically, Rockne Tarkington first came into the public eye as the ill-fated slave in the short-lived 1962 Broadway version of Kyle Oscott's novel *Mandingo* (1957) — a far cry from the role of college-educated Flip Conroy.)

According to David Marc, the "progressive feel" of *The Dick Van Dyke Show* is "due in part to the inclusion of black actors as extras in crowd scenes at public places and private events, such as museums and parties."[4] If so, Mayberry is only slightly less progressive than New Rochelle, the New York suburb where Rob and Laura Petrie live. Marc also points out that the appearance of Godfrey

Cambridge as a guest star in one episode of *The Dick Van Dyke Show* was exceptional, for "African-Americans were otherwise never seen on sixties sitcoms as guest stars." If so, TAGS is no less exceptional. The fact is that the almost total absence of blacks in Mayberry or New Rochelle is typical for the TV shows of this period, be they litcoms or corncoms. Perhaps the most egregious example is *Riverboat* (1959–1961), an NBC action series about a riverboat paddling up and down the Mississippi in the 1840s, which didn't show a single black person in forty consecutive weeks.[5]

During TAGS's original run, the absence of black actors did not go unnoticed. In 1966 the NAACP complained to CBS, not quite accurately, that the show had "never shown a black face on camera."[6] In the *New Journal and Guide*, a black weekly from Virginia, Griffith formulated a hesitant reply:

> I don't think I've ever made a statement on this subject before. I'll have to be very honest and I hope you'll quote me that way. The problem we face is simple: we have to remain honest to the types of people depicted in the small, rural town of Mayberry, North Carolina. In a series like *Dr. Kildare*, for instance, you can have any number of Negro doctors. It's logical; it's a big hospital in a big city. But put a Negro doctor in a town like Mayberry and the people most probably wouldn't go to him.
>
> A story like ours, which is set in a small Southern town, just naturally leaves itself open for problems — especially when the show is comedy. We wanted to do a story centered around a Jewish family, but it just didn't work because it turned out to be drama; it wasn't funny at all.
>
> We're not trying to avoid anything. It's just that the show has to remain honest. If we stretch the point just to accommodate certain groups, then things could easily become ridiculous. It goes without saying that all of us on the show would like it just fine if we could portray people of all races on the show regularly.[7]

He adds that the episode featuring Rockne Tarkington, which was about to air, was designed to address this criticism. This episode, however, would turn out to be the only one featuring a black actor. Perhaps to compensate, the sequel, *Mayberry R.F.D.*, would have a recurring black character, Ralph Barton (Charles Lampkin), a farmer like Sam Jones. Ralph appears in a half-dozen episodes, though his character amounts to little more than a token black clone of the show's protagonist. Twenty years later, in *Return to Mayberry* (1986), the town remains as white as it had been in the 1960s. The only blacks are a few extras in crowd scenes.

Griffith's discomfort in discussing the issue of race, palpable in his carefully worded explanation, arises from his awareness that the embrace of difference, racial or otherwise, is not a Mayberrian virtue. As he suggests, Jewish Americans would be no more welcome than African Americans. What Griffith insinuates but doesn't say outright is that the portrait of the South in *TAGS* reflects his upbringing in Mount Airy, a town that was almost entirely white. In Griffith's day the inhabitants of Mount Airy, like those of the Appalachians generally, did not descend from slaves or slave-owning planters but from the yeoman class that Frank L. Owsley described in *Plain Folk of the Old South* (1949). The South of Mayberry is that of the plain folk, subsistence farmers who owned few or no slaves and grew potatoes and corn rather than tobacco and cotton.

In 1960 about a quarter of the population of North Carolina was African American, but in Surry County, where Mount Airy is located, the figure was less than 6 percent. For Mount Airy, the number was lower: less than 5 percent. Thirty years earlier, African Americans made up less than 8 percent of the population. By contrast, in 1960 more than 25 percent of the residents of Greensboro, an hour away, were black.[8] Since it was not until 1965 that Mount Airy High enrolled its first black student, when the Mayberry Union High class of 1945 (or 1948) has its reunions, there are no black alumni. It is not true, then, that *TAGS* takes place in a "surreally all-white world."[9] The world of *TAGS* is no more surreal than the world of North Carolina novelists Doris Betts and Lee Smith, both of whom place much of their fiction in the Appalachians. Betts explains: "I come out of yeoman farmers and Piedmont red clay country. There weren't many slaves there and there wasn't an aristocratic tradition at all." Smith is more categorical: "In the county that I grew up in [Buchanan, Virginia], there were no black people . . . I remember being taken by my parents to Richmond when I was a little girl and they said, 'Now you are going to see some Negroes; don't point.'"[10]

The lack of black Mayberrians, as well as the cultivation of anachronisms, makes it unsurprising that there is little in the episodes to remind the viewer of the racial tensions of the 1960s. Of course, before *All in the Family*, sitcoms rarely made more than a token nod, if that, to what was going on in the real world. *I Love Lucy* made countless references to Cuba, and not once acknowledged the turmoil on the island during the 1950s. *Gomer Pyle, U.S.M.C.* takes place on a Marine base, and yet the Vietnam War is never mentioned. I've found only one oblique but disturbing reference to racial issues in *TAGS*. In "Mountain Wedding" (3.31), about Ernest T. Bass's relentless pursuit of Charlene Darling, Dud Wash tells Andy that Ernest T. "went off into the woods to kill a mockingbird." This episode was broadcast in October 1963. Harper Lee's novel about racial injustice in the South had been published three years earlier; the movie version had been released in 1962. Both in the novel and in the movie, the mockingbird is Tom Robinson, a black man who, though guiltless, is convicted of rape and shot while trying to escape from prison. Everett Greenbaum, who cowrote the episode, has said that the line was a joke: "We thought it was clever to use 'to kill a mockingbird' in the script. It was the title of a hit movie that year."[11] It's hard to imagine that the idea of a "redneck" like Ernest T. killing a mockingbird did not strike Greenbaum as provocative, especially given the similarity in name between Harper Lee's Maycomb and Mayberry. The most charitable interpretation is that the joke represents a rare moment of tone-deafness. The least charitable, well . . .

TAGS's avoidance of racial subjects, however, does not preclude allusions to the Civil War, which is regarded not as a dispute over slavery but as a regional conflict between North and South, the unfortunate result of what Owsley, a conservative Southern historian, termed "egocentric sectionalism."[12] Allusions to the Civil War span the entire run of the series. Old Frank Myers's most precious possession is a picture of his great-grandfather shaking hands with Robert E. Lee (2.4). Briscoe Darling mentions that to reach his cabin one has to cross the "Robert E. Lee natural bridge," an oak tree that fell across a creek (3.31). Gomer talks about Lover's Leap Rock, where a Confederate colonel plunged to his "everlasting calling" after being spurned by a Yankee woman (4.6). For one of the Founder's Day celebrations, Warren intends to fire the old cannon that, according to Andy, hasn't been fired in a hundred years — which would put the date of its last firing during the Civil War (6.11). The nickname of Floyd's ancestor was "Stonewall" Lawson (6.29); Goober's ancestor belonged to the North Carolina Seventh Cavalry, a Civil War unit (6.29). Legend has it that Ross's Treasure, $100,000 in gold stolen from Union troops by Ross's Raiders, is buried near Hopkins Creek (7.16), an echo of similar legends about caches of gold hidden throughout the South.

The episode that dwells most explicitly on Mayberry's Confederate past is "Mayberry Goes Bankrupt" (2.4), in which Frank Myers — whose last name links him to an iconic site, Myers Lake (which, like the character, was named after Frank E. Myers, the production manager for *TAGS*) — tries to avoid eviction by redeeming a $100 savings bond issued by the town to his great-grandfather in 1861. The accrued interest on the bond brings its total value to $349,119.27, a sum that would bankrupt the town. Mayor Pike and the members of the Town Council don't know what to do until they realize that the bond was issued when Mayberry was part of the Confederacy. Since it was bought with Confederate currency, it's worthless, no more than a "sentimental relic." Relieved, the Town Council forgives Myers the back taxes on his property. In the epilogue, Andy and Frank go to the mayor's office to show off another of Frank's possessions — a letter from "the President." Mayor Pike is impressed; he thinks it's a letter from the current U.S. President (who would have been John F. Kennedy). But no — it's a letter from Jefferson Davis, where he regretfully declines an invitation to visit because of "current critical events." Earlier, when Myers

Andy shows Mayor Pike the Confederate bond.

had shown Andy a picture of his great-granddaddy with Robert E. Lee, Andy had replied: "Well, who else would a Southerner pose with?"

It cannot be a coincidence that this episode was broadcast in October 1961, the centenary year of the beginning of the Civil War. After Andy has served Frank Myers the eviction notice but before the existence of the bond becomes known, Aunt Bee and Andy are sitting on the porch discussing Frank's predicament, while Opie plays with toy soldiers. The camera moves to a close-up of Opie's battlefield. Some of the soldiers, on horses, brandish swords; others kneel with rifles, wield bayonets, or man a couple of old-fashioned cannons. It's clear that they are not imitations of twentieth-century soldiers. In the late 1950s and early 1960s Confederate toy soldiers became very popular. To mark the centennial of the Civil War, Marx Toy Company, which had begun to make Confederate soldier sets in 1958, released two large sets in 1961, which prompted Sears and Montgomery Ward to make sets in competition with Marx.[13] Opie could well be staging a Civil War battle.

If Opie's reenactment foretells the crucial plot twist—the discovery of Frank's Confederate bond—the battle will end in a kind of stalemate. On the one hand, even as the episode flaunts Mayberry's Confederate past, it attests to its obsolescence. Frank, a descendant of Mayberry's Confederate mayor, lives in his ancestor's dilapidated house, an "eyesore." His anachronistic occupation, making berries for women's hats, is no more valuable than the bond. On the other hand, by the time the Town Council realizes that the bond has no cash value, they have restored Frank's shack, making it a "valuable landmark." The value of a landmark, like that of the bond, is symbolic, sentimental—but this is the currency that Mayberry, a community rich in yesterdays, trades in. To Opie, the box where Mr. Myers keeps his "valuables" is a "treasure chest." And so is Mayberry, as quaint as the 1906 World's Fair Medallion in Myers's wonder box. That the St. Louis World's Fair actually took place in 1904 increases the rarity of the keepsake.

The South of Mayberry is certainly not that to which Walker Percy's Will Barrett returns in *The Last Gentleman*: "happy, victorious, Christian, rich, patriotic and Republican."[14] Happy and Christian, yes; patriotic, maybe; victorious, rich, and Republican, definitely not. It's not Republican because there are no political parties in Mayberry, but if there were, most Mayberrians would have been Southern Democrats, like the majority of North Carolinians at the time. It's not rich because all of the townsfolk share the same standard of living, modestly middle-class. And it's not victorious because, as the story of Frank Myers suggests, the legacy of loss is ingrained in the Mayberrian psyche. Nonetheless, if Mayberry is not yet the New South, it's not quite the Old South either. Before Myers's shack is renovated, Mayor Pike complains that it is the first place that people see "when they drive in from the north." His statement hints at the historical significance, perhaps the historical origins, of the town's xenophobia. The unwelcome intrusion by outsiders, the vast majority northerners like Danny Williams and Dr. Harrison Everett Breen, is itself a reenactment of what Southerners used to call "The War of Northern Aggression." This sense of "being encircled and menaced on all sides," as C. Vann Woodward described the mind-set of the South during and after the Civil War, persists in Mayberrians.[15] Their xenophobia is a second-order phenomenon, a defensive response to what they perceive as a history of aggression.

In an episode from the third season, "The Loaded Goat" (3.18), Barney receives a call from Miss Vickers, who fears that the explosions she hears signal the approach of the Yankees. Barney tries to reassure her, but every time another blast goes off, the courthouse phone rings again; Miss Vickers is sure the Yankees are advancing upon Mayberry. Like other locals, she has a lively sense of the pastness of the present. Even as the Frank Myers episode makes clear that the Confederacy lost, "The Loaded Goat" suggests that, at least for some of the townspeople, the Lost Cause is not lost. A hundred years after the conflict, in the midst of a flood of Civil War–themed books and memorabilia, *TAGS* offers a different end to the conflict. During the eight seasons that the show was on the air, the "Battle of Mayberry" was fought many times, and the Yankees were usually turned back. In this respect *TAGS* is alternate history, like those narratives that speculate about what would have happened had Lee's plans for the invasion of the North not been accidentally discovered or, as James Thurber said, had Grant been drunk at Appomattox. The most popular of the many alternate histories of the Civil War, MacKinlay Kantor's *If the South Had Won the Civil War*, was published in the November 22, 1960, issue of *Look* and released as a book the following year. Mayberry is not only a backwoods Brigadoon, but a historical hallucination: an embodiment of the neo-Confederate fantasy of Dixie unbowed.

What Mrs. Vickers hears is not the din of war, but detonations from the work on the new underpass, Mayor Stoner's sounds of progress. The superposition of the Civil War and the "dynamitical poppings" of modernity, to use Donald Davidson's phrase, reinforces the implications of *TAGS* as alternate history. Like many a neo-Rebel historian, Miss Vickers makes the point, unintentionally, that modernity threatens Mayberry no less than the Union forces threatened the South. This was the thesis of The Twelve Southerners, Davidson among them, apostles not of progress but of tradition, in the essays collected in *I'll Take My Stand* (1930), where they argue for the preservation of the region's agrarian culture. Evidently they lost the argument, since the Old South has been, if not demolished, at least diminished by the New South, a franchise of Yankee civilization — but not in Mayberry, at least not yet.

What about the underpass? Well, some of the dynamite to clear the way for the new road is eaten by Jimmy, a billy goat belonging to a local farmer. The "loaded goat" then wanders around town, ready to go "blooey" at any moment. To prevent a chain reaction were Jimmy to explode, the building of the underpass is suspended. For the moment, an old goat has stymied the inroads of change. The last time that Miss Vickers — another old goat — phones the courthouse, Andy calms her nerves by telling her: "Yes, ma'am, we're still holdin' on to Richmond." Richmond, the Confederate capital, will fall, just as surely as the underpass will be built. At the end of the episode, after Jimmy has been led safely out of town, Andy tells the engineer that the "blasting" can resume. But like the fall of Richmond, the blasting away at tradition occurs outside *TAGS* time. Sooner or later Mayor Stoner or some other scalawag will have his way. Like the Confederacy, Mayberry cannot hold on indefinitely, but during the half-hour segments the South rises again and again.

CHAPTER FIVE

From R.F.D. to R.I.P.

*F*OR THE VAST MAJORITY OF *TAGS* FANS, THE 159 EPI-
sodes of the first five seasons, all done in black and white, contain the truest incarnation of Mayberry. It must have been a shock to turn on
the television set at 9:00 p.m. on Monday, September 13, 1965, and see Andy
and Opie strolling to Myers Lake in color. The greenery was green! The dirt
road was dirt-colored! Opie's blue jeans were blue—just like Myers Lake!

For five years Andy and Opie walked to the fishing hole seemingly untouched
by the passage of time. Opie was growing up, but the opening sequence tended
to belie this, since his attire and behavior didn't change. The new sequence looks
very much like the old one. Andy and Opie carry fishing poles on their shoulders. The familiar tune is heard in the background. Except for three large boulders (where did they come from?), the landscape hasn't changed—pine trees
in the background, nondescript bushes on the sides of the path, a fallen trunk
in the foreground. As in the original sequence, Opie strays from his father to
throw pebbles into the pond, but since Opie is five years older than he was at
the beginning of the show, he no longer grabs his father's hand when he returns.
Instead, Andy puts his arm around him. What makes less sense is that an eleven-
year-old should be walking barefoot. To judge by how gingerly Opie steps, he's
not used to it. Something is amiss here (those boulders, again), as it is also in
the final credits, where the sketch of the lake scene has been replaced by that
of a row of two-story buildings. The only pole in the new sketch is a light pole.

The shift to color in television programming, which by 1965 was widespread,
did not serve *TAGS* well. Black-and-white film matched the town's conservative
temper. In Mayberry B.C. (Before Color), daily life was predictable, mono-
tone. Since the directors rarely exploited the stark chiaroscuro effects of some
black-and-white films, most of the daytime scenes were evenly lit; in the evening, the Taylors' front porch was pleasantly dark. Beginning with the first epi-

sode of the sixth season, the viewer is exposed (I'm tempted to say, subjected) to an ever-changing kaleidoscope of color: red cars, brown roads, green lawns, white houses, yellow sunlight. When the camera pans Main Street, every storefront has newly painted signs. As Rudolf Arnheim pointed out, color film obscures the gap between nature and art by undermining the illusion of illusion, the "welcome divergence from nature," as he phrased it.[1] Andy's living room now looks like any other living room: the flowered curtains, the pink chairs, the beige sofa, the green cushions, the Blue Willow china on the pine sideboard. When we see that Goober's beanie is dark brown, it loses its charm — no longer an iconic object, like the magical cap of fairy tales, it now looks like a tattered hat of an excremental hue. The same thing happens to Floyd's Tonsorial Parlor, brightened up, but also vulgarized, by the addition of a green fern and the rotating red, white, and blue stripes of the barber pole.

With the sixth season further changes — that dreaded word — come to Mayberry. Reliable Barney Fife moves to Raleigh. Although he would make several stellar visits over the next three years, the town was not the same without him. His antics were missed; but even more glaring was the absence of those quiet moments when he and Andy sat on the porch or in front of the courthouse. Barney's departure led to the disappearance of the Fun Girls, who apparently didn't think a Fife-free Mayberry was worth the drive from Mt. Pilot. Also missing was the mountain contingent, Ernest T. Bass and the Darlings. To fill the void left by Barney's departure, the producers and Griffith replaced him with a new deputy, Warren Ferguson (Jack Burns), said to be Floyd's nephew. It wasn't a good fit. Warren's Boston accent was grating; his bumbling was not funny, not even to Andy, who had infinite patience with Barney but a very short fuse with Warren. In Warren's first episode (6.5), Andy calls him an "idiot deputy," an opinion he would not revise. The combination of Barney's absence and Warren's arrival seemed to bring out the worst in the peaceable sheriff. Later in the episode Andy storms out of the courthouse and throws a rock through a window, à la Ernest T. Bass. Though Barney was the same way, Andy gets so fed up with Warren's by-the-book approach to law enforcement that he chases Warren around the courthouse screaming, "I'll kill you!" Andy liked to rib Barney, sometimes a little too much for my taste, but he never threatened to kill him.

In scenes like this one Andy is channeling Lonesome Rhodes, the nasty, egotistical character Griffith played in *A Face in the Crowd*. In the first episode of the season ("Opie's Job"), several weeks before Warren appears, Andy is already uncharacteristically ill-tempered. He comes home in a sour mood because he's had a bad day at the office. First, the marsh caught fire again; then someone kept calling the courthouse asking for Ethel; to top things off, Otis got "gassed" and drove his car through the Harpers' rose garden. When Andy tried to arrest him, Otis challenged him to a fist fight. Although it's dinner time, Opie isn't home. He finally arrives, having just smashed his new bike into a tree. Andy chews out Opie for riding no-handed, and then—another rare event—chews out Aunt Bee for interfering. This is not the unflappable father and benign patriarch of old:

> Opie, I've told you a dozen times to keep your hands on the handlebars. . . . I wanna tell you something. Money is a very valuable thing. Now I'm what's called the breadwinner around here and I don't mind paying for things that have to be paid for but when it's carelessness, like tearing up the front wheel and fender on your bicycle, I don't know what that's liable to cost me—fifteen, twenty dollars. I don't know what to do with you.

Andy's anger at Opie is scary in the way that Lonesome Rhodes's rages were scary. Opie has messed up before, but Andy had never concluded that he didn't know what to do with his son. Sometimes his parenting methods backfired or were shown to be ill-conceived, but he always knew what to do. If Opie misbehaved, he would take him aside, explain what he did wrong, and point out the punishment to be meted out and the lesson to be learned. Later in this episode, when Opie gets fired from his job at Mr. Doakes's market, Andy has another temper tantrum. This time he tells Opie that he's ashamed to be his father, another unprecedentedly harsh judgment.

What Andy is really upset about—the unspoken backstory of his tantrums—is Barney's departure. The reason he has a rough day at the office is not because someone keeps calling the courthouse or because Otis gets drunk. Otis is always drunk. All kinds of people call the courthouse, including old ladies who think that the Civil War is still raging. The difference is that Barney is no longer there. As Griffith missed Don Knotts's contribution to the show, Andy misses Barney. Had Barney been around, Otis would have challenged *him* to a fist fight.

In the early episodes of *TAGS*, Griffith played Andy Taylor as Will Stockdale, his character in *No Time for Sergeants*, a hayseed with an exaggerated drawl and an annoying habit of finding a homespun saying for every occasion. By the middle of the first season, Griffith realized that the show was funnier if he played straight man for Barney, and he cut back on the drawl and the idioms. Five years later, Griffith again does not seem to know how his character should behave. Warren Ferguson's arrival as deputy only makes matters worse. For one thing, Warren and Andy were alike physically, tall and robust, so that it is incongruous for Warren to engage in Barney-like antics, many of them based on Barney's puniness. For another, Warren, a Massachusetts native, is an outsider, one of those exotics whom Mayberry shuns. When Barney gives the townsfolk a hard time, he does it as one of them. Warren harasses them as an outsider would harass them. It makes no difference that he's Floyd's nephew. We already know that kindred matters more than kin. In essence, Warren and Mayberry do not understand one another. His departure, the common fate of outsiders, was inevitable.

After Warren joins the ranks of the disappeared halfway through the season, Andy calms down and reverts to his good-natured old self. But the absence of a deputy brings about further changes. The courthouse can no longer serve as agora. Andy begins to wear plain clothes more often. His sheriffing recedes in favor of his role as father and suitor. In "The Bazaar" (6.5), after Warren arrests all of the members of the Ladies' Auxiliary (the reason Andy wants to kill him), the ladies' husbands come to Andy's house to complain. Dressed in ties and jackets, these men belong in the nondescript suburbs of *The Donna Reed Show* or *Father Knows Best*, not in rural Mayberry. Since plots could no longer be constructed around Barney, the other characters were also given more to do, and TAGS became more of an ensemble show. Many of the stories are now domcom staples: Aunt Bee experiments with new occupations; Opie joins a band, falls in love, learns to dance; Andy and Helen break up and make up.

Another change: not only do Mayberrians now begin to foray into the outside world—the Taylors to Hollywood, Aunt Bee and Clara to Mexico, Howard to an island in the Caribbean—but they also welcome the outside into their world. In "Aunt Bee and the Lecturer" (8.10), the Mayberry Women's Club invites Prof. Hubert St. John, the noted author of *I Know South America*, to speak about that dark continent. After the lecture, Aunt Bee says that Prof. St. John has "brought South America to Mayberry." In Mayberry B.C., the townsfolk could not have cared less about South America and anyone who brought it to them. Later that season, in what would be Barney Fife's last appearance, the Taylors' home serves as the site for a summit of Soviet and American diplomats, another indication that Mayberry's hermeticism is cracking. In the middle of the seventh season (7.19), a train station mysteriously appears in town. Equally mysterious, between the seventh and the eighth season, the population triples from 1,800 to 5,360.[2] Cracks foretell catastrophes.

During Prof. St. John's visit, he invites Aunt Bee to dinner at Morelli's. All he wants to talk about is the uncanny resemblance between Bee and his late wife Ethel. To change the subject, Aunt Bee asks him, "Hubert, what do you think of the situation in Asia?" This episode was aired in the fall of 1967, when the increasingly unpopular war in Vietnam dominated the news (and the vice president of the United States happened to be named Hubert). Had Aunt Bee found herself with Prof. St. John two or three years earlier, she likely would have asked him about Antietam rather than Vietnam, or perhaps she would not have asked anything other than whether Hubert wanted another piece of rhubarb pie. In the next episode (8.11), Aunt Bee is writing a card to a friend's son who is going off to college. She needs to complete the sentence "Knowledge is . . ." Andy suggests that she complete it, "Knowledge is power." "No," Aunt Bee says, "that sounds too military." She writes instead "Knowledge is the tool of life." When did Aunt Bee become a peacenik? Never before had Mayberry been a microcosm of American society.

In the four-month hiatus between the last episode of the fifth season and the first of the sixth, life in Mayberry became more complicated, as Mayberrians joined the sixties. As Opie reminds his father, "things are different now than when I was a kid" (6.26). Mayberry now includes a neighborhood of well-to-do families, Walnut Hills, whose pastoral name sounds like the cognomen of a suburban subdivision. Time was when the only rich person in the county was Ben Weaver, the town Scrooge, and he wasn't truly rich. In the episode in which Opie befriends a boy from Walnut Hills, "Opie Steps Up in Class" (8.5), the wordplay in the title introduces a distinction foreign to Mayberry B.C., that of socioeconomic classes. In old Mayberry there were different kinds of people — hillbillies and townsfolk — but their differences were portrayed as primarily cultural rather than economic. The faux-antebellum mansion where the rich boy lives, with its pillared porch, marble stairway, and crystal chandelier, is as different from Opie's house as Tara is from Mayberry. Aunt Bee walks in to the strains of *Tales from the Vienna Woods*. Something else she hasn't seen before: a servant. An Aunt Bee look-alike, the maid could have been her sister. Understandably, Aunt Bee doesn't quite know how to react.

The last *TAGS* episode introduces yet another group familiar to most Americans but foreign to old Mayberry: immigrants. Sam Jones hires an Italian family, the Vincentis, because "farm life doesn't seem to appeal to many people around here anymore" (8.30). The foundations of Mayberrian society are agrarian. Farmers are a common sight. The town has a feed and grain store. Cows and goats have been known to wander down Main Street. Those Mayberrians who aren't farmers or moonshiners work in the service sector: barbers, mechanics, grocers, druggists. The surest sign that the times they are a'changin' is that the children of farmers are no longer interested in farming.

WHEN ANDY GRIFFITH ANNOUNCED, BEFORE THE EIGHTH season of *TAGS*, that this would be his last year as Sheriff Andy Taylor, he was going to take Mayberry with him. But the show's producer at the time, Bob Ross, got the idea that the town could survive the loss of its sheriff as it had survived the loss of Gomer, Barney, and Floyd. Both CBS and General Foods, the show's sponsor, were keen on having the series continue. And so the decision was made to prolong the town's life in *Mayberry R.F.D.*[3] The producers of RFD, among them Griffith, made a point of establishing continuity between the two shows, which included convincing CBS to put RFD in TAGS's Monday night time slot. To take the place of Andy and Opie, they came up — surprise! — with another widower and his young son: Sam Jones and Mike, who in RFD are the same age as Andy and Opie at the beginning of TAGS (turn the clock back). Sam had been introduced in the last few episodes of TAGS as a member of the Town Council and farmer-about-town. The original idea was to build the show around him and the Vincentis: son Mario (Gabriele Tinti); his pretty sister, Sophia, (Letitia Roman); and their querulous father, Papa Vincenti (Bruno Della Santina). When CBS balked at this plan — the network wanted less pasta and more corn — the Vincentis vanished and some of the townsfolk returned.

For the first two seasons, Aunt Bee joins the Jones household as their housekeeper. Goober remains at the filling station, Emmett at the Fix-It Shop, and Howard in the County Clerk's office. Clara Edwards (Hope Summers) continues as Aunt Bee's best friend. Millie, Howard's old flame (Arlene Golonka), resurfaces with a new last name to play Sam's girlfriend. Mr. Schwump,[4] a familiar but enigmatic figure who appears in many TAGS episodes, puts in a couple of appearances, as does Reverend Tucker. Andy is still the town's sheriff, though he is seldom on camera. Not least, the switchboard operator, Sarah, gets several mentions. The knot between the two shows is tied by a literal marriage: Andy and Helen's, which takes place on the inaugural episode of RFD. Like Andy, Helen also makes a few appearances, but after the first season she and Andy move to Charlotte, where Andy goes to work for the State Bureau of Investigation. After the second season, Aunt Bee also leaves (to live with her sister) and is replaced by Sam's cousin, Alice (Alice Ghostley), the newest housekeeper. As a final touch, "The Mayberry March" became the theme of the show, confirming what the title conveyed: that this was a show about a familiar place, "the town that feels like everybody's home."[5]

But it was not the same place, not really. If Mayberry B.C. derives spiritually from the Old South, Mayberry R.F.D., in spite of the quaint acronym ("Rural Free Delivery"), is an outpost of the New South. When Sam replaces Andy, the clock in Barney's stomach strikes midnight. A new day has dawned in Mayberry, no longer just a town in North Carolina but a "part of the global picture," as Howard brags when Sam hosts a Russian agricultural expert ("The Farmer Exchange Project"). In TAGS Howard also represented the outlook of a forward-looking bureaucrat, but he was a minority of one. With his suit and bowtie, he was a square among oddballs, corporate rather than cornpone. But in RFD he speaks for the community. The trend toward expansiveness begun toward the end of TAGS continues with increasing impetus in RFD. Even if the Vincentis disappeared before the show even debuted, the town does have an immigrant population, albeit a tiny one: a struggling music teacher, Professor Wolfgang Radetsky (played by Leonid Kinsky, the bartender in Rick's Café in *Casablanca*), who teaches Alice how to play the harp. At Howard's urging, Mayberry takes up the State Department's offer and pairs up with a Mexican town of similar size and interests, "Portobello" (like the mushroom), as part of the Sister Cities program. New Mayberry even has a movie house that shows foreign films, the Bijou Theater. When a moon rock is displayed in the town, Howard sums up the progressive temper of the New Mayberry: "One small step for man, a giant leap for Mayberry" ("The Moon Rocks"). We can imagine what the boys in the barbershop, who longed for the days of covered wagons, would have had to say about the moon rock.

As head of the Mayberry Town Council, Sam succeeds Andy in running the town, but his approach to governance is cooperative rather than patriarchal. Instead of the courthouse, the physical center of the show is the Town Council's office. More of an administrator than a farmer, Sam occupies most of his time attending to town affairs rather than tending to his crops. Since he is not in law enforcement, the plots no longer revolve around troublemaking strangers. Gone are Andy's rifle cleaning and Barney's gun play. Gone are the crooks, vagrants, ex-cons, impostors. As Aunt Bee once joked, Andy and Barney resemble Matt Dillon and Chester; Sam and the Town Council are more like the PTA.[6] Allan Melvin, a frequent face in 1950s and 1960s television series, shows up often in TAGS playing a heavy. With such roles in scarce supply, Melvin reappears in RFD as the feckless town barber—Floyd's successor!—who tells Emmett that he needs a toupee. Everyday life in the New Mayberry is dull, not peaceful. Rather than by *philia*, bonds of affinity and affection, the townspeople are brought together by their pursuit of civic goals.

Sam Jones's usual attire—his "uniform"—is a neatly pressed blue shirt and chinos, a contrast not only to Andy's sheriff's uniform but to the overalls of Rafe Hollister, Jeff Pruitt, and the other farmers in TAGS. When Sam dresses up, which he often does, he wears tailored suits. Athletic and handsome, he looks every bit like the leading man that Andy never was. Sam's syntax and enunciation are nonregional Americanese. Although he was born and raised on the family farm in Mayberry, his speaking voice, a mellow baritone, has none of the folksiness of Andy's drawl. He's intelligent rather than wise, affable rather than warm. If Andy was a good ole boy, Sam is Mr. America, as Howard calls him ("Sensitivity Training"). With Sam as the town's leading citizen, mid-American niceness replaces Southern charm.

The reduced role of music also blunts the Southern flavor of the show. The original Mayberry was a music box. It boasted a choir, a barbershop quartet, a marching band, a couple of dance bands, and a guitar player who had a hit record, "Rock 'n' Roll Rosie from Raleigh." Andy and Barney liked to harmonize. Aunt Bee and Clara composed "My Hometown." Floyd composed "Hail to Thee, Mayberry." The Mayberry Union High anthem was sung several times.

Gomer sang beautifully, as did Rafe Hollister, the moonshiner with the operatic voice. Otis's drunken warblings brightened many a Saturday night. Briscoe Darling summed up the importance that Mayberrians attach to music: "You have time to breathe, you have time for music" (3.31). New Mayberry is not nearly as sonorous as its predecessor. Ken Berry, a fine singer and dancer, could have perpetuated the town's musical tradition, but his talents are rarely used. Every once in a great while he will do a soft-shoe routine or sit on the porch and croon "Carolina Moon," but these scenes are throwaways. Alice playing "Believe Me If All Those Endearing Young Charms" on the harp can't compete with the Darlings belting out "Dooley," about a man who owns a forty-gallon still; and even if Johnny Mercer's "Moon River," Sam and Millie's favorite song, was inspired by a creek in Georgia, it's nothing like "Never Hit Your Grandma with a Great Big Stick," which always made Charlene cry.

Something else that is missing from New Mayberry: leisure, the fine art of settin' and starin'. A busybody like Aunt Bee, Sam is in perpetual motion, as befits a character played by an actor who grew up wanting to be Fred Astaire. Only rarely does Sam find the time to sit on his porch, which appears only in a few episodes, a melancholy reminder of the way things used to be. Compare Floyd's Tonsorial Parlor, where the boys hung out, with Emmett's Fix-It Shop, which occupies the same locale: Emmett's shop has none of the airy, laid-back atmosphere of the barbershop; it's dark, disorderly, and full of junk (*Sanford and Son* avant la litter). The counter at the entrance blocks access. There are no chairs on which to sit. When Sam and Howard are in the shop, they are always doing something, handing Emmett a tool or taking something off the shelf. Temperamentally Emmett (Paul Hartman) is Floyd's opposite: dedicated rather than distracted, a sourpuss rather than a sweetie, down-to-earth rather than philosophical. Floyd wore a white barber's coat; Emmett, a dirty apron. Just as the neat barbershop was a reflection of Floyd's personality, the cramped, messy shop reflects Emmett's. A Mt. Pilot native, he never recalls local lore or quotes Calvin Coolidge. He doesn't sit outside his shop perusing the *Mayberry Gazette* and watching the world go by. He is too busy fussing over a toaster.

As Jack Dodson recognized when RFD was on the air, the new-look Mayberry is no longer a Southern town.[7] Mayberry needs its gadflies, its bluegrass, its hillbillies, its moonshiners. Without them, the town feels too much like a suburb, the sister city not of Portobello but of Walnut Hills. Taking on the personality of its star, Mayberry morphs into "Kenberry," an all-American nowhere, as likely to be in California as in North Carolina. In fact, in one of the last episodes, "Howard the Swinger," the location all but becomes California. Howard moves into an apartment building in Mt. Pilot that has a pool. Around the pool is a bevy of bikini-clad maidens, none of them with even a whisper of a

Southern accent. Where did these girls come from? What would Aunt Bee and Clara think of them? What happened to the fishing hole?

Less Southern, New Mayberry is also less solid, less circumstantial. None of the most prolific writers of TAGS—Harvey Bullock, Everett Greenbaum and Jim Fritzell, Bill Idelson and Sam Bobrick, Jack Elinson and Charles Stewart—wrote for RFD. With a different group of writers, the custom of dropping the names of people and places is abandoned. Less aware, perhaps, of the town's history, the new writers don't insert references to local holidays into the scripts. There are no Mayberry Union High reunions, no Founder's Day celebrations, no Confederate relics (old times there are all but forgotten). The town remains, but the environment is gone. No longer do the locals spend their time reminiscing. No longer is the landscape inscribed with the names of residents present and past. Deprived of their yesterdays, the townspeople occupy themselves with what-happens-next. More reliant on plot than on place or character, RFD offers a Mayberry stripped of much of its Mayberrianism.

In this tame new world, poor Goober looks lost. He gets arrested in Mt. Pilot, is beaten up at Morelli's, can't find his way out of a cave. When a letter from the State Department arrives, he asks, "What does the U.S.A. want with us?" Goober's is a Mayberry B.C. question. Howard provides the New Mayberry response: "This gives the Incorporated City of Mayberry a golden opportunity to become part of the big picture" ("Sister Cities"). When Andy, Barney, Floyd, and Otis were around, Goober was an insider, not as bright as the rest maybe, but no less a part of the community. Indeed, he served as the gatekeeper of the town lodge, The Regal Order of the Golden Door to Good Fellowship. Now that the old-timers have vanished, Goober doesn't fit, not least because he is now the only regular with a Southern accent. His constant arguing with Emmett and Howard betrays his discomfort. A Mayberry B.C. survivor adrift in what has become, in effect, a post-Mayberrian world, Goober has little to do in R.F.D.

In another episode from the first season, "New Couple in Town," New Yorkers Frank and Audie Wylie rent a house for three months. Word gets around that Mr. Wylie is a writer, which prompts the Mayberry Literary Club (there was no such organization in the old town, not a bookwormish community) to invite him to speak. What Aunt Bee and the other members of the Club don't know is that Mr. Wylie writes comic books about monsters, Goober's favorite reading material. Discussing Mr. Wylie's work-in-progress, Goober suggests that, for once, the monster should be the hero of a story. His suggestion is thinly veiled autobiography. In Mayberry B.C. the monsters came from elsewhere: Mars, Minneapolis, or simply Out of Town. In the New Mayberry, Goober is the monster. The bumpkin has become the exotic.

RFD's title sequence makes evident the distance between original and spin-off. Obviously intended to evoke TAGS's opening, RFD episodes also begin with a father-son scene. But that's where the resemblance ends. Sam and Mike are not walking in the woods but standing in front of their house. The family car is parked in the driveway. Instead of going fishing, they are playing catch. Baseball is a national pastime; pond fishing is a rural one. In contrast to baseball, which was invented a century and a half ago, fishing goes back to the beginnings of human history. Tossing the baseball, Buddy is practicing for his Little League game or daydreaming about the Major Leagues; trying to catch the biggest trout in Myers Lake, Opie is not practicing or pretending. Throwing a baseball back and forth is an activity; sitting by a pond with a fishing pole is an exercise in inactivity. Rather than re-creating a simpler and older way of life, the title sequence of RFD portends a show about middle-class America.

The game of catch ends when Buddy busts a barn window—a symbolic blow against agrarianism? Perhaps. More importantly, it's unexpected, the antithesis of uneventful routine. Two seasons later, in the next-to-last episode of the show, the Town Council invites a representative from a Raleigh firm, City Planners Incorporated, to advise Sam about the possibilities for commercial development in and around the town. The plot centers on Millie's jealousy toward Terry, the winsome city planner, but what stands out is the makeover of Mayberry that Sam and Terry propose. As they tour different spots—Grover's Woods, Paradise Acres (another Walnut Hills?), the filtration plant ("our pride and joy")—they come to Myers Lake. Terry floats the notion that it could be turned into a tourist attraction by adding a boathouse and concessions. Amazingly, Sam does not object, though he recognizes that "just about everybody who grew up in Mayberry has a warm spot in his heart for Myers Lake" ("The City Planner"). Never mind that the very idea of luring outsiders to town is anti-Mayberrian. How can Sam consider messing with the lake where Andy and Opie went fishing, where Barney and Andy used to take girls to skip rocks? And how can the Town Council want to turn Mayberry into a theme park? It's too bad that Floyd is no longer around to set these people straight. As he once said, presciently, "The minute you start increasing the commercial zoning in Mayberry, it'll be the beginning of the end" (7.23).

It is a testament to Mayberry's magic, diminished as it was, that RFD was still drawing a large audience in its last season. Its cancellation resulted from CBS's decision to take off the air "everything with a tree in it," in the words of comic Pat Buttram. Other "hillbilly" shows on CBS—derided at the time as the "Country Broadcasting System"—also fell victim to the "rural purge": *The Beverly Hillbillies, Green Acres, Petticoat Junction, The Jim Nabors Hour, Hee Haw,* and *The New Andy Griffith Show,* with Griffith as the mayor of another North Carolina town. *Lassie* was also put to sleep by the rural purge, as was (on ABC)

The Lawrence Welk Show, not a rural show but one that didn't appeal to hip urban audiences.[8] In their place CBS put smartcoms like *The Mary Tyler Moore Show*, which premiered in 1970, and *All in the Family*, which went on the air the following year.

But Mayberry did not go away permanently. Fifteen years after RFD was cancelled, the town made one last appearance in *Return to Mayberry*, the most-watched TV movie of 1986. Significantly, the movie passes over RFD, as if Mayberry had disappeared on April Fool's Day, 1968, when the last TAGS episode was broadcast. Never mind that the last episode was entitled "Mayberry R.F.D." None of the characters specific to the sequel—Sam and Mike Jones, Alice the housekeeper, Ralph Barton—made it into the movie. The son whom Helen and Andy christened in an episode of RFD ("Andy's Baby") was retroactively aborted. The only RFD incident that *Return to Mayberry* acknowledges is Helen and Andy's marriage, which had been anticipated in the original series. By erasing RFD, the movie undoes the makeover of Mayberry as a progressive, New South community. The goal of the return is regress. In the opening scene, as Andy drives into Mayberry, he stops by Myers Lake and gets out of the car. His mind wanders back to the past, and we are treated to a replay of the original black-and-white title sequence, when Opie was six years old. Even if the movie is in color, the town to which Andy returns is Mayberry B.C.

Written by two TAGS veterans, Harvey Bullock and Everett Greenbaum, the movie includes most of the old characters: Andy, Opie, Barney, Otis, Gomer, Goober, Helen, Thelma Lou, Howard, the Darlings, and the indomitable Ernest T. Bass. Sarah remains at the switchboard; and Juanita is on the other end of Barney's serenades. Only Floyd, Emmett, and Aunt Bee are missing—Floyd and Emmett because Howard McNear and Paul Hartman had passed away; Aunt Bee because Frances Bavier, at the time well into her eighties and living in retirement in Siler City, North Carolina, was too ill to appear. In what is perhaps the only cruel moment in a Greenbaum or Bullock script, they write a scene where Andy visits his aunt's grave. (Greenbaum recalls that during a wrap party for TAGS, Frances Bavier said to him that the show was great except for the writing, which was "vile." The graveyard scene may be payback, two decades later).[9]

The plot: after many years away from his hometown, first in Charlotte and then as a postal inspector in Cleveland, Andy plans to run for his old job, not knowing that Barney, who has come back from Raleigh and has been serving as Acting Sheriff, is also running. Comic complications ensue, the principal one having to do with a monster—in Myers Lake, no less. Gullible as ever, Mayberrians have no problem believing that a monster has taken up residence in their fishing hole. Always skeptical, Andy discovers that the monster is a fake: a pink rubber dragon, formerly part of the sign at the Shanghai Gardens, the restaurant that Aunt Bee had owned for a brief time. The whole thing is a publicity stunt dreamed up by Wally Butler, the owner of Butler's Pantry and Inn, a refurbished version of the old restaurant. Another man in a hurry, Butler has changed the menu to "continental," added a sixteen-room motel, and given the place a suitably homey name. Like the members of the Town Council in New Mayberry, he wants to turn the town into a tourist attraction, the main stopping point between New York and Florida. At the end of Lee Smith's novel, *Oral History* (1983), one of the characters, Almarine Cantrell, plans to build a theme park called Ghostland in Hoot Owl Holler, a mountain community with a supposedly haunted homeplace. Like Cousin Al, Wally Butler is a pitchman for the New South. If he had his way, Mayberry would become Monsterland.

But in Mayberry B.C., the truly "strange creatures" are outsiders like Wally Butler, the New South entrepreneur. After Barney manages to whip the townspeople into a frenzy, Andy unmasks the hoax. Then, at an election rally, Barney finds out that Andy had intended to run for sheriff. In a moving speech, he resigns from the race and endorses his old boss. He does get the girl, however, and the movie ends with Barney and Thelma Lou's long-awaited marriage. Andy serves as best man; the entertainment is provided by the Darlings, who show up bearing gifts—dumplings and bluegrass music.

Though Mayberry resists the temptation to modernize, to get with the times, change does come. Andy and Barney may have reunited as sheriff and deputy, but the old order cannot be restored. Andy is now a grandfather. Opie has grown up into a balding yuppie who plans to leave Mayberry for a more lucrative job in New York. The town itself looks different. Two-story buildings with air-conditioning line Main Street. The bus stop has expanded into a bus station. The town now has a filtration plant and a solid waste pump. A sober Otis has evolved (or devolved) from town drunk into ice cream man. Howard dyes his hair (Gomer does too, but he doesn't admit it). The Mayberry Manor, a retirement home, is going up next to Goober and Gomer's filling station.

In the epilogue scene—the last tag to *TAGS*—it's late afternoon and there's no one on Main Street. Barney and Andy walk over to the flagpole at the center of town to take down and fold the American flag. As the camera pulls back into a long shot of the two men, with shadows lengthening around them, we realize that something is coming to an end here, and not just the day or the movie, but a vision of what used to be small-town America. Once the friendly town, Mayberry is now the deserted village. It is not only Aunt Bee who has passed away: Mayberry, R.I.P.

Interlude

THE ROAD TO MAYBERRY

Nobody's from no place.

ANDY TAYLOR, "STRANGER IN TOWN" (1.12)

T HE DEBUT EPISODE OF *THE ANDY GRIFFITH SHOW* was broadcast on October 3, 1960. Two weeks later, in Havana, my family's food wholesaling business—we called it *el almacén*, the warehouse—was confiscated by the Castro regime. A few days after that, on October 24, 1960, I left Cuba with my parents, my two brothers, and my sister on an overnight ferry to Key West called, of all things, *The City of Havana*. I was eleven years old. My parents were in their late thirties. That evening CBS broadcast the fourth episode of *TAGS*, "Ellie Comes to Town." It strikes me as fitting and a little eerie that as Ellie was settling into Mayberry, I was beginning my own road to the Friendly Town. The story of how I became an undocumented Mayberrian, the town's resident alien, began on that Monday.

Like hundreds of thousands of other Cubans, we settled in Miami. Except that we didn't truly settle, since we were planning to return to Cuba to pick up where the island's turbulent history had left us off. We saw ourselves as people passing through, transients rather than settlers. Unlike immigrants, we didn't come to America looking for a better life. We had a good one in Cuba. America was a rest stop before we turned around and headed back home. The immigrant lives in the fast lane. He is in a hurry—in a hurry to get a job, learn the language, lay down roots. If he arrives as an adult, he squeezes a second lifetime into the first. If he arrives as a child, he grows up in a hurry. Not so with the exile, whose life creeps forward one disappointment at a time. If the immigrant rushes, the exile waits. He waits to embark on a new career, to learn the new language, to start a new life. If immigration is a second birth, exile is a refusal to be born again. To the forces that push him forward, the exile says: I'm not budging. For the exile, every day is delay, every day is deferral. If his life were a painting, it would have to be a tableau. If it were a piece of music, it would have to be played lentissimo.

This is what it was like to grow up in Little Havana in the 1960s. We spent our days in a state of alert, waiting for the bridge across the water. Talk of Cuba was constant, and constantly hopeful. By the end of the 1960s, the rest of the country was in the throes of turbulent social changes, but for us the only thing that mattered was Cuba. This attitude, a variety of insularism, extended into the 1970s and 1980s. Many of the Cuban old-timers in Miami still feel this way today. They continue to wait. They cannot acknowledge that their homeland is no longer their home.

For myself, I came to accept, slowly and grudgingly, that our exile was irreversible, a steady state rather than a temporary condition. I was no longer an exiled Cuban, I was a Cuban exile. The noun, the substantive, was "exile." Location trumped nationality. Residence preceded essence. At the end of Andy García's movie *The Lost City*, his character, Fico Fellove, newly arrived in the United States, says to a friend: "I'm only impersonating an exile. I'm still in Cuba." I don't think Fico would say the same thing were he still in New York fifty years later. Perhaps he would say instead: "I'm only impersonating a Cuban. I've always been an exile."

Probably the first inkling that exile from Cuba was becoming chronic came with the Bay of Pigs invasion in April of 1961. When it failed, my parents no longer talked with the same optimism of our imminent return to Cuba. In the decades that followed, the cycle of booms of hope followed by busts of disappointment kept repeating itself. Year after year, on New Year's Eve, we would intone the toast: "El año que viene estamos en Cuba." "Next year in Cuba." But as the years went by, the expectation of return waned, though no one talked very much about it. The once hopeful toast had become mournful—words for a dirge rather than for a celebration.

The last time when it seemed to us that the end of exile was at hand was at the beginning of the 1990s. The collapse of the Soviet Union had made Cuban exiles, once again, hopeful of return. As a popular song of the day put it, "Nuestro día ya viene llegando." "Our day is coming." With the disappearance of Soviet subsidies, conditions in Cuba became dire indeed, but the dictatorship continued to hang on.

When someone spends decades nourished by the anticipation of *regreso*, return, it's not easy to accept that finally the time has come to be born again. The cultural newborn greets his new world kicking and screaming. If he could, he would crawl back into the womb of memory and hope. But he also knows that memory and hope can no longer sustain him because the promise implicit in them cannot be fulfilled. I understand that this will sound bizarre, but what helped me accept the fact of chronic exile, the midwives of my second birth, were two American TV shows. One was *I Love Lucy*, a sitcom from the 1950s that centers on a ditzy redhead and her Cuban husband; and the other was TAGS. I'm not sure how many literature professors regard sitcoms as equipment for living, but I have to confess that, much as I love literature, *I Love Lucy* and *The Andy Griffith Show* have had a greater impact on my life than any book I've ever read or written. Without them, I might never have cut the umbilical cord to Cuba.

The two shows could not be more different. The Ricardos live in a one-bedroom apartment in midtown Manhattan; the Taylors in a two-story bungalow in a small town in the Piedmont. *I Love Lucy* centers on a couple, Lucy and Ricky; TAGS on a single father and his son, Andy and Opie. Ricky's accent is no less noticeable than Andy's drawl, but that's where the resemblance ends. Music is also prominent in both, but in TAGS it's hymns and bluegrass, while at Ricky's Club Babalú all roads lead to rumba. *I Love Lucy*'s theme song is a Latin-tinged big-band number. Andy and Opie stroll to the fishing hole while a simple, whistled melody plays in the background.

Growing up in Little Havana, I didn't watch either of these shows because they didn't seem relevant to my life. Had I watched TAGS, I probably would have been baffled by Andy's drawl, not to mention Gomer's and Goober's. Had I watched *I Love Lucy*, Ricky would have seemed like a caricature of the Cuban men around me. For American baby boomers, classic TV shows like TAGS and *I Love Lucy* make up the sound track of their childhood, as Robert Thompson has remarked.[1] The sound track of my childhood was Cuban-exile talk radio as exemplified in a station that called itself "La Cubanísima," a station more Cuban than which none could be conceived.

It was not until thirty years later, as I was coming finally to the realization that we were here to stay, that *I Love Lucy* became relevant to my life. Return to Cuba seemed more remote than ever. To make matters worse, my family had entered one of those periods of contraction that bedevil all families. In the early decades of exile, my parents and grandparents and aunts and uncles were all alive, and those of us who had arrived as children were growing up and starting families of our own. It seemed to me then that nobody ever died in Miami. By the 1990s, however, the first generation—those for whom return to Cuba would have been most meaningful—had begun to pass away, taking with them the memories of life before exile. With each death, Cuba grew a little more distant. It was clear that we were reaching the point of no return, an expression that, for a family of exiles, acquires a unique depth of meaning.

At the time I was going through changes of my own. I had recently married an American (second marriages sometimes accompany second births). As we were getting to know each other, Mary Anne told me that before meeting me the only Cuban she knew well was Ricky Ricardo. As she phrased it, I was Ricky Ricardo with a Ph.D. Since Mary Anne was the first American I had gotten to know well, in spite of having lived in the United States for three decades, we were curious to see how a Cuban man and an American woman made a life together. *I Love Lucy* reruns came on every afternoon on TBS. I would tape the episodes onto our now-obsolete VCR and we would watch them together in the evening. *I Love Lucy* became our version of foreplay.

It also provided the inspiration for my book called *Life on the Hyphen*. Much of what I say there about the pleasures, perils, and possibilities of a bicultural life, of a life on the hyphen, I learned by watching Ricky love Lucy. In one memorable episode, Lucy decides that Ricky misses Cuba and decides to dress up like his mother. Or like her idea of Ricky's mother. When Ricky returns from a long day of rehearsals at the Babalú Club, he walks into the apartment and utters those immortal and problematic words, "Lucy, I'm home." She emerges from the bedroom dressed like Carmen Miranda singing a song in Portuguese. Befuddled, Ricky wants to know what's going on. Sounding every bit like the American he isn't, he says, "Lucy, have you gone off your rocker?" She explains that she wanted to remind him of his happy childhood in Cuba. Ricky's reply turned into the mantra of my cultural rebirth: "Lucy, honey, if I wanted things Cuban, I would have stayed in Havana. That's the reason I married you, cause you're so different from everyone I'd known before."

Fast-forward a decade. After teaching at Duke University for many years, I had taken a position at Columbia University. As I mention in the introduction, once I became a part-time northerner, an unexpected thing happened. Instead of looking forward to next year in Cuba or to the next vacation in Miami, as I had done for all of my life, I now looked forward to Christmases and summers in the Tarheel State, where we had kept our house. To mitigate my Carolina blues, I began to watch reruns of *TAGS*, as we had done years earlier with *I Love Lucy*. Each episode was like an anti-exile pill. For as long as it lasted, I was no longer a Cuban exile; I was a Mayberrian. Like Ed Sawyer, "the stranger in town," I found in the townspeople a warmth, a *philia*, absent from my everyday life. Identifying with those anonymous passersby that we see strolling down Main Street, I felt at home in Mayberry.

After a while, the y'alls and drawls of the characters became music to my ears, sounds as sweet as sourwood honey. We speak of people being comfortable in their own skins; but we should also speak of people being comfortable in their own mouths. That's how Mayberrians sounded to me. Exiles have uncomfortable mouths. My Cuban accent is a symptom of unease, a disturbance caused by the clash between my two languages. But the Southern accent of Mayberrians testifies to the harmony of word and mouth. Whether it's Andy's soft drawl or Gomer's comical twang, words flow from their tongues without a hint of difficulty or unease. Even the Darling sons, who never speak a word, have comfortable mouths, as becomes evident when they start to sing. Just as there are no travel agencies, there are no mumblers in Mayberry. The marriage of person and place is matched by the fit of tongue and mouth.

At the same time, I realized that the Mayberry of *TAGS* was not so different from the Little Havana where I grew up. Both were tight-knit, self-sufficient communities of like-minded people. When Mayberrians get together in Floyd's barbershop or at the church social, every sentence they utter to one another, whatever its specific meaning and context, also says: we are alike. If Andy and Barney spend quiet moments on the porch or in the courthouse without speaking, the reason is that among intimates, people with a shared history and outlook, almost everything goes without saying. To be understood without explanation is the sure indication that you are among kin or kith. That's the way things are in Mayberry, and the way they used to be in Little Havana in the 1960s. Everyone didn't know everyone, but everyone knew about everyone, as in *TAGS* when Barney and Andy share recollections of a high school teacher, or when Floyd recalls some bit of Mayberrian lore. The Little Havana of those years also seemed to be full of Aunt Bees and uncle Floyds (he's not literally an uncle, but he behaves like one). My own uncle Floyd was Tío Mike, who used to take us to the side and entertain us with wild stories about the time when dinosaurs roamed Cuba. My Aunt Bee was his wife, Tía Mary, restless and never at a loss for words. Barneys also abounded. When they weren't working for $35 a week as security guards or janitors, they were hatching grandiose schemes for toppling Fidel Castro. And like Mayberrians, we had our own southern dialect, Cuban Spanish, much faster than a drawl but just as unintelligible to outsiders.

The other thing that Little Havana had in common with Mayberry was the conviction of loss, a conviction seldom verbalized but firmly embedded in the psyche of the group. Few communities are more tightly knit than a community of losers. Growing up in Miami, I belonged to such a community. I was surrounded by apostles of a Lost Cause, a romantic legend whose site was not the Old South but Old Cuba, the *Cuba de ayer* of my parents and grandparents. I was an apostle myself. The historical circumstances are quite different, of course, but the sentiments were similar. Indulging our nostalgia, we engaged in some of the same embellishments as did Southerners for decades after the Civil War. Like the advocates of the Lost Cause, we never tired of evoking a place that no longer existed, that perhaps had never existed. The Franco-American novelist Julien Green, who grew up in France as the descendant of Confederates, recalls that his mother looked upon him and his siblings as "the children of a nation which no longer existed but lived on in her heart." He adds: "We were eternally the conquered but unreconciled — rebels, to employ a word dear to her."[2] Cuban exiles felt the same way, conquered but unreconciled. Some of us still do.

Right now I am doing what Mayberrians do. I am "settin' and starin.'" Throughout the couple of years that I have been thinking and writing about Mayberry, it has often appeared to me that there is something Mayberrian about the birds that patronize the birdfeeders at our home in Chapel Hill. When I first watched the 249 episodes in sequence, I would look up from my computer screen, and there they would be, an avian Mayberry: the woodpeckers (Barn and Floyd), the blue jays (Goober and Gomer), the melodious finches (the Darlings), the tufted titmice (Ellie, Helen, Thelma Lou), the chickadees (Opie, Leon, and Johnny Paul), the cardinals (Aunt Bee and Clara), the wrens (the Fun Girls), the nuthatches (Ernest T. Bass), the scrawny robin (Judd), the occasional grackles (Mayors Stoner and Pike), the even rarer bluebird (Sharon DeSpain). There is a time-lessness to birds in a birdfeeder, as there is to Mayberry. They always look like the same birds, though obviously they aren't. A month, two months, go by and you look up from your work and there it is, that cardinal, that nuthatch, that you were looking at months ago, or last year . . . Nobody's from no place, as Andy says, and some people are lucky enough to stay in their place.

Part Two

THE PEOPLE

What a town is depends on its people.

MILLIE HUTCHINS, "HOWARD'S MAIN EVENT" (8.6)

CHAPTER ONE

Sheriff without a Gun (Andy)

ONE OF THE BOYS, ANDY IS ALSO A MAN AMONG BOYS. A father not only to Opie, Andy extends his parental solicitude to Barney, Floyd, Otis, Gomer, Goober, and other Mayberrians. In the pilot, Andy was sheriff, justice of the peace, and editor of the town newspaper. His journalism career was dropped from the series, and he acted as justice of the peace only rarely, but the diverse occupations do suggest his multiple responsibilities. Most things to all the townspeople, Andy acts as midwife, marriage counselor, matchmaker, town psychologist, and village guru — as well as big brother, surrogate father, Dutch uncle, and best friend. As early as the second episode, "The Manhunt," it is clear that Andy's personal and professional lives are inextricable. Myers Lake, where he and Opie go fishing at the beginning of the episode, is the setting for the capture of the bad guy, who tries to flee in Gertrude, Andy's leaky rowboat. If Andy is the sheriff without a gun, he is also a father in uniform.

In addition, he is the town's most eligible bachelor, a status often addressed but never dealt with satisfactorily. Early in the first season, Ellie Walker, the new druggist, becomes Andy's steady girlfriend. Played by Elinor Donahue, who had starred as the eldest daughter in *Father Knows Best*, Ellie resembled her earlier character: a smart, educated, occasionally flirtatious young woman. Ambitious, Ellie was the first woman elected to the Town Council. She was also instrumental in getting Barney and Thelma Lou together, as well as in imbuing farmers' daughters with a sense of fashion. Her lively personality made for interesting episodes, but it also shortened her fictional life. At the end of the first season, Donahue asked to be released from her three-year contract, hoping that she would be asked to stay. To her chagrin, Griffith and the producers did not object because they felt that the chemistry between Andy and Ellie wasn't right.[1] Yes: Ellie was too spunky, too blunt, too assertive. Her toothy grin prob-

Ellie in Andy's grip.

ably sent shivers up the sheriff's spine. In "The Beauty Contest" (1.16), which turns on Andy's mistaken belief that Ellie expects him to pick her as Miss Mayberry (another of his jobs: judge of beauty), the two of them are walking along Main Street arm in arm. Rather than letting Ellie hold on to him, he grips her arm as if afraid that she's going to assault him. In another episode, Andy concludes—mistakenly—that Ellie is a "desperate hunter" (1.5), which is why she is not far wrong when she calls him "a horrid suspicious-minded mistrustful cynic" (1.16).

In the second and third seasons, other women took Ellie's place as Andy's love interest, but the sexier the woman, the more uncomfortable Andy looked. In the second season, he was paired with Thelma Lou's cousin Karen Moore (Gail Davis, a veteran of Gene Autry westerns) and the county nurse Mary Simpson (played by two different actresses, Julie Adams and Sue Ane Langdon). The following season, a third county nurse arrived: sultry Peggy McMillan (Joanna Moore), who also proved too much for Andy. In the second episode of the season, Andy and Peggy double-date with Barney and Thelma Lou. After leaving the diner, they drive to the lake. Barney and Thelma Lou stay in the car while Andy and Peggy walk to the edge of the lake. Barney tries frantically to make out with an embarrassed Thelma Lou. Andy has a different notion of what to do with a girl: he shows Peggy how to skip pebbles on the water. At the end of the episode, after Peggy has convinced Andy that her father's wealth should not be a hindrance to their relationship, they are back at the lake, skipping stones across the water. When Andy dated Thelma Lou's cousin, his idea of a date was to shoot crows at Finnegan's Flats. As it happened, Karen was a better shot than Andy.

It was not until the end of the third season that Andy acquired a permanent girlfriend, Helen Crump. Having failed to light the spark with lady druggists, shooting champions, and county nurses, he settles upon an elementary school teacher, pretty but plain, halfway between comely and homely. Usually dressed in loose, shapeless suits, Helen didn't wear sweaters and seldom put on slacks or jeans. Her last name, Crump, suggests "frump," even though the actress in the part, Aneta Corsaut, was anything but frumpy. Left to her own devices, Helen could have been Mayberry's Mary Richards, but the writers never gave her a chance, which made it difficult for Corsaut to conceal her frustration. Helen's ever-present smile is as inauthentic as her fondness for Andy. As she says, her relationship with Andy is "so wonderful—and so dull" (5.28). In spite of her killer looks, Peggy McMillan did seem like someone who would have been content to spend her life skipping rocks across Myers Lake. When Aunt Bee goes away for a few days, she takes to the job of Bee-to-be with such gusto that Andy gets scared off. Given the number of attractive women who failed to awaken Andy's dormant libido—to "catch fire," as producer Aaron Ruben put it[2]—the question is not what rocks Andy's boat, but why is Andy's boat so unrockable.

In an uncharacteristically self-revealing comment, Andy Griffith attributed the problems in finding Andy Taylor a suitable mate to his own "difficulty" with women:

> We never knew how to write for women. We never did know, and because of my peculiar nature, and my personal relationship with women, and the difficulty I've always had with them—it became even more difficult for us to write for women. Elinor Donahue was a regular in the company before we ever started, and we were so lucky to get her, we thought. Well, it didn't work out at all. It wasn't her fault. It was our fault. It starts with me. [. . .] But we knew that there was a whole area in which we *needed* something. So we tried this one and that one and tried the other one, and finally realized that it wasn't any of their faults. It was our fault.[3]

On screen, Andy Griffith's difficulty came across as Andy Taylor's ineptness. Compared to Andy, even John Wayne's cowboy characters, who were barely able to utter a complete sentence in front of a woman, come off like silver-tongued seducers. Singing with Opie or Barney, Andy is a delight, but watching him croon a romantic song to a girl is another story. He does fine with humorous or folksy tunes like "The Crawdad Song" and "Old Dan Tucker," but he has a hard time negotiating "I Wish I Was a Red Rosy Bush," a ballad he sings both to the county nurse and to Helen. He can't even bring himself to look into the girl's eyes. Were Barney singing about wanting to be a red rosy bush, the scene would be funny. With Andy, it makes one squirm. The only time he looks comfortable with a ballad, "Down in the Valley," Peggy does most of the singing, with Andy accompanying her on the guitar.

Even more awkward are those rare moments when the script calls for what he calls "kissy-kissy" (1.22). Peggy McCay, who played Sharon DeSpain, Andy's high school sweetheart in "Class Reunion" (4.19), relates the conversation she had with Griffith before they played their romantic scene: "He said to me, 'Do you really think we need to kiss?' I said, 'Andy, I *really* do, because it's a real love scene and I think we'd better do it.' And he said, 'Well, all right.'"[4] Others were not so lucky. In "Christmas Story" (1.11), he turns away when the script calls for him to kiss Ellie goodbye. And he doesn't do much more or better with Helen, who may have launched a thousand ships but couldn't squeeze a tender kiss out of Andy. Griffith said that what he liked about Andy and Helen's relationship was that it was "natural" and didn't require a courtship, which would have been a "hump."[5] A hump! Almost imperceptibly, Helen became Andy's fiancée, but anytime someone assumed that they were soon to marry, he promptly disavowed it. Although he claimed that he missed being married, that he wanted to have someone to come home to, talk of marriage invariably upset him. As he says to Barney in one of the many Andy-doesn't-find-a-wife episodes, "that subject is closed" (3.29).

In 1967 Griffith told *TV Guide* that more went on between Helen and Andy than met the viewer's eye: "They are a couple of adult human beings — unwed. What they do offscreen as adults we indicate occasionally by a look or a touch."[6] If such looks and touches happened, they were so subtle as to escape the viewer's detection — perhaps one reason why Helen usually looks not only bored but frustrated. The only thing that gets a rise out of her is the suspicion, always unfounded, that Andy is seeing someone else. And my surmise is that the underlying reason for her anger is not jealousy but envy: if only she could be that other woman! Analogously, the only times Andy shows real interest in her is when he thinks that Helen is falling for another man. But given his tepid feelings, one would think that he'd be relieved if someone took Helen off his hands.

"The Hollywood Party" (6.9) illustrates the difference between his "natural" relationship with Helen and the way he relates, or doesn't, to women more overtly sexual. In Hollywood for the filming of "Sheriff without a Gun," the movie about his life, Andy is asked to do publicity shots with Darlene Mason (Ruta Lee), who plays the doubly fictional sheriff's leading lady (the sheriff is played by none other than Gavin McLeod, the captain of *The Love Boat*). Andy is invited into Darlene's dressing room for the photography session. Sitting on the couch while Darlene primps, a nervous Andy confesses that he's never been in a lady's room. Once the photo shoot begins, Andy can't seem to get "cozy" enough. When she puts her arm around him, he moves away. His excuse is that he doesn't want to be unfaithful to Helen. Fortunately for him, Helen doesn't dress seductively or whisper in his ear. If she did, he'd be put off by her too. A good number of *TAGS* episodes deal with the shyness toward women of Gomer, Goober, Warren, or Howard, but Andy beats them all because he's not merely bashful, he's reluctant.

In this respect, as in others, the sharpest contrast is with Barney, a secret subscriber to *Love*, a *Playboy*-type men's magazine. In "Barney Comes to Mayberry" (7.19), when *he* gets the chance to date a movie star, he makes pass after pass, fruitlessly of course. In spite of occasional bouts of insecurity, Barney is the town's wolf. During his five years as deputy, he ran through a gallery of girlfriends: Miss Rosemary, Hilda Mae, Melissa, Phoebe Gilbert, Thelma Lou, and, of course, Juanita. Any time he and Andy double-dated, Andy drove so that Barney could smooch with his date in the back seat. His tousled hair and lipstick-smeared face became a running gag. In *Return to Mayberry*, Thelma Lou recalls that because of Barney's "friskiness," she had to slap him to keep him in line. And one steady girl wasn't enough. He had no compunction about two-timing Thelma Lou with Phoebe Gilbert or Juanita or going out with Daphne and Skippy, the Fun Girls. Always on the prowl, he's as aggressive as Andy is awkward. The only other character who matches Barney's libido is Ernest T. Bass, the mountain wolf. No wonder Ernest T. falls for Barney in drag (3.31).

The Taylor household suits Andy's personality because it rests on his and Aunt Bee's monastic marriage. In several episodes, the studio portrait of a beautiful young woman hangs from a wall in the living room. It would be reasonable to assume that it's a photograph of Andy's deceased wife, though in fact it's the young Frances Bavier's studio portrait.[7] If Bee's last name is Taylor, it's not only because she is Andy's father's sister but because she is, chastely, his spouse. Unlike the bonds between spouses, those that link the residents of this home are intergenerational, vertical rather than horizontal. As Andy says any number of times, he is perfectly happy with this arrangement: "Rule around here has got to be no marrying unless it's absolutely of a overwhelming nature" (2.26). No woman ever overwhelmed him.

In an episode from the first season, "The New Doctor" (1.24), Andy proposes to Ellie, fearing that he is going to lose her to the handsome Dr. Benson. But when Ellie demurs, Andy is relieved. She turns him down, citing the reason that Andy himself gives any time the subject of marriage is broached: the time's not right. But the real reason Andy doesn't get hitched is that his marriage would shatter the anaphrodisiac atmosphere of the Taylor household, and hence disrupt Mayberrian order. Sheldon Leonard once remarked that Andy needed a girlfriend so that viewers would not suspect him of being homosexual.[8] The subtle point behind this bizarre remark is that sexuality, of whatever kind, is antithetical to Andy's role in the community. He is a sexless sovereign — the sheriff without a gun — who stands above and apart from the people over whom he lords.

Technically Andy holds an elective office, but he governs Mayberry like a monarch. Andy at his desk is a king on a throne, with the buffoon, Barney, at his side, and his retinue of nutty knights — Floyd and Otis and Gomer and Goober — not far away. After Andy helps Floyd out of a scrape, he says that Andy is a "prince." As prince, Andy is the upholder of the law, but also the one who decides when the law does not hold. It doesn't come as a surprise that Mayberry was almost named "Taylortown" in honor of Andy's ancestor, Carlton Taylor, one of the purported heroes of the Battle of Mayberry. For all practical purposes, Mayberry *is* Andy Taylor's town.

As a sexless sovereign, the ruler over what political theorists have called "a state of exception," Andy cannot marry. He must remain autonomous and unentangled. I realize that my description diverges from the image that *TAGS* fans have of him. I don't deny that Andy is the glue that makes Mayberrian society stick, a personification of community-building *philia*. His kindness and sobriety give the town a stable anchor. Without its sheriff, Mayberry would be a nuthouse. But it's also true, in my view, that Andy remains an enigma, as monarchs are enigmas. In contrast to Barney, who likes to talk about the traits he inherited from his mother and father, including the clock in his stomach, Andy never talks about his parents or his childhood. This is all the more striking given that Aunt Bee is his father's sister, and thus would be likely to talk to Andy about her brother. But she is as unmemorious as her nephew. Other than what we find out in the Mayberry Union High reunions, we know remarkably little about him. Especially surprising is the absence of any mementos from his deceased wife, whom he never talks about. Aunt Bee has her kitchen and Opie has his room, as does Barney, but Andy has no space of his own. His bedroom will have a significant role in only one episode, "The Rumor" (4.29), which ends with him ceding it to Aunt Bee. His willingness to part with the room where he has slept for many years, presumably the room he shared with his wife, underscores the irrelevance to the show of Andy's inner life — his memories, his dreams, what he says to himself when no one is listening. The space that defines him is the venue where he holds court, the appropriately named courthouse, which he shares with the town.

Most of the other characters express their excitement or worry by fidgeting — Floyd being the fidgeter-in-chief. But Andy tends to keep his own counsel. His defining feature is the amused, benevolent smile with which many an episode ends. The one crucial exception to his reserve is his relationship with Opie, the only kinship bond in the show that really matters. Disinterested in women, he relishes physical closeness with his "young'un" — putting him on his lap, tucking him in at night, hugging and kissing him. (Andy's expressions of affection rarely extend to Aunt Bee, who is almost as unaffectionate as he is.) Embarrassed by all the PDAs, eleven-year-old Opie asks his father not to kiss him in front of company. But as the title sequence suggests through small gestures—the clasping of hands, the arm around the shoulder—Opie is the one person in Mayberry whom Andy cares about in a way that goes much deeper than *philia*. It's not the lessons he teaches Opie or the lessons he learns from Opie that are most meaningful, but Andy's love for his son. Only Opie could ever break Andy's heart.

A recurring theme, Andy's devotion to his son is nowhere clearer than in "Opie's Rival" (3.10), an episode in which Andy is dating Peggy McMillan. In the opening scene, Andy and Opie are fishing in Myers Lake—a telltale sign, since this is one of only a handful of episodes whose first scene is continuous with the title sequence. Father and son are having a grand time, chatting and joking about the biblical Jonah, who caught a fish from the inside. Opie hooks a fish, the biggest fish, Andy says, ever caught by anyone of Opie's size and weight. "If I didn't know better, I'd swear you were kin to Isaak Walton, the man who wrote the book about fishing." Opie replies that not even Walton can fish better than his paw. Opie: "I bet you're the best fisherman in the world." Andy: "I'll bet you something else, I'll bet you're the best fishing partner in the world."

The outing is topped off by a fish fry in the woods. Opie: "Paw, we sure have a lot of fun together, don't we? It's always going to be like this, ain't it?" Andy: "If I have anything to do with it, it will." Opie then proposes that he and his father make a pact so that they are never separated. His idea is that they become blood brothers by cutting their wrists with a knife, the way the Indians do on television. Andy suggests that they make a cross on their wrists with ashes from the fire and rub their wrists together, which works even better than blood. With Opie and Andy, exceptionally, kin and kindred coalesce.

The next day, they run into Peggy in front of the courthouse. She also likes to fish, so Andy invites her to come along with them. Clearly not happy, Opie gives many reasons why Miss Peggy wouldn't want to go fishing, but the next scene finds the three of them in the boat. While Opie sits by himself in the back, Andy teaches Peggy the rudiments of fishing. When Opie lands an even bigger trout than the day before, his father doesn't notice. That evening, as Andy is preparing to go out with Peggy, Opie pretends to be sick so that Andy will call off the date. The following day, Opie prevents his father from seeing Peggy by not relaying her messages, which makes her think that Andy is giving her the brush-off. After Opie sees Peggy going off in a huff, he comes out to the porch and confesses that it's all his fault. He's scared that with Peggy around, "you won't want me anymore."

Andy puts Opie on his lap. "I wanna tell you something, Ope, and I want you to listen real careful, 'cause this is important. You're my young'un, and I love you more than anything or anybody in the whole world. And nothing or nobody can ever change that. You know, it's hard for me to tell you just how much you do mean to me, 'cause you're a part of me." Even if he were to get married one day, he continues, "nothing or nobody will ever change things between me and you. Because you're my son and we're buddies, right?" It scarcely matters that, in the epilogue, Andy, Opie, and Peggy are enjoying a fish fry together. (With a cross of ashes on her wrist, Peggy has become a blood brother too). As it turns out, this will be Peggy's last appearance, one more indication that Opie will never have a rival. Andy's relations with women, Helen included, are profoundly un-eventful, like the plot-generated complications. The one true event at the heart of *TAGS* is a father's unconditional love. Alone with Opie, fishing in the lake or talking quietly on the porch, Andy is most entirely himself.

CHAPTER TWO

Imagination (Mr. McBeevee)

SOME OF THE MOST INTERESTING PEOPLE WHO PASS through or live in Mayberry appear in only one episode. They include Ed Sawyer, the stranger who knows as much about Mayberry as the locals (1.12); Clarabel and Jennifer Morrison, moonshining sisters (1.17); Frank Myers, the Confederate bond holder (2.4); manicurist Ellen Brown, the sexiest woman ever to set foot in Mayberry (2.16); Henry Bennett, the town jinx (2.17); Barney's inept cousin Virgil (2.30); Regis, a hillbilly who carries around a sign calling for the elimination of the gold standard (4.7); and luckless Newton Monroe, played by Don Rickles (5.29). But my favorite is Mr. McBeevee, Opie's invisible friend, who opens the fourth season.

Nine-year-old Opie comes home one afternoon with a hatchet that he says was given to him by Mr. McBeevee, a man he met in the woods. Andy thinks that Mr. McBeevee, like the imaginary horse Blackie, is a figment of his son's overactive imagination. He asks Opie to put the hatchet back where he found it. The following day Opie shows his father a quarter given to him by Mr. Mc-Beevee. Interrogated by Barney, Opie claims that Mr. McBeevee lives up in the trees, wears a shiny silver hat, has twelve hands, jingles when he walks, and blows smoke out of his ears.

As the second act begins, Andy is wandering around in the woods. He's obviously in turmoil — something that nobody but his son can do to him. He wants to trust Opie, but also wants Opie to recognize the difference between reality and make-believe. Exasperated, he calls out Mr. McBeevee's name. Unexpectedly he gets a reply — "Hello, did somebody call me?" — and a man climbs down from a tree. Andy can't believe his eyes. There *is* such a person! Mr. McBeevee is a lineman working on the telephone poles in the woods by Myers Lake. His twelve hands are the tools in his tool belt, which jingle when he walks; his large silver hat is a tin helmet; and the smoke that comes out of his ears is a trick that he performs with a cigarette.

At the courthouse, Andy tells Barney that he has just seen Mr. McBeevee and invited him over for supper. Barney thinks that Andy has lost his mind. Is Barney right? Does Mr. McBeevee really exist? Nobody but Andy and Opie has seen him. We have seen him too, but then again, we believe that shadowy figures on a small screen are real people. There *is* something magical about this man who spends his days in trees and speaks with an Irish brogue. Shiny hat and all, he seems an oversized and benevolent leprechaun, an emanation of the sociable woods of Mayberry, where one is as likely to encounter a band of gypsies as a group of campers. Mr. McBeevee—in the original script his name was "McTeevee"—embodies the suspension of disbelief required of us, invisible visitors to Mayberry. He is every bit as real as the town itself.

CHAPTER THREE

Life Imitates Fife (Barney)

Aunt Bee: For heaven's sake, what's happening to this town anyway?
Andy: Barney!

"THE CASE OF THE PUNCH IN THE NOSE" (5.25)

*A*S THE ANDY GRIFFITH SHOW WAS ORIGINALLY CON-
ceived, Sheriff Andy did not have a sidekick. Don Knotts, who
had appeared with Griffith in *No Time for Sergeants*, suggested to Griffith that
he needed a deputy. Griffith and Sheldon Leonard liked the idea, and Barney
Fife was born, a role that earned Knotts five Emmys and TV immortality. Although Knotts had a long and successful career, nothing he did after leaving
TAGS—movies such as *The Ghost and Mr. Chicken* (1966), *The Reluctant Astro-
naut* (1967), and *The Love God* (1960); the sitcom *Three's Company*, where for
five seasons he played the lecherous Mr. Furley—lived up to his brilliance as
Barney Fife. As everyone connected with TAGS realized, Griffith was the titular
star, but Knotts's Barney was the main attraction.

Alone among Mayberrians, Barney Fife knows defeat, his weekly bread.
Time after time he hatches a scheme that goes awry, arrests the wrong man,
or lets the right one escape. Skippy, one of the Fun Girls, calls him Bernie. *The
Mayberry Gazette* gives his last name as "Fike," which sounds too much like
"fake." His occasional moments of redemption, usually orchestrated by Andy,
hardly compensate for his lifelong losing streak. In an early episode, "Andy the
Matchmaker" (1.7), Barney decides to resign from his position—another running gag—because the people don't respect him: "Folks around here think of
me as a failure, sort of a nobody." The final straw is the limerick that a couple of
boys write on the bank wall:

There was once a deputy called Fife
Who carried a gun and a knife.
The gun was all dusty,
The knife was all rusty,
'Cause he never caught a crook in his life.

Barney's sense of inadequacy—when he gets drunk, he walks around repeating, "I'm no good, I'm no good" (3.15)—will be a recurring motif, the subject of episodes such as "Barney Gets His Man" (1.30), "Barney's Replacement" (2.2), "Lawman Barney" (3.7), "Barney and the Cave Rescue" (4.13), "Barney's Sidecar" (4.16), and "The Legend of Barney Fife" (6.18). Two things protect Barney's frail ego: Andy's affection and Barney's almost boundless capacity for self-delusion, which allows him to flatter himself with epithets as if he were some kind of epic hero: Reliable Barney Fife, Subtle Barney Fife, Eagle-Eyed Barney Fife. Or, in Andy's words: Barney the Beast and Fife the Fierce. It's fitting that he plays the cymbals in the Mayberry Band, for he's all sound and, for the most part, no fury. As Andy says, "that boy weighs about 100 pounds and 50 of it is proud" (2.2).

Barney's pride is rendered all the more risible by his looks: stooped shoulders, sunken chest, thin neck, protruding Adams apple. Athletic, he's not: when he runs, he waddles. Courageous, he's not: confronting ruffians, his trembling hands can't retrieve the bullet from the shirt pocket. Well-off, he's not: he rents a room in a boarding house. Articulate, he's not: a master of the malapropism, particularly when he tries to show off his knowledge of psychology. He turns "therapeutic" into "therapetic," "introvert" into "innervert," "compulsion" into "compelsion," "kleptomaniac" into "kleptominerac," and Cole Porter's "roaring traffic swoon" becomes a "roaring traffic spoon." For sure, Barney is not the only simpleton in Mayberry, but he differs from the others in that he seems to have no compensating gifts. Ernest T. rhymes. The Darlings pick. Gomer sings. Goober can take apart a car and put it back together in a day. Barney's talent is his pride. He sticks his thumbs in his gun belt, sniffs, and proclaims: "You know, Andy, there's no greater feeling than knowing you're perfect" (4.20).

As a comedic type, Barney descends from the miles gloriosus, or "vainglorious soldier," a stock character in Roman comedy. But the braggart is usually a secondary character, mere comic relief. During the years he serves as deputy, Barney is the catalyst for most of the action, the town's center of levity. Pumping himself full of hot air, he floats above the ground only to be inevitably deflated. A stickler for detail, he seems to know every law and regulation in the book but always misapplies them. Even when Andy cushions the fall, it is often painful to watch Barney make a fool of himself. In "The Clubmen" (2.10), he and Andy are being considered for membership in an exclusive gentlemen's club in Raleigh.

Barney is beside himself with happiness. Spiffy in his salt-and-pepper suit, he accompanies Andy to the Esquire Club. Andy doesn't put on airs, but Barney pretends he knows all about golf and the stock market. As he makes one dumb remark after another, comedy verges on cruelty. The saving grace is that he is too deluded to see himself as the others see him. Predictably, Andy is invited to join and Barney is turned down. Believing that it was Andy who got rejected, Barney writes a letter of resignation. Andy does not disabuse him. Once again, "Andy Saves Barney's Morale," the title of another episode (1.20).

The core of Barney's character is a precarious equilibrium between self-delusion and self-awareness. In most episodes, as in "The Clubmen," his blindness seems total: acute comic hubris. Barney catches a bad guy by mistake and acts as if he had planned it all along, bragging that he's "Barney the Bulkhead," whose body is a lethal weapon. In "Barney and the Choir" (2.20), the first of several episodes about his lack of musical ability, the first tenor falls ill and Barney takes his place. The problem is that he can't carry a tune. Not wanting to hurt his feelings, Andy figures out a way to have Barney think he is singing while another choir member does the tenor part. Although that booming voice could never come out of a Fife, Barney's surprise is only momentary. Since it's the voice he'd like to have, it's the voice he thinks he has. The scene is hilarious, with Barney energetically mouthing the words into a dead mike, his fifty pounds of pride in full flower. The next day, still oblivious, Barney tells Andy that if his law enforcement career doesn't work out, he has an ace in the hole: show business.[1]

But there are also moments in *TAGS*, admittedly less frequent, when Barney acknowledges the truth about himself. The genius of Don Knotts's acting is not to let these flashes of self-awareness sink in too deeply. Then Barney would become only pathetic. But just as he fights the low opinion others have of him, he fights the low opinion he has of himself, and usually triumphs. Barney knows that he's not up to the job of sheriff. (When he sits in Andy's chair, his head barely rises above the desk.) He knows that he's not reliable, cunning, or eagle-eyed. He knows that he's cowardly. He knows that he's high-strung and senti-mental. He knows that he is not big, strong, or handsome. The only reason he passes the physical exam required of deputies is because Andy attaches a heavy chain to Barney's ID tag, which brings his weight up to 145 pounds. After the weigh-in, Barney takes the chain off and says to Andy: "Isn't it amazing what it takes to hold one of them little tags?" (5.2). It's not clear to us whether, when he says this, Barney knows what really happened. The ambiguity—the fine line between blindness and insight—defines his character. But whether Barney real-izes it or not, his ID—his identity—needs ballasting. After an unsuccessful run for town sheriff, he wallpapers his room with leftover campaign posters so that he can bask in his multiplied image.

Unlike most Mayberrians, Barney is not content with his lot. His off-key singing in a town full of musical people accentuates the difference. Not for nothing is his last name Fife: high-pitched, thin as a reed, repeatedly sounding discordant notes. But this makes him the only individualist in town, someone who marches to the offbeat of his own drum. In "Barney and the Choir," he stands apart from the group and is given his own microphone. It's a trick, but it also conveys his individuality. Barney studies karate, takes voice lessons, reads up on new law enforcement methods, tries his hand at real estate. He dreams of making it big, whether the big time is Broadway, the Esquire Club, or the front page of the *Mayberry Gazette*. At a hotel in Raleigh, he registers as "Bernard Fife, M.D." (M.D. stands for "Mayberry Deputy"). Barney fights for lost causes, not the antebellum South but himself: the ninety-pound weakling who stares into the mirror and sees Charles Atlas looking back. Ortega y Gasset once wrote that a man's greatest endowment is "el don de insatisfacción," the gift of being unsatisfied. Barney incarnates this gift in excess, a trait all the more noticeable because he is surrounded by people who want nothing more than what they have. Andy refuses several jobs to remain sheriff of Mayberry; Barney doesn't turn down opportunities—he muffs them. When he auditions for the Ladies' League Musicale, he is asked to sing "a capella." He sings "Acapella, Acapella" to the tune of "La cucaracha" (3.20).

Rushing in where fools fear to tread, Barney upsets the status quo. But he differs from the con men who pass through Mayberry in that he doesn't con anyone but himself. In another episode about his singing voice, "The Song Festers" (4.20), his spot as the soloist in the choir is taken by Gomer, who, all agree, has a much better voice. Barney knows it too, though he is loath to admit it. Andy arranges it so that all three—Barney, Andy, and Gomer—will sing the solo, thus avoiding embarrassment for his deputy. Reluctantly Barney agrees to share the spotlight. Unlike Andy, who's happy being a sheriff, and Gomer, who's happy being a mechanic, and Floyd, who was born to be a barber, Barney is only happy imagining himself as someone he is not. Cary Grant, who was born Archie Leach, once remarked that he dreamed of the man he wanted to be until he became that man. Barney also dreamed, but he remained Barney.

His decision to move to Raleigh is consistent with his aspirations. But contrary to what he has told Andy—that he has "a big job, a terrific future"—in the Raleigh Police Department Barney is little more than a gofer (one of his big jobs is to replace the paper towels in the bathroom). What is more, his incompetence almost gets him fired. He lives in a rundown boarding house with a family of burglars, "Ma and the boys," who are pulling off a string of supermarket robberies thanks to Barney's inadvertent complicity, as Andy realizes. He sets the Parkers up so that Barney catches them in the act of robbing another store. Impressed by Barney's acumen, Captain Dewhurst changes his mind about firing him. The episode, "A Visit to Barney Fife" (7.18), is difficult to watch not only because of the disdain of his Police Department colleagues but also because we can imagine what will happen to Barney once Andy goes back home. How long before he messes up again and really gets fired? How long before he's back to living at the Y? The scenes at the Parkers' recall those at the Taylor household, with everybody dining together and relaxing on the porch. But the external similarities bring out the contrast between the two families and, by extension, the two towns. Ma Parker is no Aunt Bee, and her "boys" are nothing like Floyd, Gomer, and Goober. When Barney shows Andy his bachelor "pad," a cramped room with a rickety bed, a tawdry armchair, and no view, he speaks as if he were living in luxury. But Barney knows that it's not true and Andy plays along. If the Parkers' household is nothing like the Taylors', the room lacks the homey feel of the one he rented from Mrs. Mendlebright, who reminded him of his mother. During an earlier trip to Raleigh, Barney had bragged: "You know, Andy, this is where I belong. Barney Fife in the asphalt jungle!" (2.25). As a jungle, Raleigh is a breeding ground for nasty critters such as the Parkers, against whom Barney is defenseless.

I don't think that many viewers of *TAGS* can identify with Andy. Too modest, too wise, too perfect a father, he is a role model impossible to emulate. But we can identify with Barney: proud but fragile, restless but leery of change, easily roused, and just as easily demoralized. And yes, like us, sometimes Barney rises to the occasion, fleetingly incarnating the man he wants to be.

In one memorable episode, "Lawman Barney" (3.7), a couple of tough-looking strangers are selling produce from their truck, which violates Section 17b, Article 4, of the town ordinances. When Barney confronts them, they scare him away. He returns to the courthouse sullen and depressed. It's not, as Andy thinks, because he had a fight with Thelma Lou or because the laundry put too much starch in his shirt. It's because he knows that he has behaved like a coward. Meeting the strangers, Andy tells them to watch out for Barney, a wolf in sheep's clothing who is setting them up "for the kill." Andy then orders Barney to get the farmers to leave town. In the meantime, the strangers find out from Floyd that Barney is not the "beast" that Andy portrayed, and they go back to their roadside stand. Against Andy's advice, Barney insists on confronting the strangers anyway. For once, his hands don't tremble, his voice doesn't crack. He walks up to the two men, full of fear yet resolute, informs them that he is an officer of the law, and proceeds to stare them down (or up, since both are a head taller than he is). Once the strangers drive away, Barney nearly collapses.

Moments like this give us a peek into his tumultuous inner life. Appealing as they are, most Mayberrians are not prey to inner conflict. Barney is a warehouse of self-doubt decked out like a store at Christmas. Andy's bedroom has no relevance to his role; Barney's rented room is a projection of his personality, an inner space turned outward. In "Up in Barney's Room" (4.10), a title that would not make any sense apropos of Andy, Barney points to the "touches that reflect [his] personality": family pictures, the Mayberry High pennant, clippings from the *Mayberry Gazette*, and issues of *True Blue Detective* magazine going back to 1959. The salt-and-pepper suit, his pretension to elegance—someone calls him "the Adolph Menjou of Mayberry"—is hanging in the open closet. Barney even has his secrets: the subscription to *Love* magazine, an issue of which Andy finds while rummaging through a garbage pile. When Mrs. Mendlebright asks Barney to move his old trunk out of the cellar so that she can grow mushrooms, Barney stores it in Andy's garage. The trunk is full of mementos: books, notebooks, trophies, a tennis racket, cleats, a Mayberry High bullhorn, a yearbook, and his most prized possession, a rock that his father kept on his desk, on which a young Barney used to strike matches to light his father's pipe. In contrast, Andy didn't even keep his high school yearbook, which Aunt Bee gave away.

Unlike his boss and cousin, Barney enjoys talking about himself and his parents. A sickly child who suffered from nosebleeds, though not as frequently as his father, he was taught to sew and crochet by his mother, from whom he inherited his delicate stomach, "low blood sugar content," and the repulsion toward hats that have been on someone else's head. As a teenager, he was so thin that he could reach into a milk bottle and retrieve an egg. Always an outstanding student, in high school he would get bad marks on purpose so that the other students wouldn't hate him. "An IQ can be a mixed blessing. Some people want it and can't get it. I had it and had to get rid of it" (4.8). In high school Barney participated in the Spanish Club and the Tin Foil Drive. He was also a Hall Monitor and a member of the Volleyball Court Maintenance Crew, but didn't make it into the Philomathian Society, he says, because someone blackballed him. After graduating, he joined the armed forces and worked in the PX library on Staten Island, where he commanded several thousand books, his contribution to whipping "the dreaded Hun."

Because of the disparity in temperament, Barney and Andy have a complicated relationship. On one level, Barney is the grown-up son who never grew up. In his dealings with Opie, Andy can act like a disciplinarian who is ready to give his son a "whippin'" (or at least threaten to do so). With Barney he takes a different approach. Barney's usual punishment is being the target of Andy's ribbing, which always hits the mark. Barney: "Never know when to stop, do you? Just go on and on and on. It's a kind of sickness with you, I guess" (1.26). There are times when Andy's teasing comes off as a little sadistic, the verbal equivalent of bullying—as if Griffith, the star, were getting even with Knotts, the upstart. For the most part, however, the sheriff accepts his deputy's foul-ups with biblical forbearance.

As one would expect, Barney does not cut his boss the same slack. Not only does he boast that he is a better police officer; he is not above thinking that

Andy is trying to steal his girl or take credit for his deputy's accomplishments. When Barney runs for sheriff, he accuses Andy of malfeasance in office. In "Andy on Trial" (2.29), he makes similar accusations to a reporter sent by the publisher of a Raleigh newspaper to dig up dirt on the town's sheriff as retaliation for a traffic ticket. Posing as a student researching her thesis, the beautiful reporter (Ruta Lee) has no trouble getting Barney to brag about how he would improve the town's law enforcement. "The kid is a little lax," Barney admits. Not only does Andy "mollycoddle" the town drunk, he allows jaywalking and uses the squad car for personal business. After the story appears in the newspaper under the headline, "Does the Sheriff Run the Town, or Does the Town Run the Sheriff?," a state investigator shows up. At the hearing, Barney is called to testify against Andy. When the statements he made to the reporter are quoted back to him, Barney has to agree that they're all true: Otis checks himself in and out of jail; Andy tears up jaywalking tickets and uses the squad car to deliver groceries. But once the questioning is over, he refuses to get off the stand.

> This is a hearing, ain't it? Well, then I think you should hear more than a bunch of yesses. Sure I said all them things. But the truth is sometimes I get carried away with myself. When I was talking to that young lady there, well I got to bragging a little bit. I guess that's one of my faults. But I sure didn't think it was going to backfire and be used against Andy. Why, Andy is the best friend I got in the whole world. And as far as I'm concerned he's the best sheriff too. You gotta understand, this is a small town. The sheriff is more than just a sheriff. He's a friend. And the people in this town, they ain't got a better friend than Andy Taylor. You ask me if Andy runs a taut ship. Well no, he don't. But that's because of something he's been trying to teach me ever since I started working for him. And that is that when you're a lawman and you're dealing with people, you do a whole lot better if you go not so much by the book but by the heart.

For once, Barney acknowledges in public what he usually says only to himself. Instead of Andy stepping in before reality crashes in on his deputy, as usually happens, Barney intervenes on Andy's behalf by confessing the truth about himself: he brags, he gets carried away. As befits his personality, the epiphany is short-lived. A bit later, on the phone with Thelma Lou, he reverts to his normal self, bragging that he "made a monkey" out of the prosecutor and "pulled Andy out of a mess." Nonetheless, Barney's flashes of self-awareness, though rare, are among the most poignant moments in the show. His recognition that he is smaller than life makes him compellingly lifelike, reliably human.

In *Return to Mayberry*, Andy explains to Opie why he is going to withdraw from the race for sheriff: "Opie, please understand. I won't run against Barney. I should have figured he'd be running. I don't expect he's had too many high spots in these last years. Everyone deserves one. This may be his big one. I won't stand in his way." But in the end it is Barney who bows out because he knows that he's not cut out to be top dog, though this does not stop him from barking.

Mayberry is a queer town full of queer people. Except for Andy and Opie, all of the show's regular characters are, well, characters. As one of the outsiders who comes upon Mayberry remarks: "I've never seen such a bunch of kooks in my whole life" (2.15). Yet from this rare congeries of kooks we learn a great deal about human nature. And no one teaches us more than Barney, the odd-ball who is Everyman.

CHAPTER FOUR

A Face in the Crowd (Mr. Schwump)

U NLIKE CHARACTERS WHO, LIKE MR. MCBEEVEE, APPEAR once and then move on, never to be heard from again, some Mayberrians seem to be always hanging around but never say a word. Since they have names, they can't be called "extras," though they never are given much to do. One of them is Leon, the little boy in a cowboy suit who exemplifies the dictum that children should be seen and not heard. In "The Shoplifters" (4.21), he almost gets into the act when he extends his hand to Barney, offering to share his peanut butter and jelly sandwich, while Barney is trying to catch a shoplifter by pretending to be a mannequin at Weaver's Department Store. Barney shoos him away.

Another prominent silent character is Mr. Schwump, a heavy-set man in late middle age with an over-the-top toupee. Usually dressed in a suit and a tie, he walks on Main Street, mills about in a crowd, attends a party or a meeting of the local lodge. Like Leon, Mr. Schwump never utters a word. Thought up by Jim Fritzell and Everett Greenbaum, the creators of Mayberry's weird-est denizens, Mr. Schwump materializes in the middle of the fourth season in "My Fair Ernest T. Bass" (4.17). After Ernest T. has crashed Miss Wiley's party, Mr. Schwump is standing outside the house next to Mrs. Wiley. When Andy asks whether anybody made an effort to stop Ernest T., she replies that "Mr. Schwump tried to pinch him." The next time Ernest T. breaks up one of Mrs. Wiley's parties, in "The Education of Ernest T. Bass" (5.4), Mr. Schwump is there again, dancing away.

In fact, cutting a rug seems to be a favorite activity, for he is also very much in evidence at a dance where Andy and Barney show up with the Fun Girls. Before agreeing to take Daphne, Andy tells Barney that he has no intention of standing "in the stag line with Mr. Schwump" (4.27). But Andy underestimates him. The scene at the dance begins with the camera tracking Mr. Schwump as he walks

Mr. Schwump with Andy and Barney.

across the room with two bottles of soda pop. He sits down at a table and hands one of the bottles to his companion, a pretty brunette (no stag line for him). A few moments later, when Andy arrives with Daphne, Mr. Schwump is standing in the middle of the dance floor. Andy says hello and Daphne playfully tickles Mr. Schwump under the chin.

Never on screen for more than a minute or two, Mr. Schwump is memorable because of his silence. As we have seen, Mayberrians love to gab. Mr. Schwump furnishes a silent counterpoint to all the chatter. His idea of sitting and staring is literally to sit and stare. No verbal whittling for him. Occasionally he will say something to someone, but always out of earshot. In this respect, his presence is a little spooky, like the unfamiliar face in a family photograph. And an unfamiliar face he is, for no one connected with the show — Griffith, producers, directors, actors, writers — has been able to remember the name of the actor who played Mr. Schwump, though he appeared, however briefly, in more than twenty episodes.

When you least expect him, there he is: sitting next to Andy and Barney on the bench outside the courthouse (5.15); listening to Rev. Tucker's sermons (6.14); sneaking into the summit meeting between Americans and Russians (8.21); attending a Civic League meeting (8.30). Like other Mayberrians, he lived on into *Mayberry R.F.D.*, where he appeared in a few more episodes, including the first one, as one of the guests at Helen and Andy's wedding.

My theory is that the mask is the face: Mr. Schwump played Mr. Schwump. He is no more an actor's persona than Mayberry is a fictional Mount Airy.

CHAPTER FIVE

Growing Up, Growing Old (Opie and Floyd)

W HEN *TAGS* WENT ON THE AIR, OPIE WAS SIX YEARS old, and so was the actor who played him, Ron Howard. By the end of the series, Opie was no longer a little boy but a teenager. In *My Three Sons*, when Chip became a teenager the Douglases adopted Ernie (played by the real-life younger brother of Stanley Livingston, who played Chip Douglas); in *The Donna Reed Show*, the Stones adopted Trisha (played by the real-life younger sister of Paul Petersen, who played Jeff Stone). Following this tradition, the Taylors could have taken in Leon the waif, played by Ron Howard's little brother, Rance. But an enlargement of the Taylor household would have gone against the spirit of *TAGS*, which is not a "family" show in the mold of *My Three Sons* or *The Donna Reed Show*. Opie needs to be an only son. The village patriarch cannot be a father to anyone but Opie.

By the same token, Opie cannot be a son to more than one parent. Andy needs to be a widower. Although Opie's motherlessness is occasionally mentioned, particularly in episodes that allude to the possibility of Andy getting married, it is never given much prominence. The one time that Andy and Opie discuss the death of Opie's mother, in the pilot, Andy consoles Opie for the loss of his pet turtle by reminding him that his mother passed away when Opie was just a baby. "We have to learn to live with our sorrows," he says, offering to go down to the creek and get Opie a new turtle; but Opie wants Wilford. When Andy tells him not to be stubborn, Opie comes back with a zinger: "You didn't get a new Ma." What we don't know yet, but will find out in the first episode of the series, is that Andy also grew up an orphan—in his case, motherless and fatherless.

Only in one *TAGS* episode "Opie the Birdman" (4.1) does the subject of Opie's orphanhood constitute a crucial, if unstated, element in the plot. While playing with his new slingshot, Opie kills the mother of a brood of fledglings.

Seeing the lifeless bird on the lawn, he can't hide his remorse. He begs the bird, "fly away, please fly away," but it doesn't move. At supper Opie is not himself. Aunt Bee wonders whether he has "a touch of the pip," and in a sense he does, for the "pip," old-fashioned slang for a cold, is also the name of an avian disease. Andy, who saw a dead bird on the lawn as he came into the house, knows what's wrong. He goes upstairs and asks Opie whether he killed that bird. Opie confesses, expecting a whipping. But Andy elects a more subtle punishment. He opens the window in Opie's room. The fledglings are chirping away. "That's those young birds chirping for their mama that's never coming back. Now you just listen to that for a while." The expression on Opie's face suggests that, at some level, he realizes that he and the orphan birds have something in common. In an earlier episode, Aunt Bee had told Andy not to let Floyd cut Opie's hair too short because it made the boy look "like a baby bird." Opie replied: "I didn't know that I looked like a bird" (3.4). He may not look like a bird, but he now finds that the birds resemble him, for they too are motherless.

The next day Opie adopts the three "young'uns," whom he baptizes Winkin, Blinkin, and Nod, names taken from a lullaby poem. At first he worries that he won't know how to care for them, but Andy reassures him (after all, he too is a single parent: if the fledglings' predicament reflects Opie's, Opie's predicament reflects his father's). All of the birds thrive, even the smallest one, Nod. Soon the day comes when the birds get too big for the cage. Andy tells Opie that they are now "grow'd up" and he must let them go. Opie fears that they won't be able to fly because he hasn't raised them properly. Again Andy reassures him, perhaps anticipating that one day *he* will have to let Opie go. Opie takes each bird out of the cage. They fly away.

> *Opie*: "Cage sure looks awful empty, don't it, Paw?"
> *Andy*: "Yes, son, it sure does. But don't the trees seem nice and full?"

Adding poignancy to the exchange is its location, the porch, usually a place of stability. Here it becomes a platform for change. As Winkin, Blinkin, and Nod fly away one by one, the viewer, like Opie, realizes that things don't always stay the same, no matter how much the Mayberrian world, an aviary where almost nobody flies in or out, creates the opposite impression. After the birds have flown into the trees, the camera switches from a close-up of Andy and Opie to a long view of the two of them in the front yard surrounded by trees full of chirping. The distancing created by the switch from close-up to long shot highlights the theme of the episode. Parents die. Children grow up. People move away. When this episode was reviewed in *Variety*, the writer remarked that, like the series itself, it appealed to people who "like to look backward sentimentally

Nod about to fly away.

and escape the complexities of life as it has been lived and is being lived."[1] This statement may apply to other TAGS episodes, but not to "Opie the Birdman," one of the most quietly complex in the entire series.

TAGS kept track of Opie's maturation by having the first episode of each season mark the stages in his path from childhood to adolescence. If the fourth season begins with Opie infatuated with his new slingshot, the fifth season opens with Opie infatuated with his teacher, the sixth with Opie getting his first job, and the seventh and the eighth with Opie in the throes of adolescent crushes. (Apparently the younger Taylor did not inherit his father's difficulties with the opposite sex.) In the first episode of the sixth season, Floyd asks Opie whether he wants a shave. It's intended as a joke, but signals that Opie, now twelve years old, is about to leave childhood behind. By the last season of TAGS, Opie is a teenager and in the eighth grade. He goes on dates, learns to dance, plays in a rock band, makes plans for college, and explores the world beyond Mayberry.

It's not pleasant to watch Opie getting older, at least for me. If one of God's greatest creations is the little boy, one of his least successful is the male adolescent. As a teenager, Opie loses (or suppresses) the range of feeling evident in "Opie the Birdman," "The New Housekeeper," "Mr. McBeevee," and other early episodes. Toward the end of TAGS, he's on the way to becoming Richie, the character Ron Howard played in *Happy Days*. Like Opie, Richie has a good heart, but unlike the young Opie, Richie can be obnoxious, conceited, and self-absorbed, much like Ronald Bailey, the spoiled adolescent who gets arrested while speeding through Mayberry in "Bailey's Bad Boy" (2.15) or even like Barney, who has the emotional makeup of a sixteen-year-old. If the Fonz is Barney as Thug Almighty, Richie is Opie as Barney. Neither in the last couple of seasons of *TAGS* nor in the whole run of *Happy Days* does Howard match the naturalness and sensitivity of his performances as a grade-school boy. Ronny was a better actor than Ron.

HOWEVER SAD IT MAY BE TO SEE OPIE GROW UP, IT DOES not compare to seeing Floyd grow old. Unlike Aunt Bee, who never seemed to get any older, Floyd was not so lucky. Initially played by Walter Baldwin, Floyd appears for the first time in "Stranger in Town" (1.12). An episode later, when Floyd appears again, Howard McNear has taken over the role. A veteran of film, radio, and television, McNear began his career playing a variety of dramatic roles, including Doc Adams in the radio version of *Gunsmoke*. But for several years before joining *TAGS*, he had already been playing the jumpy, distracted, and somewhat sanctimonious character that he brought to perfection in Floyd. In *I Love Lucy*, he played little Ricky's fussy music teacher; on *The Donna Reed Show*, he played Mr. Wilgus, the Stones' neighbor; in *Leave It to Beaver*, he played a finicky barber—a snippet of clips to come.[2] According to McNear, the character for which he became famous was a caricature of himself, a view shared by his coworkers on the show.[3]

As everybody's barber and member of the Town Council, Floyd is one of Mayberry's leading citizens. Like Andy, he is a "founder," one of those townspeople who can trace their lineage back to Mayberry's earliest settlers. The first time we see McNear, Floyd is in a meeting of the Town Council along with Mayor Pike, Orville Monroe, and Andy. Typically, he is in a tizzy, this time over the prospect of having a movie filmed in Mayberry. Floyd's barbershop has occupied the same location next to the courthouse for twenty-eight years. Even though his barbering skills are often called into question, especially by Barney, he has been cutting hair ever since Andy was a boy. Barbering was his childhood dream: "I always did want to be a barber, even when I was a little kid. I used to practice on cats. I'd catch them in the alley and then I'd clip them. We had the baldest cats in the county" (1.13). His motto: "Every head a walking testimony" (3.8).

Andy is surrounded by eccentrics, but Floyd is in a class by himself. A master of the non sequitur, his sentences start in one direction, hang in the air, and finish on a different track altogether. When he does complete a statement, his voice trails off into a sigh. He is not beyond making his point, whatever it may be, by quoting a Latin proverb that he was taught at barber college: "tempus edax rerum" (time, devourer of all things). Garrulous, he likes to tell corny jokes, like the one about the zebra who fell in love with the convict. In the Mayberry Band Floyd plays the trombone, loudly and badly—a perfect complement to Barney's cymbals. In a couple of episodes he is given a wife and a son, but it's difficult to imagine Floyd as a husband or father. He needs so much guidance himself that it's not likely that he could raise a son or function as a suitable mate. If anything, he is avuncular: the crazy uncle of Mayberry, Aunt Bee's matching opposite.

Though mostly an interested bystander, Floyd sometimes gets caught up in hijinks. As easily duped as any Mayberrian, he allows a bookie to run his gambling operation from the barbershop. On another occasion, captured by three female convicts, he doesn't object to being held prisoner, even going into town for groceries with one of the women. After the bad gals have been apprehended, an oblivious Floyd can only worry that the hamburgers they were having for dinner will overcook. But only one episode, "Floyd, the Gay Deceiver" (3.9), features him as the protagonist. According to producer Aaron Ruben, when McNear found out that he would be the focus of the episode, he went into a panic, as Floyd himself would have done: "Howard was a dear, dear man, and very modest. I didn't realize it at the time, but he was absolutely terrified about doing that show. Shortly before we were to shoot, he called me up, and said, 'Oh, oh, oh, I don't think you should . . . uhm, uh, make me the ah, ah, star of that story. I . . . I . . .' He was scared silly."[4]

Nonetheless, this episode contains one of McNear's best performances. As a member of the Lonely Hearts Club, Floyd tells the woman he has been corresponding with that he is a wealthy widower. When he finds out that she is coming to meet him, he feels like "a miserable, deceitful wretch" and considers moving to Nashville to join a monastery. Andy agrees to help him out by letting him use the elegant home of a family on vacation and convincing Aunt Bee to pose as Floyd's maid. Andy will pretend to be Floyd's son, Andrew Paul Lawson. As Andy had suspected, Floyd's flame is a phony who sponges off rich widowers. Once she discovers that Andy is on to her, she leaves in a hurry. Floyd thinks that she has left because she knows he's a fraud. Keeping the truth to himself, Andy tells Floyd that she wasn't upset, that she understood. As clueless as ever, tenderhearted Floyd is relieved that he didn't hurt her feelings.

For the most part, however, Floyd plays a supporting role, often on stage but seldom in the spotlight. He sits in his barber chair or on a bench outside the barbershop and gabs with the townsfolk. Unlike Andy, he's not wise. Unlike Barney, he doesn't want to be a hero. Unlike Aunt Bee, he feels no urge to roam. Although Floyd criticizes another member of the Town Council member for being "a maybe man, no action" (7.8), Floyd is himself Mayberry's maybe man, indecisive to the point of inertia.

Even so, his place in Mayberry is crucial. The official record keeper in Mayberry is Howard Sprague, the county clerk, who keeps tabs on births, deaths, marriages, and property transactions — "facts and figures, facts and figures" (6.26). Distracted but not forgetful, Floyd is the repository of communal memory. Rather than computing statistics, he retells stories. As a consequence, those who don't remember the past are condemned to have Floyd repeat it. Beginning many a conversation by asking, "Do you remember?," he goes on to expound on the time that Honey Tewilliger, Efrem and Martha Tewilliger's youngest girl, dumped Hollis Putney for his brother, or when Agnes Drumhiller—the talk of the town in 1949—took to nipping elderberry wine because she was stood up at the altar by Horace Frizzy. He remembers that Bobby Gribble wrote in the wet cement of the sidewalk that he hated Emma Larch, and that Fluffy Johnson wore fake nails and eyelashes. He tells these tales with an attention to detail that is both absurd and astounding. Fluffy Johnson's nails and eyelashes fell off when she was on a date with Orville Portnoy, the night man at the bakery, and he never got over it. Eleven years after writing the graffiti on the sidewalk in front of the barbershop, Bobby married Emma. Agnes and Horace also married eventually, and she dyed her hair orange to get back at him. Floyd carries inside his head a history of everyday life in Mayberry compared to which Howard Sprague's records are meaningless scraps of paper.

Equally important is the barbershop itself. Along with Andy's porch and the courthouse, it is the other principal venue for verbal whittling, but—unlike them—an exclusively male domain. As a female Mayberrian says, "A lady never goes into a barbershop" (1.17). When Floyd moves out of the shop because of a dispute over the rent, chaos ensues. The fellows now gather at the courthouse to chat and play checkers, which doesn't allow Andy to get any work done. Aunt Bee has to chase Opie around the living room to give him a haircut. Life doesn't get back to normal until Floyd and his landlord, Howard, agree on the rent. A space between the Taylor home and the courthouse, the barbershop is not encumbered by the entailments of either of those places and lacks the connection that house and courthouse have between them. Instead it's an informal version of the Esquire Club, where, as Opie puts it, the men "just sit around and play checkers and talk and grunt" (7.22).

Halfway through the third season, Howard McNear suffered a stroke that made it difficult for him to walk and left him with a partially paralyzed left arm. By then McNear had appeared in roughly one-third of the episodes. His role had kept increasing, with the last episodes before he fell ill some of the ones where his character was most involved: "The Mayberry Band" (3.8), "Floyd, the Gay Deceiver" (3.9), and "Convicts at Large" (3.11). As a result of the illness, he was absent from the show for over a year. Returning toward the end of the fourth season in "Andy Saves Gomer" (4.23), he remained a fixture through the seventh season, appearing in well over half of the episodes during that span.

But the Floyd who came back was and was not the same man who had disappeared without explanation a year earlier. In one respect, he was more like himself than ever—more distracted, more jittery, and hence, even funnier. He also appeared more frequently, particularly after Don Knotts left the series. In his last season, he appeared in twenty of the thirty episodes. In effect, Floyd replaced Barney as Andy's sidekick, his main conversation partner. Episodes that earlier in the series would have opened with Andy and Barney in the courthouse, now begin with Floyd and Andy sitting in front of the barbershop. Just as he had been straight man to Don Knotts, Andy now does the same thing for McNear, as Floyd becomes Mayberry's foremost clown prince:

> *Floyd*: I'm kinda looking forward to these next two Sundays.
> *Andy*: A new preacher, huh?
> *Floyd*: Yeah! Get a little new blood up in the pulpit.
> *Andy*: Of course, I always thought Rev. Tucker did a fine job.
> *Floyd*: Yeah, except I knew every one of his sermons by heart. . . . Of course, a lot of that is our fault.
> *Andy*: Our fault?
> *Floyd*: There's too few sins in this town. We never gave him much to work with.
> *Andy*: Well, is that bad?
> *Floyd* [aroused]: I didn't say it was bad! You missed my point completely!
> *Andy*: No, no, what I meant . . .
> *Floyd* [interrupting]: You're not listening.
> *Andy* [resigned]: OK, go ahead, Floyd.
> *Floyd*: As I was trying to tell you. . . . What were we talking about?
> *Andy*: Reverend Tucker.
> *Floyd*: Ah, yes, fine man. Now Andy, you can tell me. What do you have against him? (7.5)

In exchanges like this one, Floyd was never better. But the aftereffects of McNear's illness changed his appearance and limited what he could do. His face was thinner, his hair grayer, his glasses thicker, and he developed a twitch that made him blink. His barber's smock didn't sit well on his stooped shoulders. His speech, as distinctive as ever, was less vigorous. The old Floyd was spry and potbellied. He marched in the front row of the Mayberry Band. When he became agitated, he would pace up and down, arms flailing. In "Floyd, the Gay Deceiver," when he finds out that his long-distance paramour is coming to see him, he runs back and forth across the barbershop to the wall mirror to berate himself. Anytime he drifted off and left a sentence hanging in midair, a flick of the tie or a wave of his scissors would complete his thought. After the stroke, he could do none of these things. For the most part he sat in the barber chair, his left arm resting awkwardly on his lap. At times the directors would create the illusion of mobility by having the audience hear footsteps before showing Floyd sitting, as if he had just walked in. At other times, in long shots, a double was used so that he appears to be driving a car. The prop men devised a contraption that allowed Floyd to stand, but only in a couple of scenes does he manage to take a few halting steps with Helen or someone else holding him by the arm. For the most part he was stationary, an inert observer of human folly, including his own. His immobility, which became more pronounced as the years went by, gave Mayberrian sedentariness an unexpectedly tragic dimension.

Most viewers who saw the show in its original run were probably unaware of McNear's failing health, which of course, was not written into his character. The travails of growing up are sitcom fodder; the infirmities that come with growing old are not, especially in Mayberry, a world committed to stasis. Aging and its calamities happen to the inhabitants of the lands beyond Kelsey's Woods, not to Mayberrians. As in Brigadoon, so too in Mayberry. Before McNear's illness, no one embodied the anachronistic temper of TAGS as thoroughly as Floyd, whose idea of a political slogan is "Tippecanoe and Tyler too," which he thinks has something to do with someone tipping over a canoe. But this makes his aging all the more wrenching. As a throwback to another era, an old-timer even when he was young, Floyd seemed ageless. In his later appearances, he seemed ageless no longer.

With every season, he looked more gaunt, less energetic, his voice reduced at times to little more than a whisper. We see him for the last time in "Goober's Contest," the last episode of the seventh season, broadcast in March of 1967. Though he tries hard, McNear is no longer able to express Floyd's liveliness. By this point McNear struggled to remember his lines, and his performance bears it out. Rather than distracted, Floyd looks blank. Slurring his words, he delivers them with only a semblance of his impeccable timing and modulation. McNear passed away two years later, on January 3, 1969.

Unlike other characters who disappear without explanation, at the beginning of the last season Floyd was written out of the show. Too prominent a Mayberrian for his absence to go unnoticed, Floyd has decided to retire, as Andy mentions in "Goober the Executive" (8.16). He is replaced by Emmett, the fix-it man. As a barber, Floyd was a logical relay for gossip. But broken-down cuckoo clocks and overheating toasters do not reveal juicy bits of gossip, like the fact that a client's cowlick is really a scar put there by his wife's broom. Floyd had a bulletin board where Mayberrians posted job openings, a metaphor for the circulation of information that the barbershop enabled. A handyman Floyd was not; his uselessness was part of his appeal. But what Emmett was really supposed to fix—Floyd's absence—he never did because he couldn't have.

Genial Floyd embodies Mayberry's gentleness. You can tell by the way he cuts hair. A snip here, a snip there, and a dash of witch hazel at the end. A traditionalist, he never uses a clipper, only scissors and a comb. He dislikes electric lather makers because they don't make the "klep, klep, klep" sound of the shaving brush in the mug. Yet Floyd's unremarked but visible decline reminds us that it will not always be May in Mayberry. Time passes with a vengeance. Tempus edax rerum.

CHAPTER SIX

Old Geezers (Judd and Asa)

T HE WORLD OF MAYBERRY DOESN'T COUNTENANCE
aging, but it does allow for being old. Other than Opie and his
occasional friends, few young people ever appear on the show. (The absence
of children, of course, is more than made up for by the infantile behavior of
the grown-ups.) The young men about town are Andy and Barney, both well
into their thirties. By contrast, the town does have a substantial contingent of
seasoned citizens, among them Aunt Bee and Clara, Majors Pike and Stoner,
Orville and Floyd, Ben Weaver and Emma Brand. Two of the oldest are Judd
Fletcher and Asa Breeney, the quintessential geezers. Played by Burt Mustin,
Judd is an old man with time on his hands. Appearing in a dozen episodes between the first and the seventh seasons, he sits on a bench whittling, shoots
the breeze with Floyd, and plays checkers outside the Mayberry Hotel with
another old-timer, Chester Jones. Although Judd is usually referred to as Judd,
his name (if not his identity) is variable. He is also called Jubal, Burt, and "old
man Crowley." In "Goober's Replacement" (6.28), the cast credits identify him
only as "old geezer." Seventy-four at the beginning of the series, Judd may have
been around so long that even the scriptwriters have forgotten his name. (Burt
Mustin, who was born in 1884, was even older than Judd.)

Unlike Mr. Schwump, Judd is more than a face in the crowd. With a hooked
nose and pursed lips, his visage tapers into a beak, which he uses to squawk.
He's not above upbraiding Aunt Bee for her squeaky voice, flirting with Goober's girlfriend, or getting into a tussle. When he calls Chester a "two-faced
cheating liar," Barney arrests him for disturbing the peace. Judd's defense is that
he hasn't had the energy to disturb the peace in thirty years. Seeing a gum wrapper on the sidewalk, Barney predicts that littering will spur a crime wave. Judd
agrees: another gum wrapper, and Mayberry is liable to turn into Dodge City.
He then tricks Barney into ticketing the governor's car for parking in front of

Asa sleeping on the job.

a No Parking sign. A couple of years later, when Barney deputizes Judd to help out in Andy's absence, Judd thinks that, as a deputy, he's entitled to free fruit.

Unlike Judd, Old Asa is not a troublemaker, though trouble still comes his way. He appears in five episodes between the third and the fifth seasons. Played by Charles P. Thompson, who was born in 1901, he's a tall, slender man in his seventies, with thinning white hair and a mustache. "The Bank Job" (3.13) is best remembered for Gomer Pyle's debut; but it's also the episode where we meet Asa. An elderly guard at Mayberry Security Bank, he sleeps on the job, unmindful of crooks or clients. Though he wears a gun belt, when he tries to draw his Spanish American War–vintage pistol, it falls apart. He reappears the following season, first as the clerk at the Mayberry Hotel, and then, with a different last name (Bascomb), as the night watchman at Weaver's Department Store, who does no better at staying awake at Weaver's than he did at the bank. When Barney is straining to pass the physical exam for deputies, Asa lends him the harness that he uses to relieve the pinched nerve in his back — "the misery" — because the harness added half an inch to his height. It does the same for Barney, who grows an inch. For his last appearance, Asa is back at the bank and back to his habit of dozing on the job. Oblivious to all the funny business around him, he illustrates the sleepiness of a sleepy town. As Mr. Weaver points out, Asa is Mayberry's Rip Van Winkle. But unlike what happens to Rip, when Asa wakes up, nothing has changed.

CHAPTER SEVEN

Mayberry Maidens (Aunt Bee, Helen Crump, and Thelma Lou)

Men you can slap in jail, but women—what can you do?

BARNEY FIFE, "AUNT BEE THE CRUSADER" (4.15)

*A*UNT TO HALF A COUNTY BUT MOTHER TO NO ONE (to paraphrase Faulkner on Ike McCaslin), the most important woman in *TAGS* is Mayberry's Beatrice, Aunt Bee. During the early years of the series, Aunt Bee didn't do much other than serve breakfast in the mornings and supper in the evenings. Frances Bavier, a New York stage actor who studied at Columbia University and the American Academy of the Arts, chafed at her modest role, which she blamed on the writers. As the show developed, and especially after Don Knotts left, the writers began devising more stories for her. By the end of the series, she was the most visible character after Andy and Opie.

Many of the episodes about Aunt Bee depart from an unusual premise for *TAGS*: role restlessness. Although she hides it fairly well, spinsterhood weighs heavily on her. Among Mayberrians, only Barney is as unhappy with his lot. The difference is that Barney shouts his discontent, whereas Bee muffles hers; yet she too yearns for a "big moment," the title of the episode where she learns to fly (8.23). As she says, after listening to Andy, Howard, and Goober recount their exploits, such as they are, "What have I ever done?" (8.23). Most often, her restlessness arises from loneliness, which provides material for the half-dozen episodes that, in one fashion or another, explore the possibility of Aunt Bee finding a mate. In "Aunt Bee's Romance," after her old beau leaves Mayberry, she's glad to see him go: "Fun is fun, but there's a limit to everything" (5.5). Even as she says this, we sense that Aunt Bee would prefer a life with fewer limits.

At other times her restlessness manifests itself in activities that get her out of the house: owning a restaurant, working at a print shop, learning to drive, flying a plane, composing songs, doing commercials, hosting a cooking show on TV, traveling to Mexico, serving as a juror, running for Town Council (as Ellie had done years earlier). The earliest episode with this theme, "Aunt Bee on TV" (6.10), doesn't occur until the sixth season, once the other malcontent, Barney, is no longer around to stir things up. During the Taylors' visit to Hollywood—a trip undertaken at Aunt Bee's urging—she appears on a game show, winning the sweepstakes. Back in Mayberry, she flaunts her prizes, which include a mink coat from "the furrier of the stars." What is worse, her winnings leave Andy with a hefty tax bill of $1,138.72. In the end Aunt Bee gets rid of all of the prizes (except for the TV set and the garbage disposal), reasoning that it's more important to keep her friends and relieve Andy of the debt.

Every time that Aunt Bee strikes out on her own, she will come to the same conclusion: her old life was better. As in her refusal of suitors, however, what's most significant is not her ultimate acceptance of limits, but the recurring desire to transgress them. When Andy questions the wisdom of investing in a restaurant, she retorts, "Why should a woman not go into business?" (7.21). Aunt Bee is an interesting character to the extent that she defies the image that most viewers have of her, that of everybody's favorite aunt. Much like Frances Bavier, who never warmed up to the cast and crew, Aunt Bee is a tough cookie. As Briscoe Darling points out, "She's got an awful lot of sheriff in her" (4.5).

Does Aunt Bee actually *like* children? The evidence on this score is, at best, ambiguous. For someone who has devoted her life to raising children, her lack of tenderness is puzzling. About all she ever says to Opie is to take a bath or do his homework. According to Andy, when he was a boy Aunt Bee hugged him so hard that he turned purple, but there is little evidence of this warmth in the way she treats her nephew's son. Significantly, after the show's inaugural episode, "The New Housekeeper," Aunt Bee's and Opie's affection for each other was never again the subject of another episode. If anything, the show sends the message that Opie does not need Aunt Bee for anything other than keeping him clothed and fed.

In the last episode of the first season, "Bringing Up Opie," Aunt Bee is alarmed that the boy is picking up bad habits from spending too much time in the courthouse: "His head is being filled with criminals and sheriffing. I wouldn't be surprised if at Opie's next birthday party he shoots out the candles." Andy doesn't want to declare the courthouse off-limits to his son, but finally he agrees with Aunt Bee that "a home is a more proper environment than a jail." The episode thus pits divergent models of parenting and their respective locations: Aunt Bee and Andy, house and courthouse. In "The New Housekeeper," Aunt Bee comes to live with Andy because, presumably, he cannot raise a son by himself. Now, in the last episode of the first season, the topic of Opie's upbringing is revisited, but with a different outcome. Aunt Bee realizes that Opie belongs with his father, bad influences or not, and gives up on the plan of keeping him under her ample wing.

Had Aunt Bee taken a larger role in Opie's upbringing, she would have been a stronger character, but at the risk of diluting the intensity of the father-son bond, which may be why she and Opie never develop any emotional closeness. Lukewarm and fussy rather than warm and fuzzy, Aunt Bee is more housekeeper than homemaker. Thus she was able to move from the Taylors' kitchen to the Joneses' without missing a beet. She treated Sam and Mike, mere acquaintances, no differently than she treated her own kin. I know it's *TAGS* blasphemy to say this, but episodes like "Aunt Bee Learns to Drive" (6.21), "Aunt Bee's Restaurant" (7.21), or "A Trip to Mexico" (8.3) make me think that Opie and Andy were better off with Rose, their old housekeeper: equal efficiency and fewer headaches.

After Aunt Bee the most visible woman in Mayberry is Helen Crump. By the time Aneta Corsaut was hired to do a one-off appearance as Opie's third grade teacher, Griffith and the producers had all but given up their quest to find Andy a suitable romantic interest. The character's comical last name suggests that the writer of the episode, John Whedon, thought of her as little more than a schoolmarm. Unexpectedly the chemistry between Griffith and Corsaut was good, and after a few more appearances she was kept on as Andy's steady girl. A Kansas native like Corsaut, Helen stands apart from the other regulars in that she wasn't born or raised in Mayberry. Thanks to what Andy calls "the Mayberry telegraph," there are no townspeople whose entire lives are not well known to their neighbors. Not so with Helen, a woman with a past, as in one of the last episodes of the series, "Helen's Past" (8.24).

Looking for a history outline in a box full of Helen's papers (among them letters from her old boyfriend, tied together with a pink ribbon), Andy comes upon a clipping from a Kansas City newspaper that shows Helen being arrested. Wearing a tight dress and a fur stole, she looks like a moll rather than schoolmarm. Without her knowledge, a puzzled Andy takes the clipping from the box. The next day Howard and Goober find the clipping on his desk at the courthouse. He swears them to secrecy while he investigates. A reporter for the *Kansas City Chronicle* tells him that on August 4, 1959 — several years before moving to Mayberry — Helen was charged with illegal gambling, possession of a concealed weapon, and being in the company of a known hoodlum. The Mayberry telegraphers make sure that word about Helen's "wayward youth" soon reaches the Mayberry School Board, which decides to fire her. Just in the nick of time, Andy discovers from the court records that Helen's activities were part of the research for her master's thesis about organized crime.

Initially furious that Andy suspected her of having a shady past, Helen gets over it after Andy apologizes, and the episode closes with Helen and the Taylors, a happy quasi-family once again, sitting on the porch enjoying a quiet eve-

ning. Though the overt lesson is that the people we care about deserve the bene-
fit of the doubt, the episode demonstrates once again the extent of Mayberrian
distrust of outsiders, including someone who by this time has lived in Mayberry
for six years. Even Andy, Helen's fiancé, doesn't trust her enough to ask directly
about the newspaper clipping. Though this episode is one of the few that revolves around Helen, the real focus is on the reaction of Mayberrians to her
supposedly criminal past. Corsaut once complained that most of what she did
on *TAGS* was ask whether somebody had packed the salt and pepper.[1] But had
Helen been more assertive, as Ellie and the county nurses were, she would not
have been compatible with Andy, who had all he could handle with Aunt Bee.

The truth is that there isn't much for women to do in Mayberry other than
pass the salt. With the exception of Helen, whenever a regular character was
added to the show he was always male: Gomer, Goober, Warren, Howard,
Emmett. Eccentrics all, they were easy to write for. Helen is not an oddball, and
the effort to make her unthreatening to Andy made her less distinctive still. It's
hard to imagine what Helen did with her time when she wasn't grading papers
or packing the picnic box.

Well, not exactly. Helen does have one big moment, but only one. In Corsaut's favorite episode, "Helen, the Authoress" (7.24), Helen writes a children's
book, *Amusing Tales of Tiny Tots*, for which a Richmond publisher gives her an
advance of $1,000. Andy can't handle Helen's success. He becomes the butt of
Floyd and Goober's jokes, who kid him that once he marries Helen his address
will be Easy Street. To make matters worse, Helene Alexion Dubois (Helen's
pen name), spends her evenings working on rewrites with her publisher. To get
back at her, Andy does something unprecedented: he picks up with Mavis Neff
(Elaine Joyce), Juanita's rival for the title of town floozy (who, nonetheless,
can't get Andy to kiss her). By the end of the episode, Andy has apologized and
he and Helen have made up, but her twenty-five minutes of fame quickly fade
into oblivion. By the following week, Helene is back to being Helen. Her writing career is never mentioned again.

A more interesting character than Helen is Thelma Lou (Betty Lynn), in
large measure because she has to put up with Barney, which entails managing
his moods, massaging his ego, accepting his idiosyncrasies. Seeing the same
Barn whom the others see, she smiles rather than mocks. Barney brags: "She's
crazy about me" (5.28). Thelma Lou understands why he brags, as she understands why, in contrast to Andy, he is not given to apologizing. One could say
about her what Sherwood Anderson says about Elizabeth Willard, one of the
residents of Winesburg: that she "was forever putting out her hand into the
darkness and trying to get a hold of some other hand."[2] For Thelma Lou, that
other hand was Barney's. None of Andy's serial girlfriends ever mustered for
the sheriff the affection that "Thel" exhibits toward his deputy. She loves his

Thelma Lou and Barney window-shop.

feistiness and allows for his frailties. When Barney thinks that he is going to be fired, she intercedes in his behalf. When he sings, she shields him from ridicule. It doesn't matter that he is a 100-pound weakling or that their dates are Dutch treat. Although she gets angry when Andy and Barn hook up with the Fun Girls, if Barney pretends to make a date with someone else in her presence, she plays along with him. She even overlooks his catting around with Juanita—"everybody's Juanita"—because she realizes that even if the dates are real, they are inconsequential. She is not far wrong when she tells him that she is "the most understanding person in the whole world" (5.28).

Unlike Helen, native Mayberrian Thelma Lou (her last name is never mentioned) was a member of Andy and Barney's graduating class at Mayberry Union High. But such are the ways of fictional worlds that she and Barney didn't meet until 1960 at Wilton Blair's funeral. In her first episode, "Cyrano Andy" (1.22), she and Barney have been dating for a while, though he hasn't gotten up the nerve to ask her to be his girl. After they become a couple, he will hound her like a hormone-crazed adolescent. Thel herself is no less amorous, as Barney's lipstick-smeared face attests. She even kisses him in public, to his dismay. It's impossible to picture Andy and Helen in an intimate moment, but it's not hard to picture Barney and Thel going beyond frisky.

A few weeks after Helen and Thelma Lou catch the boys in the squad car with the Fun Girls, Thelma Lou finds out that Barney has been bragging about having "the little girl right in my hip pocket" (4.30). She decides to make Barney jealous by dating Gomer, who thinks that he has to marry Thelma Lou because she kissed him on the cheek. Thanks to Andy, the kiss gets taken back, Gomer is let off the hook, and Thelma Lou apologizes to Barney. In the opening scene of the episode, walking home from watching a Cary Grant movie, Barney and Thelma Lou stop to window-shop at the furniture store. They begin to fantasize about what their home will be like. Barney wants a den with a leather chair, good books, the aroma of pipe tobacco, and maybe a dog. The den will be his own private domain, where not even Thelma Lou can intrude. For her part, Thelma Lou wants a nice living room with a blue and green sofa, a welcoming room to host the ladies. After daydreaming for a while, they realize that they are talking like a couple about to get married.

> *Thelma Lou:* Look at us, you'd think we're ready to set up house-keeping tomorrow.
> *Barney:* Yeah, the way we're talking. Well, you know, that's out of the question. I mean, like we've been saying for a long time, marriage isn't something that you just leap into.
> *Thelma Lou:* I certainly hope you don't think I'm pressuring you.
> *Barney:* Oh, heck no, no. I've known you long enough to know better than that. Besides, I'm not the kind of guy who can be pressured.
> *Thelma Lou:* I know.
> *Barney:* But, if after we did all this thinking, we did decide that . . . You know . . . If we got this house and if we had this den, there'd be no ladies in it, right?
> *Thelma Lou:* Right. (4.30)

Barney differs from Andy in that he is not averse to marriage. His reluctance is only a front. If Thelma Lou pressures him, and she does, gently, it's only to get him to do what he really wants to do. Thelma Lou has a hip pocket too.

Later in the episode Barney tells Andy that since he is not going anywhere and Thelma Lou is not going anywhere, there's no rush for them to tie the knot. Ironically, a year later Barney would leave for Raleigh and, a month after that, Thelma Lou would move to Jacksonville, North Carolina, where she meets the man she eventually marries, the head of a wrecking crew. Barney finds out the news at a class reunion during one of his return visits to Mayberry. He becomes so distraught that he gets drunk on nonalcoholic punch. (What the wrecking crew wrecked was Barney's heart.)

But if Thelma Lou marries someone else, it's only because Barney left Mayberry without her. Recalling the class-reunion episode, "The Return of Barney Fife" (6.17), Betty Lynn remarked that she played her part as if she had not really married: "I decided that Thelma Lou didn't actually get married. She knew this fellow at work and when they had the reunion and everyone would be coming back, she said to this fellow, 'Listen, I don't want to go back to Mayberry like I was. I'm going to tell them I got married. Would you do me a favor and come with me?'[3] Her actress's intuition did not betray her.

Another reunion, twenty years later, set things right. Barney finally got his man cave and Thelma Lou her living room, as well as a resonant last name.

CHAPTER EIGHT

Beasts of the Southern Wild
(Ernest T. Bass and the Darlings)

Nature has a place for the wild clematis as well as for the cabbage.

HENRY DAVID THOREAU, "WALKING"

MAYBERRIAN SOCIETY IS ARRANGED IN CONCENTRIC circles. The innermost circle embraces townies like Floyd, Aunt Bee, Helen, and Thelma Lou. The next circle includes the farmers who live on the outskirts of town, among them Rafe Hollister, Jeff Pruitt, the Wakefields, and the Carters. Usually dressed in a hat and overalls, farmers make trouble by distilling white lightning or feuding, but only rarely do their actions threaten the town's order. They and the townsfolk are the cabbages of Mayberry. For the wild clematis, we need to move to the outer circle, the mountains, where Ernest T. Bass and the Darlings hold sway. Oblivious to town mores, mountain people live in caves or cabins, not houses. They have no social graces but, like European royalty, they "pledge" their children as soon as they are born. Even more superstitious than Barney, they put great stock in omens, from owls to phantom riders. From the point of view of polite society, these people are "creatures," as Mrs. Wiley dubs Ernest T. Bass, yet they too are an integral part of *TAGS*.

Anchoring these circles is the courthouse, whose influence extends to the whole of Mayberry County, as the map behind Andy's desk suggests. Like Wallace Stevens's jar in Tennessee (in "Anecdote of a Jar"), the courthouse centers and takes dominion of the territory that sprawls around it, though the farther we wander from Andy's desk, the center's center, the more the "slovenly wilderness" tends to take over.

And no one is more slovenly or wild than Ernest T. Bass. Although he appeared only in five episodes between the third and the sixth seasons, he left an

"It's me, it's me, it's Ernest T.!"

indelible imprint on Mayberry. Whether it was throwing a rock through a window, wrapping his legs around somebody's neck, or whimpering like a chimp, one could always count on Ernest T. for improper conduct:

> Wrong or right,
> I'm here to fight.
> And if you're wondering who I be,
> it's me, it's me, it's Ernest T!

Not that Ernest T. is evil, depraved, or even unfriendly. When Andy meets him, he remarks that Ernest is a "strange and weird character." "He's a nut!" echoes Barney, who should know. But Ernest's eccentricity, his nuttiness, has a humane, endearing side. His habit of throwing rocks through windows is not only a form of aggression but a way of communicating—mountain telegraphy. Like his rhymes, which are also double-edged, rocks through a window can signify anger or affection. Beneath his simian demeanor, Ernest T. is a sentimentalist, a dreamer. Charlene Darling marries another man, yet he believes that he can still win her heart. When he falls in love with Ramona (he pronounces the name "Romeena"), he is willing to learn to read and write so that she will consent to marry him. Receiving the diploma for "larnin'," he is genuinely moved (and so are we). If the courthouse is where King Andy holds court, Ernest T. is the knight-errant of the mountains, a misembodied Quijote brandishing hillbilly chivalry.

Some of the characters in TAGS—Andy, Floyd, Aunt Bee—resemble the actors who played them. Not Ernest T., brought to life by Howard Morris, a New Yorker who was as different from Ernest T. as Don Knotts—by all accounts, a serious fellow—was from Barney. Yet it proved to be an inspired casting choice. According to Morris, when Griffith and the producers were getting ready to shoot "Mountain Wedding" (3.31), the first episode in which Ernest T. appears, they didn't know what to do with the character. Aaron Ruben asked Morris, whom he knew from Sid Caesar's *Your Show of Shows*, to take a look at the script. Morris did, and the rest is *TAGS* hysteria. It was Morris who invented the mannerisms that define the character—the hopping, the rhyming, the bizarre pronunciation and speech patterns, and that unmistakable manic voice. Years later, asked where the character came from, Morris replied that it "stirred something in my groin."[1] Yes: Ernest T. is groin-engendered, a creation of the lower body.

If Barney is a belated avatar of the miles gloriosus of classical comedy, Ernest T. derives from the medieval *uomo selvatico*, the wild man of the woods. Based on mythological figures such as satyrs and fauns, the wild man exists at the edge of civilization, physically and socially. Uninhibited, his behavior verges on the animalistic. Uncultivated, his feelings are indistinguishable from his instincts. Usually pictured as hirsute, another of his names is *pilosus*, which explains why Floyd says that when he cuts the hair of "one of those boys from the hills," he keeps going until he sees scalp (5.15). Frequently the wild man is shown carrying a club, the equivalent of which is Ernest T.'s sack full of rocks. According to Richard Bernheimer, this figure is associated with "madness, passion, and violence."[2]

Though hardly as fearsome as his predecessors, Ernest T. injects a pinch of madness, passion, and violence into Mayberry. When Andy and Barney go to the Darling cabin to see what to do about his unwillingness to accept Charlene's marriage, Ernest T. comes out from behind the bushes with a shotgun and tells them that since Darlene wasn't married by a preacher, the marriage doesn't count: God's law, not man's. To prevent him from abducting her on the day of the preacher wedding, Barney dresses like the bride. Thinking that Barney is Charlene, Ernest T. drags him off into the woods. Barney's reaction to Ernest T.'s advances: "I wouldn't marry you even if you were the last man in the world." Ernest T.'s retort, which unfortunately was edited out: "Try it, you might like it."[3]

Andy does his utmost to correct Ernest T.'s aberrant behavior, but fails utterly. In *TAGS*, makeovers tend not to work out because the Mayberrian world is an essentialist one. People are what they are. To change is to pretend to be someone you're not, not a good thing. What Barney says apropos of Ernest T. applies to everyone else: "his behavior patterns are a permanent fixture of his behavior" (4.17). In "My Fair Ernest T. Bass," his third appearance, scriptwriters Everett Greenbaum and Jim Fritzell take their cue from the hit Broadway musical, *My Fair Lady* and narrate such a makeover. Playing Henry Higgins to Ernest's Eliza, with Barney tagging along as Colonel Pickering, Andy tries to socialize the wild man. He cleans him up, teaches him proper manners, corrects his speech. Marveling at the transformation, Barney says, "You know, if you wrote this into a play nobody would believe it." Once the lessons are finished, the big night arrives: a party at Mrs. Wiley's home, a scene modeled on the embassy ball in the musical. Ernest T. makes a grand entrance. Instead of grimy jeans and hunting cap, he is spiffy in a double-breasted suit with a white pocket square and a dapper fedora. Andy introduces him as Oliver Gossage, his cousin from Raleigh. Everything goes according to plan. Ernest T. repeats the "amenities" that Andy has taught him to say. Because of his accent, Mrs. Wiley concludes that Oliver must hail from Back Bay Boston, another echo of *My Fair Lady*, where the Hungarian linguist concludes that Eliza has royal blood. But then the plan goes awry. At the party, Ernest T. meets his Dulcinea, Romeena, who seems as taken with him as he is with her. When Romeena's dancing partner does not let Ernest T. cut in, he takes a flower vase and smashes it over the man's head. Finally recognizing Ernest T., Mrs. Wiley screams: "Oh no! It's him! That animal! That creature!" Ernest reverts to his true self—"She called me a 'creachture'! I ain't no 'creachture'!"—and starts to tear the place up.

It takes all of Andy's and Barney's strength to drag him out kicking and screaming. But he does get the girl. Romeena follows Ernest T. out of the house. As the scene ends, the two of them are running frantically down the street, jumping over tree stumps and twirling around light posts. Then they disappear into the night. Barney is surprised that a demure girl like Ramona/Romeena would "go ape" over Ernest T., but Andy reminds him that she is the granddaughter of Rotten Ray Ancrum, who came down from the hills in 1870 and burned the town down. Havoc is in her blood.

Unlike other romances in Mayberry, this one will last. In "The Education of Ernest T. Bass" (5.4), Ernest T. once again comes down from the mountains because Romeena wants him to learn to read and write. Andy's efforts to educate him turn out no better than his efforts to civilize him. But it seems that the diploma, worthless as it is, does the trick, because in his last appearance Ernest T. is saving money for his honeymoon. To help him out (a tent and a lantern cost twelve dollars), Andy gives him a job as the guard at the school crossing. The problem is that Ernest T. throws rocks at drivers who disregard his signals. He loses the job to Malcolm Merriweather, who has returned to Mayberry to settle down permanently. Hence the title of the episode: "Malcolm at the Crossroads" (6.3). A feud ensues between the grit and the Brit, the valet and the caveman. Malcolm is all manners and fine talk; Ernest T. is as ornery as ever. Apparently of Irish ancestry, Ernest T. gets even angrier when he discovers that Malcolm is an "Englishter." Lying, Andy tells Ernest T. that Malcolm is really Irish. Ernest T. jumps into Malcolm's arms and invites him to his cave for possum steaks. Once Ernest T. realizes that he has been tricked, the fight is on again.

When Ernest T. faces off against Malcolm, it's not only a contest between the wild and the mild, the savage and the civilized, but between like and unlike, "ours" and "not ours," to reprise Briscoe Darling's formula. Wild as he is, Ernest T. belongs; mild as he is, Malcolm does not. Their embrace cannot last. Ernest T. stays and Malcolm goes.

Is he therefore an "animal," a "creature," as Mrs. Wiley says? There is indeed something creature-like about him (not for nothing are his initials "E.T."), but as Helen points out, Ernest T. resembles the other Mayberrians in that he has a "good soul." The genius of the character, like that of Barney Fife, lies in its contradictions. His high regard for his looks clashes with his slovenliness. His self-proclaimed feats of physical strength—twenty chin-ups with one hand— do not mesh with his scrawniness. His boorish behavior overlays depth of feeling. If Ernest T. is a savage, he is a noble one. If he is a Southern grotesque, his ingenuousness compensates for it. And he is hardly the dullard that he seems. Though he can't read or write very well, he devises clever coinages such as "femaling" (his term for courtship) and "hermitize" (what he will do if the femaling fails). Even as his strange speech conveys his discomfort with language, his knack for rhyming shows his ability to manipulate it.

An outsider within, Ernest T. embodies the unruliness that lurks at the outer reaches of Mayberry. In contrast to the true outsiders, the crooks and the con men, he doesn't undermine the community's order. Rather, he gives vent to impulses that, were they to inhabit the townspeople, would shatter the friendliness of The Friendly Town. Ernest T. embodies the "tolerated margin of mess," in Aldous Huxley's phrase, that allows a society to function harmoniously. Barney says that he "wouldn't touch [Ernest T.'s] id with a ten-foot pole" (4.17). That's right: it's the ten-foot pole that keeps the town's inner circle safely removed from behavior that, were it to become widespread, would bring mayhem to Mayberry.

Next to Ernest T. Bass, the Darlings almost seem like Rotarians. Making their debut in "The Darlings Are Coming" (3.25), they appear in six episodes. The Darling clan, headed by Briscoe (played by Denver Pyle, whose last name inspired Gomer and Goober's), includes a daughter, Charlene (Maggie Petersen), and four sons: Rodney (the fun-loving one), Mitch (strong as an ox and almost as smart), Doug (also called Jebbin), and Dean (also called "Other"). Charlene marries Dud Wash, an Army veteran who hunts possum and beaver for a living, and they have a daughter named Andelina in honor of Andy. According to Briscoe, self-described "tiller of soil and feller of trees," his is "a family of hearty-eating men and beautiful, delicate women" (4.5).

If Ernest T. is Barney's hillbilly double, Briscoe Darling is Andy's. But unlike

Ernest T. and Barney, who constantly butt heads, Andy and Briscoe are kindred spirits, or as close to kindred as a mountain man and a sheriff can be. Briscoe says: "You know something, sheriff? That haircut of yours may be city style, but your heart was shaped in a bowl" (4.5). After Briscoe eats four servings of Aunt Bee's white beans, she wants to know why he doesn't praise her cooking: "Eatin' speaks louder than words," he responds, repeating the same pearl of wisdom Andy had uttered earlier in the evening, also after gorging on Bee's beans. Wifeless patriarchs both, Briscoe and Andy enjoy a special rapport. It's obvious that they like each other, in spite of their differences. Whenever Briscoe shows up in town, Andy is glad to see him. Whatever the complications that ensue from the Darlings' rustic habits, Briscoe and Andy can settle them.

The Darlings live in a shabby log cabin deep in the hills. It has an old-fashioned well pump, a barrel of water and farm tools on the porch, and farm animals in the front yard. The room where Briscoe and his boys sleep is furnished with cots, a small table with four chairs, several kerosene lamps, a rocking chair, and a pile of cut wood. The jugs on the shelves betray the Darlings' taste for moonshine. Inside the front door, a tattered sign announces, "Home, Sweet Home." Like Aunt Bee, Charlene tends house and does the cooking. Her specialties are hog backbone and fish muddle. Homey the cabin surely is, but living in such close quarters is foreign to Andy's middle-class mores, not to speak of his reserve. When he spends the night at the cabin, bedded down in the same room with the Darling men, the snoring gets so loud that he can't sleep a wink.

The Darlings drive into town in an ancient flatbed truck, with Charlene riding shotgun and the boys and their instruments crammed into the back. If the truck overheats, Briscoe stops at the David Mendlebright Memorial Horse Trough for eleven hatfuls of water. Except for a few scenes involving Charlene, the Darlings always appear together, as befits a clannish family. They like nothing better than to "scrub one on" (Darling-speak for a hoedown). Briscoe plays the jug, his sons play banjo, guitar, mandolin, and bass, and Charlene sings and does the mountain jig (the sons are played by The Dillards, a bluegrass band). Their jam sessions, during which they perform such fan favorites as "Ebo Walker," "Boil Them Cabbage Down," and "Stay All Night, Stay a Little Longer" provide some of the most entertaining moments in the show. Just as sweet are their unheard melodies, songs in their repertoire that go unsung because they make Briscoe or Charlene cry: "Will You Love Me When I'm Old and Ugly," "Dirty Me, Dirty Me, I'm Disgusted with Myself," and "Never Hit Your Grandma with a Great Big Stick."

Not shy about playing and singing, the Darling boys never utter a nonsinging word. Whenever anyone addresses them, they look like they're in a fog, giving yet another meaning to the fine art of "settin' and starin'." Even if the family's

The Darlings "scrub one on."

name takes off on that of the Dillards, in *Peter Pan* the last name of Wendy and her brothers is also Darling. Mute but musical, Charlene's brothers are lost boys adrift in a mental Neverland of their own.

The Darling Cycle of the Mayberry Chronicles suggests that Tolstoy was wrong: happy families are not all alike. Perhaps it is truer to say that happy families, however different, always get along. This may be why, at one time or another, all three of the Taylors are on the verge of getting "betrothed" to a Darling: Andy to Charlene, Bee to Briscoe, and Opie to Andelina. Watching the Taylors and Darlings sit around the table enjoying Aunt Bee's pot roast, and afterward playing and singing together, one begins to think that it's too bad that by the time Andy met her, Charlene was spoken for. Lively and uninhibited, she would have cured Andy of his "difficulty" with women. During one of their get-togethers, even Aunt Bee gets into the act by reciting an unintentionally revealing poem, "A Fading Flower of Forgotten Love." When she initially demurs at reciting the poem, she says that she only performs in front of family. To which Briscoe replies, "We're a family." And so they are. Clematis and cabbage, the perfect combination.

CHAPTER NINE

Otis Regrets (Otis Campbell)

O F THE MAYBERRIANS WHOM WE GET TO KNOW WELL, the saddest case is Otis Campbell, the town drunk. Floyd's decline is painful to watch, but sooner or later we all go through something similar. And when the other characters get into trouble, they overcome it in less than half an hour. But not Otis, whose trouble, chronic alcoholism, prevents him from leading a normal life even by *TAGS* standards. To make matters worse, his only brother, Ralph, is also an alcoholic — the town drunk of a different town.

Even though Otis appears in over thirty episodes, we don't know much about his life. He was booked for the first time on September 23, 1941, at two in the afternoon, for being intoxicated at the Garden Flower Show. In 1963 he celebrated a special anniversary: "Twenty-seven years ago I took my first drink and I've been in love with it ever since" (4.11). He says he works as a "glue-dipper" in the furniture factory, but it is hard to see how he can keep a job. With no children and few kin, he prefers the jail cell to his home because it gets him away from his wife, Rita, with whom he is constantly arguing. In one of his first appearances, he has thrown something at Rita and hit her mother instead. He doesn't get along any better with Aunt Bee, whom he regards as a "beast" because she makes him do household chores. His advice to Andy on how to handle Miss Ellie: "If you want results with her, hit her in the mouth with a leg of lamb" (1.10).

Unlike the other men in town, Otis is not one of the boys. Not once do we see him in the barbershop shooting the breeze with Floyd, sitting on a bench whittling, or attending a social or church function. When he's not drunk, he's invisible. Barney gives Otis a sobriety test to determine whether he can resume "his place in society" (1.25). But the point is that Otis has no place in society. Drunk, Otis is liable to do anything. One evening he rides a cow into town thinking it's a horse; another time, he is accompanied by his invisible dog, Spot.

Every Friday or Saturday night Otis staggers into the courthouse, unshaven and unkempt, locks himself in jail, and sleeps it off. More of a home than his home, the courthouse is where he gets his mail. That Otis considers Andy and Barney, his jailers, his "best friends" tells us how alone he really is.

Played by Hal Smith, a versatile actor who did many voices for TV cartoon characters, including Owl in *Winnie the Pooh*, Otis made his debut in the second episode of the first season, "The Manhunt." As the series entered its last years, his appearances became rarer, and he appeared only once in the seventh season and not at all in the last. By the mid-sixties it was no longer acceptable to make fun of alcoholics with lines such as "In a way, his drinking does a good service for the town. Otis laps it up so fast that other folks can't get to it" (2.31). Andy explains Otis's absence from Mayberry by telling Opie that Otis is now doing his drinking in Mt. Pilot. When he reappears in *Return to Mayberry*, he has become an ice cream man, not having touched a drop of booze in many years. Dressed in a clownish white suit with a cap, Otis cuts a less funny but no less pathetic figure than he did as the town drunk.

Like Helen, Otis has one shining moment. In "A Plaque for Mayberry" (1.25), the Women's Historical Society intends to honor the memory of Nathan Tibbs, a Revolutionary War hero whose lone surviving descendant lives in the town. It turns out to be Otis. Worried that he will show up "gassed" for the award ceremony, Mayor Pike orders Andy to hustle Otis out of town and find a substitute. Andy refuses. He visits Otis to tell him about the plaque, perhaps the only scene set in Otis's house. It's also the only time that Otis and Rita show any tenderness toward each other. When Rita kisses him affectionately on the forehead, Otis remarks that it's the first time that she has planted on his head anything as light as a kiss. For once his wife has something to be proud of, compensation for the "awful bad times" that he's given her.

Later that day, at the Mayor's office, Otis hasn't shown up for the ceremony. The Mayor and Andy fear the worst. Finally he and Rita appear. Instead of his usual attire — rumpled jacket, loud tie, tattered hat — Otis is wearing a dark suit over a neatly pressed shirt and a conservative tie. Clean shaven, with a new hat in his hand, he looks almost dapper. To everyone's relief, he's sober. He accepts the plaque "to Mayberry's most distinguished citizen" with these words:

> I've been thinking about the big long speech I could make here. Then I got to studying how that was all wrong. See, I don't deserve this award. I didn't do nothing. Being descended from a hero don't make you one. Shucks, a man can't take credit just for being born. So I want to give this to Mayor Pike to accept for the town of Mayberry, of which I'm proud to be a citizen.

Unlike Barney, who is convinced that he is Nathan Tibbs's descendant, Otis may be a drunk, but he's not deluded. He confuses a cow with a horse and mistakes a goat full of dynamite for his heroic ancestor, "Uncle Nat," but Otis knows who he is, a self-assessment that is nothing if not sober. Donating the plaque to the town, he becomes part of Mayberry's body politic, an upstanding citizen like Floyd or Howard, if only briefly. The next time we encounter him, the following week, Otis is drunk on his birthday. He calls Sarah from the courthouse to ask whether anyone has phoned to wish him a happy birthday. Nobody has. He has to sing "For He's a Jolly Good Fellow" to himself.

Some years ago country singer Joe Diffie had a hit record entitled "Ships That Don't Come In." The setting of the song is a bar where the speaker meets an old man. The speaker pulls up a chair and together they drink to life's losers, those who wait forever for ships that don't come in. Otis is one of those people. There are no bars in Mayberry, but if there were, Otis would be that old man. After closing time, he will stumble down the street and lock himself in Cell Number 1 of the Mayberry jail.

CHAPTER TEN

Love in the Country (Gomer, Goober, and Howard)

I N A TOWN OF BACHELORS, ROMANCE MUST BE IN THE air. But it is not in Andy's or Barney's character to instigate romance. Barney is hot-blooded rather than romantic. Andy is neither. It is up to a trio of unlikely Lotharios — Gomer, Goober, and Howard — to put themselves in the way of love's arrows.

An attendant at Wally's Service, Gomer Pyle (Jim Nabors) appears for the first time in "The Bank Job" (3.13). In his only scene, he goes over to the bank with an acetylene torch to get Barney out of the vault in which he accidently has locked himself. From this modest beginning, he would go on to become one of the town's most active citizens before joining the Marines and bedeviling Sgt. Carter in *Gomer Pyle, U.S.M.C.* After Gomer's departure, his cousin, Goober Beasley Pyle (George Lindsey), takes over at Wally's Service. Between the fourth and the eighth seasons, Goober appeared in over seventy episodes. Howard Sprague (Jack Dodson) made his debut late in the sixth season as the nerdy, conscientious county clerk; he returned for three dozen additional appearances and, like Goober, lived on in *Mayberry R.F.D.*

Although Gomer and Goober are usually lumped together as bumbling hayseeds, they are quite different. Gomer is an attention freak: ebullient, loquacious, hedonistic. His signature utterance — "Shazzam!" — which he took from Captain Marvel comics, not only stresses his cartoonish, over-the-top personality, but his knack for transformation. Not counting cousins, his first date ever is with Mary Grace Gossage, whom he plans to take to the Chamber of Commerce dance in "A Date for Gomer" (4.9). Dressed in a double-breasted suit with accessories purchased specifically for the big event — yellow socks, shoes with brass buckles, a belt with an imitation mother-of-pearl buckle, and a purple tie with "akerns" (acorns) on it — the grease monkey is unrecognizable. In "The Song Festers" (4.20), he undergoes a similarly radical metamorphosis

Gomer dances up a storm.

when the choir director discovers that Gomer's nasal twang conceals a beautiful tenor voice.

On the night of the Chamber of Commerce dance, Gomer notices that Mary Grace doesn't have a "corsayge" like Helen and Thelma Lou. He rushes out to get one. By the time he gets back, the other couples have left. Gomer and Mary Grace stay at Thelma Lou's, where they dance up a storm all by themselves. Greenbaum and Fritzell in their script indicate that in this scene "Jazz is blaring and Gomer and Mary Grace are dancing"[1]—directions that don't begin to describe Gomer's hilarious gyrations, with feet flying and arms flapping in all directions. He is oblivious to Mary Grace, who can do little more than hold onto the whirling dervish. The next time Gomer goes dancing, this time with Helen, he also prances around like a man possessed. Give him a stage, be it a dance or a concert, and Gomer assumes a different identity. Whether it's jitterbugging wildly, singing "Santa Lucia," or telling a long, involved story, he loves the spotlight. The exaggerated twang, the protruding jaw, the relish with which he throws himself into any project, the inexplicable difference between his speaking and his singing voice—all make him stand out. Other Mayberrians may be histrionic, but they can't match Gomer's unself-conscious exhibitionism. When Barney enters a house before Gomer, Gomer says, without a hint of vanity, "Age before beauty" (4.2). Declaring for Thelma Lou, he begins: "It seems that you feel about me the same as I feel about me" (4.30). Even if the mangling of pronouns arises from his nervousness, it reflects Gomer's self-absorption. Mayberry's queen is not a Bee but a Gomer. When he says "Shazzam!" you almost expect him to turn into Mary Marvel.

His cousin Goober is a different sort, not a queen but a commoner. For viewers accustomed to Gomer, Goober at first seems like watery grits, Pyle lite.

In the only episode where the two appear together, "Fun Girls" (4.27), Gomer steals every scene. But in the end Goober is more believable, and more affecting, precisely because of his commonness. His cousin is larger than life, as clowns are. Everything about Gomer is heightened. Even his shoes look too large. Goober is as plain as peanuts. Unlike Gomer, who would be equally at home in *Hee Haw* and *Aida*, he does not have a split personality or a double voice. He likes to do imitations — his favorite is Cary Grant ("Joody, Joody, Joody, Joody") — but he's too self-conscious to pull them off. His signature mannerism, clicking his tongue and softly jabbing his interlocutor in the chest, mixes shyness and sociability (Lindsey called the gesture a "knuckle cluck"). In "A Man's Best Friend" (6.12), Opie and a friend take advantage of Goober's naïveté by tricking him into thinking that his dog is talking. Goober's embarrassment when he discovers the trick reveals a vulnerability rare for a Mayberrian. Had the prank been played on Gomer, he wouldn't have noticed; had it been played on Barney, he would pretend that he hadn't noticed. More vulnerable than either, Goober doesn't hide that the boys have made a fool of him. And it's not like him to hold a grudge. In the epilogue, he's back to his normal self, agreeing to play "FBI dog" with Opie and Tommy. Goober is the boys' best friend.

Jack Dodson once pointed out that Goober is "a broad character built on very subtle touches."[2] The subtlety comes across especially in Goober's timid courting. His introduction to romance occurs in "Goober and the Art of Love" (5.20) when Andy and Barney set him up with Lydia Crosswaith so that he stops tagging along with them on their dates with Helen and Thelma Lou. Before meeting Lydia, the only woman Goober ever had a crush on is Maureen O'Sullivan, Jane in *Tarzan* movies. His inexperience shows on the first date, when he hurries out of Lydia's house after two minutes, having run out of things to say. To teach Goober the art of love, Barney has Goober take lessons from the master — Andy! Barney and Goober walk to Helen's house one evening so that Goober can see how Andy "makes his move." Peeking through a window, Barney provides the play-by-play as Andy inches closer to Helen and then puts his arm around her while they're watching TV. No thanks to Andy, Goober and Lydia finally hit it off, though it's a bit hard to imagine what their relationship will be like. She can't ride in a car because she vomits and she gets "the herpes" when she's out in the sun.

But Lydia is a passing fancy; she lasts all of one episode. Goober's true love is Flora, a new waitress at the diner — "a lulu alright," according to Floyd — who doesn't make her debut until the sixth season in "Eat Your Heart Out" (6.24). When Flora shows up in town, Goober goes crazy over her: "I finally found her, the right girl for me." But his shyness gets in the way. Talking to Flora on the phone, he throws kisses, but only after she has hung up. Goober gets Andy to accompany him to the diner to flaunt his feats, such as being the champion hand-wrestler of Mayberry. Predictably Flora falls for the wrong guy. Only when Goober begins ignoring her does Flora switch her affections. No more articulate than he is, she communicates her change of heart by giving Goober the largest portion of meatloaf. As she says, "a woman should serve her man."

The actress who plays Flora, Alberta Nelson, is perfect for the part: a little plump, busty, attractive but not exactly a knockout, and the only woman in Mayberry to wear tight jeans. Flora's wholesome farm-girl looks make a big hit with Mayberry fauna, particularly the old geezers. In "Goober's Replacement" (6.28), when she subs for Goober at Wally's Service, cars wait in a long line to be gas-pumped by the rural Venus in blue jeans. Even Floyd is smitten. Andy thinks that Goober can service cars just as efficiently; Floyd retorts: "Goober is not quite the same in slacks." She attracts so much business that Goober loses his job to her. Much as she likes working at Wally's, when Flora finds out what has happened, she gives up jeans and job for a dress and a recipe for pounded steak. She realizes that if any man's heart ever led through his stomach, it's Goober's. Wally takes him back and all's right in Mayberry.

Earle Hagen's background music for Flora's scenes is a slow-paced melody reminiscent of 1950s ballads like "A Summer Place." By February 1966, when Flora moves to Mayberry, the heyday of this kind of music had long passed, but "Flora's Theme" fits her old-fashioned outlook, as well as the town's anachronistic temper. Characters far more important than Flora—Floyd, Otis, Gomer, Howard, Helen, Thelma Lou—don't have musical themes. Andy and Opie have "The Fishing Hole"; Barney has "The Manhunt"; Mayberry has "The Mayberry March"; Ellie and Aunt Bee also have their themes. Wonderfully adept at getting to the essence of a character, Earle Hagen makes each tune describe its subject: casual and warm for Andy and Opie; tense and suspenseful for Barney; cheerful for Ellie; wistful for Aunt Bee; a little bit dippy for Mayberry. "Flora's Theme" captures the innocence of dog-loving Goober's puppy love. Upon meeting Flora, he gets a thrill from just waving hello or sitting next to her at the picture show. When Flora's hand brushes against his while putting down a plate of succotash, he's in heaven. "Flora's Theme" should really be called "Goober's Theme."

It's not clear how long Flora remains Goober's girl. She will make one more appearance in *TAGS* (8.25), but without the episode making any reference to her relationship with Goober. Something must have happened that we're not privy to, because in the next-to-last episode of the show, Goober starts dating a woman from Mt. Pilot—a Ph.D. in psychology no less—after "exhausting all the girls in Mayberry" including Juanita, who has been seen going to Myers Lake with Harold Fossett. Still, no man in Mayberry ever fell for a girl the way Goober fell for Flora. Not Gomer. Not Andy. Not Barney. Not Briscoe. Not Opie. Not even Ernest T.

Perhaps only Howard Sprague's crush on Millie Hutchins, who works at

Boysinger's Bakery, can compare with Goober's lovesickness. Howard and Goober are as different as Goober and Gomer. Goober is a bumpkin; Howard, a bureaucrat. Howard's signature is not a beanie but a bowtie. In contrast to Goober, who learned how to work on cars by trial and error, Howard relies on book learning. After all, he is a graduate of the Bradbury Business College in Mt. Pilot, an education that stocked him with an ample supply of polysyllables, words like "differential" and "flabbergasted" that would never come out of the mouth of any other Mayberrian. Fishing in Tucker's Lake, he prefers "the scientific approach" to "animal cunning." No one but Howard would notice that the menu in the Shanghai Gardens restaurant leaves off a "Chi" from Ling Chi Chi Chicken.

Howard is the exception to the rule that Mayberrians don't change. When we are introduced to him in "The County Clerk" (6.26), he is a mama's boy in a town singularly bereft of mothers. After a few more appearances by Howard, Jack Dodson suggested that the character would have more possibilities if his doting mother were written out of the show. Griffith and the producers agreed. Mrs. Sprague immediately remarried and moved to Mt. Pilot, never to be heard from again. Millie replaces mother as Howard's significant other, and goes on to play a major role in his evolution from mama's boy to one of the boys. Emboldened by his interest in Millie, Howard gets up the courage to confront her thuggish ex-boyfriend, Clyde Plaunt (Allan Melvin), in a scene reminiscent of Barney's encounter with the produce vendors (one of whom was also played by Melvin). Together Howard and Millie see a movie titled *Two in Love*, which could have served as the title of the montage—an unusual device for TAGS—during which, backed by a variation of "Flora's Theme," the two of them stroll hand in hand around town, walk in the woods, go on a picnic to Myers Lake.

After knowing Millie for only three months in a town where, as Andy once told Briscoe, courtships last five or six years, Howard does something unheard of: he proposes. But, as we have learned to expect, he calls the wedding off at the last minute when he realizes that his and Millie's "path to happiness" lies in continuing as sweethearts rather than getting married (8.12). Mayberry's spotless record of bachelorhood remains unblemished. When Millie reappears in RFD, still working at Boysinger's Bakery, she will be Sam's girl, not Howard's (apparently she's a thoroughly modern Millie). Howard hasn't forgotten their romance, however. As he tells Emmett in an early episode of RFD, "The Harvest Ball," "We were quite an item."

Howard's end: twenty years later, in *Return to Mayberry*, Howard is still single. Worried that he is losing his looks, he dyes his hair, which turns an awful shade of red. He tries a different color, Flamenco Brown, with results even more unsightly. He should have married Millie when he had the chance.

CHAPTER ELEVEN

Trashy Women (Daphne and Skippy)

I like my women just a little on the trashy side,
When they wear their clothes too tight and their hair is dyed.

CONFEDERATE RAILROAD, "TRASHY WOMEN"

N0 ACCOUNT OF ROMANCE IN MAYBERRY WOULD BE complete without at least a few words about Daphne and Skippy, the "fun girls," as Thelma Lou calls them. We see Daphne (Jean Carson) and Skippy (Joyce Jameson) only on three occasions, but their aura, like that of Ernest T. Bass, hovers over the entire series. Like the wild man, they inject a note of uninhibitedness that threatens to loosen the town's straight-laced mores. If Ernest T. descends from the mountains, Daphne and Skippy come from another kind of eminence, Mt. Pilot, the Sodom and Gomorrah of the Mayberrian imagination. The difference is that, because he is a man, Ernest T.'s behavior is outrageous only in its excessiveness. His pursuit of Romeena differs from Barney's advances to Thelma Lou in degree, not in kind. But the forwardness of Daphne and Skippy has no parallel or precedent in the modest demeanor of the Mayberry maidens.

Bleached blondes who favor tight sweaters and form-fitting skirts, Daphne and Skippy compete with Helen and Thelma Lou for the attention of Andy and Barney. Daphne, the floozy with the nymph's name, speaks with a gravelly croak that caricatures the throaty voices of Hollywood's femmes fatales. Her idea of a good time is to watch the floorshow at the Gigolo Club. Younger and better looking, Skippy, the floozy with the name of peanut butter, thinks that Barney is a "scream." Daphne is the clingy type; she likes to nuzzle up to Andy and croak, "Hello, doll." Skippy is more raucous. Any time "Bernie" cracks her up with a joke, she gets so excited that she nearly shoves him to the floor.

As usual, Barney is responsible for getting Andy into "nutty situations" with the Fun Girls. In "Barney Mends a Broken Heart" (3.6), he introduces Andy to Daphne to lift Andy's mood. Subsequently, Daphne and Skippy tend to show up at the courthouse on nights when Andy and Barney have dates with Helen and Thelma Lou. Of course, Andy wants nothing to do with the two "wild women," though this doesn't stop Helen and Thelma Lou from thinking that they are being two-timed. Although Thelma Lou never complains about Barney's flirtation with Juanita, the Fun Girls represent a different kind of threat: sexually aggressive outsiders who, were they allowed free access to the local men, would undermine the town's paradisiacal innocence.

Asked about the rarity of Ernest T.'s incursions into town, Howard Morris remarked that his character tended to "overpower" everyone around him.[1] The same can be said of Daphne and Skippy. Barney explains his dalliance with Skippy by telling Thelma Lou: "She forced herself on me" (5.28). For once, he doesn't exaggerate. Forceful women may be fun, but they need to be kept away: if not by the ten-foot pole that comes between Ernest T.'s id and Barney, then by the twelve miles that separate Mayberry from Mt. Pilot.

Old Sam

There's no disgrace in being a little fish.

HOWARD SPRAGUE, "SUPPOSE ANDY GETS SICK" (8.14)

*T*HE HOT TOPIC IN THE BARBERSHOP IS THE START OF the fishing season. Andy hasn't missed an opening day in twenty years. Opie has been to the last four. For seven years (the lifespan of TAGS at this point), Floyd has been trying to hook Old Sam, a "legendary fish," the only silver carp in the lake and perhaps in the whole state. (According to the U.S. Geological Service, the silver carp, a species indigenous to Asia, was not brought to the United States until 1973; Old Sam may be the one silver carp not only in North Carolina but in North America.) Floyd claims that he had Old Sam hooked a year earlier, but the fish—"a real fighter"—got away. Howard, who has never been fishing before, asks Floyd and Goober whether he can go with them, but they want no part of the neophyte. The next day, early in the morning, Howard tags along with Andy and Opie. As beginner's luck would have it, he hooks Old Sam, using potato salad as bait, one of his scientific discoveries.

The conundrum: what to do with the fish? While Old Sam swims around in a fish tank on Main Street, the locals argue about his fate. Cooking him is unthinkable. Since Old Sam was "born and bred" in Tucker's Lake, Floyd believes that Howard should throw him back in, a plan opposed by the Fish and Game Department, which wants Old Sam for the Raleigh Aquarium. Howard donates his rare catch to the aquarium. But when he and Opie go to Old Sam's new home, he realizes that Floyd was right. Exiled from Tucker's Lake and cooped up in a narrow tank, Old Sam is a melancholy sight—a fish out of his own water. A few days later, the boys are back at the lake. Floyd claims to see a fish that looks just like Old Sam. Howard tells him that it is indeed Old Sam. During the

Old Sam at the aquarium.

visit to the aquarium, Old Sam let him know that he missed his old friends, and so Howard put him back in the lake. Much to everyone's delight, the status quo ante is restored. Mayberrians will continue to try to snag Old Sam, who will be forever sought and forever free.

The episode marks an important step in Howard's integration into the town's inner circle. Perceived as a "strange bird," Floyd and the others are slow to take him in. But by putting Old Sam back in the lake, Howard acts in the way that Floyd or Goober would have acted. His action makes him the "big fish in the small town," the phrase that serves as the title of the episode (7.11). But Howard is not the only big fish in town; there's Old Sam, the little big fish who has baffled the local anglers for years. Like Mayberry B.C., Old Sam resists change. When Andy says that Old Sam is just a fish, an irate Floyd yells back, "No, he isn't!" What makes Sam not a fish, adds Floyd, lowering his voice, is that he has a name. By the same token, what makes Mayberry not just another small town is that it is Mayberry.

One of the episode's writers, Bill Idelson, remembers that the fish's name was chosen because it was "homey."[1] But there may be more to it than this. Andy Griffith's middle name was Samuel, a name he passed on to his son. And one of the landmarks of the campus of the University of North Carolina at Chapel Hill, Griffith's alma mater and the school that Sheriff Andy wanted his son to attend, is a statue of a Confederate soldier erected as a memorial to the alumni who fought for the South. To this day, the students call it "Silent Sam," perhaps in contradistinction to Uncle Sam. Removed to the Raleigh Aquarium, Old Sam may be a casualty of *TAGS*'s version of the War of Northern Aggression, his imprisonment a harbinger of the changes that will befall the town.

When the boys find out that Howard has given Old Sam to the Fish and Game Department, their initial outrage soon slips into melancholy.

Goober: It's like the end of something, ain't it.

Floyd: Seems like Old Sam has always been out in that lake. Saw him once in a while, but nobody ever caught him. And now he's not there anymore.

Andy: Yeah, I guess that's right.

Goober: He's been in there a long time.

Andy: I remember taking Opie down there when he was four.

Opie: Yeah, you had to bait my hook then.

Andy: It was worth it, though. Going after something special as Old Sam.

Opie: Yeah.

Floyd: Well, it's all gone now.

It may be that TAGS itself is like Old Sam in the aquarium, the rectangular glass pane of his tank reminiscent of the TV screen behind which Mayberrians act out their lives like so many strange fish. Certainly the townsfolk are "something special," as Andy says about Old Sam, and their specialness is even more pronounced now, more than half a century after the show's debut. "Big Fish in a Small Pond" is an episode from the next-to-last season. The following season another Sam will appear in Mayberry: affable Sam Jones, Andy's successor as the town's sovereign. The arrival of a young Sam signals the end of the old regime. But as long as Old Sam remains in Tucker's Lake, Mayberrians will stay in their magical fishbowl, and we will be there to watch them.

A Cuban in Mayberry

Sometimes a man hits upon a place to which he mysteriously feels that he belongs. Here is the home he sought, and he will settle amid scenes that he has never seen before, among men he has never known, as though they were familiar to him from his birth.

SOMERSET MAUGHAM, *THE MOON AND SIXPENCE*

WATCHING *TAGS* EPISODES OVER THE LAST FEW YEARS, I've kept my eye out for traces of Cuba, however faint, in Mayberry. I haven't had much luck. When Andy's rich girlfriend, Peggy McMillan, takes him to a fancy restaurant in Raleigh, the band is playing a cha-cha. Peg asks Andy whether he wants to dance, and he replies that he "can't do that." Barney can, though, as he demonstrates when he does the cha-cha with Netty Albright during a high school reunion. In fact, the cha-cha seems to be one of the specialties of Mayberry's favorite dance band, Carl Benson's Wildcats, which advertises its cha-cha chops with a drawing of a palm tree on the bass drum. In the eighth season, the entertainment at the Harvest Ball is provided by another band with a similar repertoire, Casper Tice and His Latin Rhythms. Before the Taylors head for California, Floyd suggests that they stay at a senior citizens lodge on Route 66 where they can "sway to the maraca rhythms of José González." After the Taylors return, Opie says that one of the highlights of the trip was standing in front of Cesar Romero's house and holding his newspaper. And then there is that old cannon that supposedly went up San Juan Hill with Teddy Roosevelt, and old Asa's pistol, also of Spanish-American War vintage. Years later, in *Return to Mayberry*, the hair dye that turns Howard into a redhead is called "Cuban Sunset."

A paltry yield of Cubanisms, I agree, given the 125 hours' worth of episodes, plus the reunion movie.

The most explicit reference to Cuba that I've come across occurs not in *TAGS* but in Harvey Bullock's script for "Andy's English Valet" (3.26), the first of the Malcolm Merriweather episodes. Having just met the Englishman, Barney and Andy are wondering where Malcolm comes from. Barney thinks he's "a trouble maker from another country." When Andy suggests that it may be Cuba, Barney replies: "No, not Cuba, but he's a foreigner all right. Maybe Canada."[1] In the filmed episode, the mentions of Cuba in Bullock's script were omitted, perhaps because the allusion to troublemaking Fidel Castro was too explicit. But the deletion suggests to me the sketch of the *TAGS* episode that never was—the Cuban installment of the Mayberry Chronicles—which also has to do with the arrival in Mayberry of a foreigner, but not, like Malcolm, from the British Isles.

"THE LOST BOY"

Act I: At the courthouse, Andy is riffling through old accident records while Barney, sitting by his side, is reading the "News of the World" section of the *Mayberry Gazette*. He turns to Andy. "You know, Ange, things sure have changed down in Cuba." He was there once, during his army days. "Havana was quite a town then, yes sir." Andy: "Livelier than a cow's tail in fly season, huh?" Barney puts on his man-of-the-world look and nods. "Yes, sir. That's where Juanita and me, you know . . ." Andy (surprised): "I didn't know that." Barney: "Yep, she was on a cruise down there. Once she saw the stripes on my uniform, she was a goner. She's been crazy about me ever since." Andy: "I thought you were a buck private, Barney." Barney (nervously): "Well, she saw the stripes she knew I was going to get—had I stayed in, that is."

The courthouse door opens. In comes Opie, seven or eight years old, with a boy about his age or maybe a little older. He walks up to Andy's desk. "He don't speak English, Paw." Opie came across the boy sitting on the sidewalk by the bus stop. The boy smiles at Andy, who asks him his name. The boy looks at him blankly. "You're right, Ope. He don't seem to." Barney intervenes. "Leave it to me, Ange. I can handle this." He pushes his chest out, puts his hands on his hips, and slowly circles the boy. Brusquely he turns and says, "Sprechen Sie Deutsch?" No reaction. "Parlez français?" Still no reaction. "Habla español?" The boy's face lights up and he starts speaking very fast in Spanish. Barney doesn't understand a word. "Naw, I don't think he speaks Spanish either." Andy: "Of course he does, Barn. 'Sí' means yes. I know that much." Opie: "I feel bad for him, Paw. I don't think he has any friends." Andy: "Well, I'm sure he has friends where he came from." Opie: "You mean like from England? Don't they speak English in England, Paw?" Barney (interrupting): "I bet you he came straight from Cuba. Yes, sir, he must be one of them refugee children I was reading about. Look, it's right'cheere in the paper." He gives Andy the paper. Andy (after glancing at it): "Reckon you might be right, Barn." Barney goes up to the boy again: "You coma de Coobah? Coobah?" As he says this, he stretches his arm, as if pointing in the direction of Cuba. The boy lights up. "Sí, sí, de Cuba, de Cuba."

In the next scene, Barney and Andy are in the barbershop. Floyd is resting in the barber chair, as usual. Andy is sitting on a chair against the wall, and Barney is pacing. Opie has taken the little boy to his house for Aunt Bee to look after. Andy: "I don't know what to do about that little boy. All I know is that he's from Cuba and that he has a Tía María that he keeps talking about." Barney, turning to Floyd: "That's Spanish for 'aunt,' Floyd." Floyd: "Oh, he's got an aunt. Well, that's a fine thing. Aunt Bee is a wonderful aunt, isn't she, Andy?" Andy: "Not Aunt Bee, Floyd, a different aunt. We've been all around town asking and nobody knows anything about this Tía María." Barney: "Even went up to Tom Strongbow's farm. It's a well-known fact that the Cherokees originally came from the islands. No bananas." Floyd (fascinated by the mention of islands): "Oh, the islands! Yes, a lovely place. And you say that Tom just got back from there, Barney?" Andy (talking more to himself than to the others): "I just don't know what else I can do. He's gonna have to go to the orphanage in Raleigh." Barney protests. "You can't do that, Ange. Think of the way they treat boys in those places. It's like *Oliver Twist*. Remember? Just awful." Floyd: "The twist? No, no, that would be terrible, terrible. No, Andy, you can't do that to the boy . . . (pauses). It's bad for the spine, you know."

Just then, Goober walks into the barbershop. He says "Hey" and knuckle clucks Barney, who pulls away in disgust. Goober (excited): "I hear there's a lost boy in town!" Andy grunts in assent. Goober: "Can't remember the last time we had a lost boy come through. How long's he gonna be here?" Andy (irritated): "We don't know, Goober. We don't know who he is, we don't know what he's doing here. All he keeps saying is something about a Tía María. I'm gonna have to call Child Welfare and have them take care of it." Again, Barney protests. At some level, he identifies with the lost boy. Goober: "I know Tía María." Andy jumps up from his chair. Floyd gets all ruffled. Barney (eyes popping): "*You* know Tía María?" Goober: "Sure, it's the new Mexican restaurant in Mt. Pilot." Andy (mixing disappointment with impatience): "It's not that kind of Tía María, Goob." Barney: "Wait, Andy. Think about it for a minute. Suppose you came from Cuba and you needed to make a living. What would you do?" Andy: "I don't know, Barney." Barney: "You open a Mexican restaurant, that's what!" Andy: "Oh, Barn . . ." Barney: "Don't you get it, Ange? The boy's Tía María must be the owner of that restaurant!" Andy is dubious, unlike Floyd and Goober, who are instantly convinced. Floyd (haughty): "Listen to Barney, Andy. The islands, Mexican food, a hungry boy. It all makes perfect sense." Goober: "Yeah, Andy, yeah. That has to be the answer." Andy (after reflecting for a bit): "Mebbe you're right. It *is* possible that the boy was supposed to get off the bus at Mt. Pilot and got off here by mistake." Enthused, Barney, Floyd, and Goober all express their agreement. End of Act I.

Act II begins with an exterior shot of a restaurant with a large rectangular sign that says "Tía María" under a Mexican sombrero. Inside, the restaurant is decorated in generic Latin style: serapes, maracas, and plastic palm trees; on the walls, cutouts of guitars and castanets; on each table, bongo-shaped salt and pepper shakers. In a corner, an accordionist playing mariachi music. Andy, Barney, and Goober come into the restaurant. A heavyset waiter, dressed in a white shirt and black pants with a red cummerbund, shows them to a booth. Andy sits across from Barney and Goober. Barney picks up the salt-and-pepper bongos and begins shaking them as he hums "La cucaracha." As he does, salt and pepper fly all over the table. The waiter makes a face at him. To recover, Barney again tries out the Spanish he learned at the Spanish club. Waiter: "Sorry, no Spanish. Today's special is guacamole stew. What can I get you?" Andy (tentative): "Well, we're not here to eat exactly. What we'd like is to see the owner." Waiter (looks around the almost empty restaurant): "Ok, he's in the back. I'll get him." Andy, Barney, and Goober are puzzled. Moments later, a short, bald man in his mid-fifties comes out, wiping his hands on an apron. Goober: "Don't tell me *he's* Tía María?" Owner (overhearing): "Catchy name, isn't it? Adds to the atmosphere." The owner is Dante Morelli, cousin of the Morelli of Morelli's. Since his cousin already had an Italian restaurant, Dante decided to open a Mexican one instead.

Back to the courthouse: Andy, Barney, and Goober are despondent. Andy: "Reckon I'll just have to call the Child Welfare office tomorrow." Barney: "I feel so bad for that boy. What's gonna happen to him? Can't we find him someplace to stay?" Goober: "What if I adopt him, Andy? I could teach him to speak English, how to change wiper blades, drain oil . . ." Barney (interrupting): "First thing, Goober, you can't adopt a child unless you're married." Goober: "Well, can't I get married and then adopt him?" Andy: "Please, Goob. You can't adopt this little boy." Goober is crestfallen. The three of them go back to their private thoughts. A few moments later, there's a ruckus outside the courthouse. They hear Otis screaming, "Let me go! You let me go!" The door opens and a pretty, dark-haired woman—a María Conchita Alonso look-alike—comes into the courthouse dragging Otis by his tie. Otis: "Tell her to stop, Andy, tell her to stop!" In fluent but accented English, the young woman tells Andy that Otis was sleeping under her car. Andy: "I've told you before, Otis: you *don't* sleep under people's cars. That's dangerous." Barney (making a bad joke): "Yeah, Otis, especially if you're gassed." Andy: "I apologize for this, ma'am. I hope you understand. Otis . . ." Unexpectedly, the young woman breaks out in tears. Andy tries to comfort her. Barney (officious, taking out his pad): "Can I have your name, miss . . . ?"

The young woman (getting ahold of herself): "María Martínez." Andy: "Did you say María?" She nods. Andy: "Tía María?" She nods again. She has been looking for her nephew all day. At the Mt. Pilot bus stop, the driver told her that a little boy had gotten off in Mayberry. He was sent by her sister from Cuba. Barney: "From Cuba? By bus?" Andy (before the young woman has a chance to explain): "Yes, Barn. A flying bus." Otis: "Hey, Andy! I saw one last night. You should've seen how it flapped its wings." Andy (turning to the woman, who is puzzled by the conversation): "I think I know where you can find your nephew."

Cut to Andy's house, where Aunt Bee is in the kitchen, preparing supper, while Opie and the lost boy play upstairs. They're getting along fine, in spite of the language barrier. Andy comes into the house, followed by Tía María and Barney. He calls Opie. The two boys come down the stairs. When the lost boy sees Tía María, he runs into her arms and they start speaking rapid-fire Spanish. Opie looks at his father, wondering what's going on. "What are they saying, Paw?" Andy: "I'm not rightly sure, son. I expect something about what a long way it is from Cuba. That's his aunt that's been looking all over for him." Aunt Bee comes out of the kitchen. Opie looks at beautiful Tía María and then at his dowdy Aunt Bee, who notices that she is being compared. Aunt Bee (fussy): "If that boy came all the way from Cuba he must be starved." She orders everybody to the well-set table. Barney (rubbing his stomach): "I could use a little 'mañana' myself." Turning to Andy: "That's what we used to call it in Cuba, Ange." Andy (amused): "My, aren't you a regular Spanish-speaking devil? Old Christopher Columbus couldn't have said it better himself." Barney fills up with pride. Andy: "Except that *mañana* means tomorrow, Barn. You planning to eat tonight or tomorrow?" Barney turns his back to Andy and stomps off to the table.

The tag of my imaginary TAGS episode: an exterior shot of the Taylors' front porch in the evening. Andy is leaning against a post, smoking a cigarette; Barney is slouched back on the settee, eyes half-closed. Aunt Bee and Tía María emerge from the house. A happy Tía María thanks Aunt Bee for the tasty fried chicken—*pollito frito*. Then she thanks Andy and Barney for helping her find her nephew. Aunt Bee calls out to the two boys. Opie and his new friend come out of the house. As Tía María begins to leave with her nephew, she stops, turns back, and kisses Andy and Barney on the cheek—to Andy's surprise and Barney's delight. Watching Tía María and the no-longer-lost Cuban boy walk away from the porch, Barney begins to hum "La cucaracha," but this time he hums it slowly, giving the tune a melancholy air. He and Andy begin to sing softly: "La cucaracha, la cucaracha . . ." Opie joins in, followed by Aunt Bee, with her squeaky voice. Fade out.

THE END
FIN

List of Episodes
(WITH ORIGINAL AIR DATES)

27. Ellie Saves a Female (April 17, 1961)
28. Andy Forecloses (April 24, 1961)
29. Quiet Sam (May 1, 1961)
30. Barney Gets His Man (May 8, 1961)
31. The Guitar Player Returns (May 15, 1961)
32. Bringing Up Opie (May 22, 1961)

SEASON 2 (1961–1962)

1. Opie and the Bully (October 2, 1961)
2. Barney's Replacement (October 9, 1961)
3. Andy and the Woman Speeder (October 16, 1961)
4. Mayberry Goes Bankrupt (October 23, 1961)
5. Barney on the Rebound (October 30, 1961)
6. Opie's Hobo Friend (November 13, 1961)
7. Crime-Free Mayberry (November 20, 1961)
8. The Perfect Female (November 27, 1961)
9. Aunt Bee's Brief Encounter (December 4, 1961)
10. The Clubmen (December 11, 1961)
11. The Pickle Story (December 18, 1961)
12. Sheriff Barney (December 25, 1961)
13. The Farmer Takes a Wife (January 1, 1962)
14. The Keeper of the Flame (January 8, 1962)
15. Bailey's Bad Boy (January 15, 1962)
16. The Manicurist (January 22, 1962)
17. The Jinx (January 29, 1962)
18. Jailbreak (February 5, 1962)
19. A Medal for Opie (February 12, 1962)
20. Barney and the Choir (February 19, 1962)
21. Guest of Honor (February 26, 1962)
22. The Merchant of Mayberry (March 5, 1962)
23. Aunt Bee the Warden (March 12, 1962)
24. The County Nurse (March 19, 1962)
25. Andy and Barney in the Big City (March 26, 1962)
26. Wedding Bells for Aunt Bee (April 2, 1962)
27. Three's a Crowd (April 9, 1962)
28. The Bookie Barber (April 16, 1962)
29. Andy on Trial (April 23, 1962)
30. Cousin Virgil (April 30, 1962)
31. Deputy Otis (May 7, 1962)

SEASON 3 (1962–1963)

1. Mr. McBeevee (October 1, 1962)
2. Andy's Rich Girlfriend (October 8, 1962)
3. Andy and the New Mayor (October 15, 1962)
4. Andy and Opie, Bachelors (October 22, 1962)
5. The Cow Thief (October 29, 1962)
6. Barney Mends a Broken Heart (November 5, 1962)
7. Lawman Barney (November 12, 1962)
8. The Mayberry Band (November 19, 1962)
9. Floyd, the Gay Deceiver (November 26, 1962)
10. Opie's Rival (December 3, 1962)
11. Convicts-at-Large (December 10, 1962)
12. The Bed Jacket (December 17, 1962)
13. The Bank Job (December 24, 1962)
14. One Punch Opie (December 31, 1962)
15. Barney and the Governor (January 7, 1963)
16. Man in a Hurry (January 14, 1963)
17. High Noon in Mayberry (January 21, 1963)
18. The Loaded Goat (January 28, 1963)
19. Class Reunion (February 4, 1963)
20. Rafe Hollister Sings (February 11, 1963)
21. Opie and the Spoiled Kid (February 18, 1963)
22. The Great Filling Station Robbery (February 25, 1963)
23. Andy Discovers America (March 4, 1963)
24. Aunt Bee's Medicine Man (March 11, 1963)
25. The Darlings Are Coming (March 18, 1963)
26. Andy's English Valet (March 25, 1963)
27. Barney's First Car (April 1, 1963)
28. The Rivals (April 8, 1963)
29. A Wife for Andy (April 15, 1963)
30. Dogs, Dogs, Dogs (April 22, 1963)
31. Mountain Wedding (April 29, 1963)
32. The Big House (May 6, 1963)

SEASON 4 (1963–1964)

1. Opie the Birdman (September 30, 1963)
2. The Haunted House (October 7, 1963)
3. Ernest T. Bass Joins the Army (October 14, 1963)
4. The Sermon for Today (October 21, 1963)
5. Briscoe Declares for Aunt Bee (October 28, 1963)
6. Gomer the House Guest (November 4, 1963)

7. A Black Day for Mayberry (November 11, 1963)
8. Opie's Ill-Gotten Gain (November 18, 1963)
9. A Date for Gomer (November 25, 1963)
10. Up in Barney's Room (December 2, 1963)
11. Citizen's Arrest (December 16, 1963)
12. Opie and His Merry Men (December 30, 1963)
13. Barney and the Cave Rescue (January 6, 1964)
14. Andy and Opie's Pal (January 13, 1964)
15. Aunt Bee the Crusader (January 20, 1964)
16. Barney's Sidecar (January 27, 1964)
17. My Fair Ernest T. Bass (February 3, 1964)
18. Prisoner of Love (February 10, 1964)
19. Hot Rod Otis (February 17, 1964)
20. The Song Festers (February 24, 1964)
21. The Shoplifters (March 2, 1964)
22. Andy's Vacation (March 9, 1964)
23. Andy Saves Gomer (March 16, 1964)
24. Bargain Day (March 23, 1964)
25. Divorce, Mountain Style (March 30, 1964)
26. A Deal Is a Deal (April 6, 1964)
27. Fun Girls (April 13, 1964)
28. The Return of Malcolm Merriweather (April 20, 1964)
29. The Rumor (April 27, 1964)
30. Barney and Thelma Lou, Phffft (May 4, 1964)
31. Back to Nature (May 11, 1964)
32. Gomer Pyle, U.S.M.C. (May 18, 1964)

SEASON 5 (1964–1965)

1. Opie Loves Helen (September 21, 1964)
2. Barney's Physical (September 28, 1964)
3. Family Visit (October 5, 1964)
4. The Education of Ernest T. Bass (October 12, 1964)
5. Aunt Bee's Romance (October 19, 1964)
6. Barney's Bloodhound (October 26, 1964)
7. Man in the Middle (November 2, 1964)
8. Barney's Uniform (November 9, 1964)
9. Opie's Fortune (November 16, 1964)
10. Goodbye Sheriff Taylor (November 23, 1964)
11. The Pageant (November 30, 1964)
12. The Darling Baby (December 7, 1964)
13. Andy and Helen Have Their Day (December 14, 1964)
14. Three Wishes for Opie (December 21, 1964)

15. Otis Sues the County (December 28, 1964)
16. Barney Fife, Realtor (January 4, 1965)
17. Goober Takes a Car Apart (January 11, 1965)
18. The Rehabilitation of Otis (January 18, 1965)
19. The Lucky Letter (January 25, 1965)
20. Goober and the Art of Love (February 1, 1965)
21. Barney Runs for Sheriff (February 8, 1965)
22. If I Had a Quarter-Million (February 15, 1965)
23. TV or Not TV (March 1, 1965)
24. Guest in the House (March 8, 1965)
25. The Case of the Punch in the Nose (March 15, 1965)
26. Opie's Newspaper (March 22, 1965)
27. Aunt Bee's Invisible Beau (March 29, 1965)
28. The Arrest of the Fun Girls (April 5, 1965)
29. The Luck of Newton Monroe (April 12, 1965)
30. Opie Flunks Arithmetic (April 19, 1965)
31. Opie and the Carnival (April 26, 1965)
32. Banjo-Playing Deputy (May 3, 1965)

SEASON 6 (1965–1966)

1. Opie's Job (September 13, 1965)
2. Andy's Rival (September 20, 1965)
3. Malcolm at the Crossroads (September 27, 1965)
4. Aunt Bee, the Swinger (October 4, 1965)
5. The Bazaar (October 11, 1965)
6. A Warning from Warren (October 18, 1965)
7. Off to Hollywood (October 25, 1965)
8. The Taylors in Hollywood (November 1, 1965)
9. The Hollywood Party (November 8, 1965)
10. Aunt Bee on TV (November 15, 1965)
11. The Cannon (November 22, 1965)
12. A Man's Best Friend (November 29, 1965)
13. Aunt Bee Takes a Job (December 6, 1965)
14. The Church Organ (December 13, 1965)
15. Girl Shy (December 20, 1965)
16. Otis, the Artist (January 3, 1966)
17. The Return of Barney Fife (January 10, 1966)
18. The Legend of Barney Fife (January 17, 1966)
19. Lost and Found (January 24, 1966)
20. Wyatt Earp Rides Again (January 31, 1966)
21. Aunt Bee Learns to Drive (February 7, 1966)
22. Look, Paw, I'm Dancing (February 14, 1966)

23. The Gypsies (February 21, 1966)
24. Eat Your Heart Out (February 28, 1966)
25. A Baby in the House (March 7, 1966)
26. The County Clerk (March 14, 1966)
27. The Foster Lady (March 21, 1966)
28. Goober's Replacement (March 28, 1966)
29. The Battle of Mayberry (April 4, 1966)
30. A Singer in Town (April 11, 1966)

SEASON 7 (1966–1967)

1. Opie's Girlfriend (September 12, 1966)
2. The Lodge (September 19, 1966)
3. The Barbershop Quartet (September 26, 1966)
4. The Ball Game (October 3, 1966)
5. Aunt Bee's Crowning Glory (October 10, 1966)
6. The Darling Fortune (October 17, 1966)
7. Mind over Matter (October 31, 1966)
8. Politics Begin at Home (November 7, 1966)
9. The Senior Play (November 14, 1966)
10. Opie Finds a Baby (November 21, 1966)
11. Big Fish in a Small Town (November 28, 1966)
12. Only a Rose (December 5, 1966)
13. Otis the Deputy (December 12, 1966)
14. Goober Makes History (December 19, 1966)
15. A New Doctor in Town (December 26, 1966)
16. Don't Miss a Good Bet (January 2, 1967)
17. Dinner at Eight (January 9, 1967)
18. A Visit to Barney Fife (January 16, 1967)
19. Barney Comes to Mayberry (January 23, 1967)
20. Andy's Old Girlfriend (January 30, 1967)
21. Aunt Bee's Restaurant (February 6, 1967)
22. Floyd's Barbershop (February 13, 1967)
23. The Statue (February 20, 1967)
24. Helen, the Authoress (February 27, 1967)
25. Goodbye, Dolly (March 6, 1967)
26. Opie's Piano Lesson (March 13, 1967)
27. Howard, the Comedian (March 20, 1967)
28. Big Brother (March 27, 1967)
29. Opie's Most Unforgettable Character (April 3, 1967)
30. Goober's Contest (April 10, 1967)

SEASON 8 (1967–1968)

1. Opie's First Love (September 11, 1967)
2. Howard, the Bowler (September 18, 1967)
3. A Trip to Mexico (September 25, 1967)
4. Andy's Trip to Raleigh (October 2, 1967)
5. Opie Steps Up in Class (October 9, 1967)
6. Howard's Main Event (October 16, 1967)
7. Aunt Bee, the Juror (October 23, 1967)
8. The Tape Recorder (October 30, 1967)
9. Opie's Group (November 6, 1967)
10. Aunt Bee and the Lecturer (November 13, 1967)
11. Andy's Investment (November 20, 1967)
12. Howard and Millie (November 27, 1967)
13. Aunt Bee's Cousin (December 4, 1967)
14. Suppose Andy Gets Sick (December 11, 1967)
15. Howard's New Life (December 18, 1967)
16. Goober, the Executive (December 25, 1967)
17. The Mayberry Chef (January 1, 1968)
18. Emmett's Brother-in-Law (January 8, 1968)
19. Opie's Drugstore Job (January 15, 1968)
20. The Church Benefactors (January 22, 1968)
21. Barney Hosts a Summit Meeting (January 29, 1968)
22. Goober Goes to the Auto Show (February 5, 1968)
23. Aunt Bee's Big Moment (February 12, 1968)
24. Helen's Past (February 19, 1968)
25. Emmett's Anniversary (February 26, 1968)
26. The Wedding (March 4, 1968)
27. Sam for Town Council (March 11, 1968)
28. Opie and Mike (March 18, 1968)
29. A Girl for Goober (March 25, 1968)
30. Mayberry R.F.D. (April 1, 1968)

Notes

INTRODUCTION: TO THE FISHING HOLE

1. Ella Taylor, *Prime-Time Families: Television Culture in Postwar America* (Berkeley: University of California Press, 1989), 29.

2. Bob Lucas, "Loner, Worrier and Door-Puncher," *TV Radio Mirror*, August 1967, 88.

3. I will identify episodes by the season and the order in which they were broadcast. The appendix contains a list of all the episodes along with the original airdate. I take the information about the filming and broadcast dates of the episodes from the collection of scripts in the Andy Griffith Papers, #4697, Southern Historical Collection, the Wilson Library, University of North Carolina at Chapel Hill. The series is available on DVD: *The Andy Griffith Show: Complete Series Collection*, Mayberry Enterprises Inc., 2007.

4. Originally scheduled to debut on September 26, 1960, the first episode of *The Andy Griffith Show* was delayed for a week so that CBS could broadcast the first of the Kennedy-Nixon debates. I thank Robert Thompson for bringing this to my attention.

5. Ted Reuter, "What Andy, Opie, and Barney Fife Mean to Americans, Even in the '90s," *Christian Science Monitor*, January 22, 1998.

6. Lee Pfeiffer, *The Official Andy Griffith Show Scrapbook* (New York: Citadel Press, 1994), 52.

7. Clarence Peterson, "Andy Griffith Brings a Fine Comedy to TV," *Chicago Daily Tribune*, October 4, 1960; Harry Harris, "Network Loses Hope's Voice," *Philadelphia Inquirer*, October 4, 1960; J.P.S., "Andy Griffith Show," *New York Times*, October 4, 1960; Jack O'Brian, "Andy Bandies Barnyard Fun," *New York Journal American*, October 4, 1960; *Variety Television Reviews* 7, ed. Harold Prouty (New York: Garland, 1989), October 5, 1960; Tom Mackin, "Mixup Livens Dull Show: Andy Griffith Bows," *Newark Evening News*, October 4, 1960; Marie Torre, "The Andy Griffith Show," *New York Herald Tribune*, October 4, 1960; *Variety Television Reviews* 9, ed. Howard H. Prouty (New York: Garland, 1989), September 21, 1966; *Variety Television Reviews* 8, ed. Howard H. Prouty (New York: Garland, 1989), September 22, 1965; Fred Danzig, "TV in Review," *Durham*

Morning Herald, October 5, 1960; *Variety Television Reviews* 8, ed. Howard H. Prouty (New York: Garland, 1989), September 22, 1965.

8. Andy Griffith, "We Got Lucky," *Chicago Daily Tribune*, September 23, 1961. Among the writers, the one notable exception to nonnativeness was Harvey Bullock, who was born in Oxford, North Carolina, and graduated from Duke University. He wrote thirty-one episodes.

9. To my knowledge, David Marc and Robert Thompson were the first to apply auteur theory to television comedy; see *Prime Time, Prime Movers* (Boston: Little, Brown, 1992), 13–113. Years after the series ended, Griffith remarked: "I was very protective of that show, you have to understand that . . . I'd been in on these scripts from the outset, so I had a notion, a preconceived notion as to how they should be done. I realize people say, 'Things can be done hundreds of different ways.' That's true. But if you have written it and you hear it a certain way and it doesn't come back that way, it'll drive you crazy after a while" (Steve Levin, "Andy of Manteo," *Carolina Lifestyle* 2.6 [June 1983]: 34). According to Aneta Corsaut, "Andy oversaw everything. He was always a workaholic, but a very talented one. He was able to do writing, rewrites, help direct, and produce!" (*The Official Andy Griffith Show Scrapbook*, 66). To help the writers, Sheldon Leonard kept in his office a seven-volume encyclopedia of North Carolina folklore, *The Frank C. Brown Collection of North Carolina Folklore*, ed. Newman Ivey White (Durham: Duke University Press, 1952–1964).

10. Lee Edson, "Cornball with the Steel-Trap Mind," *TV Guide*, January 28, 1961, 17–19.

11. Ken Beck and Jim Clark, *The Andy Griffith Show Book* (New York: St. Martin's Griffin, 2010), xv.

12. Gerard Jones, *Honey, I'm Home! Sitcoms: Selling the American Dream* (New York: St. Martin's, 1993), 138; David Marc, *Comic Visions: Television Comedy and American Culture* (Boston: Unwin Hyman, 1989), 106; Harry Castleman and Walter J. Podrazik, *Watching TV: Four Decades of American Television* (New York: McGraw-Hill, 1982), 144.

13. Flannery O'Connor, *Mystery and Manners: Occasional Prose*, ed. Sally and Robert Fitzgerald (New York: Farrar, Straus & Giroux, 1969), 40.

14. José Ortega y Gasset, *La deshumanización del arte, Obras completas*, vol. 3 (Madrid: Revista de Occidente, 1957), 357–358. In English: Ortega y Gasset, *The Dehumanization of Art* (Princeton: Princeton University Press, 1968), 10–11.

15. Ibid., *Ideas sobre la novela*, 409; *Dehumanization of Art*, 90.

16. As quoted in Dan Harrison and Bill Habeeb, *Inside Mayberry* (New York: Harper Perennial, 1994), 1. Griffith pointed out many times that Mayberry's atmosphere harked back to his childhood in the 1930s: "The dress is modern and people drive late-model cars, but the mood and atmosphere are in the '30s. We keep the problems small and become concerned over them." Bob Lucas, "Loner, Worrier and Door-Puncher," *TV Radio Mirror*, August 1967, 88.

17. Ortega y Gasset, *Ideas sobre la novela*, 408; *Dehumanization of Art*, 88.

PART 1: THE PLACE

1. A World unto Itself

1. Beck and Clark, *The Andy Griffith Show Book*, 40th Anniversary Edition (New York: St. Martin's Griffin, 2000), 123–125, 175–190. Stephen Spignesi compiles a similar list of named characters in *TAGS* in *Mayberry: My Hometown* (Ann Arbor, MI: Popular Culture Ink, 1991), 25–32.

2. Ortega, *Ideas sobre la novela, Obras completas*, vol. 3, 414; *Dehumanization of Art*, 97.

3. Jones, *Honey, I'm Home!* (New York: Grove Weidenfeld, 1992), 95.

4. In fact, "Mayberry" was located at "Forty Acres," the Desilu back lot in Culver City. Andy Griffith: "Funny thing about the Mayberry we know at 'Forty Acres' is that even though all the buildings are false fronts, when you're working there you get the feeling of being in a small town. You forget that on the other side of the fence is one of the biggest cities in the world. . . . I suppose the reason we're so fond of this spot is that it's kinda like going home again. . . . It's a little town like the type I have lived in. . . . I prefer to think it's like the town where I was born and raised. That way, as Sheriff Taylor, I can put color into my role, instead of something manufactured." Marion Purcelli, "All about Mayberry," *Chicago Tribune*, October 28, 1967.

5. Josephine Humphreys, "A Disappearing Thing Called the South," in *The Prevailing South*, ed. Dudley Clendinen (Atlanta: Longstreet Press, 1988), 215–216.

6. The names "Happy Valley" and "Mayberry" may have been inspired by communities near Mount Airy. About fifty miles from Mount Airy is an area known locally as Happy Valley. The valley, which has been farmed since the eighteenth century, supposedly derived its name from the whiskey, brandy, and other spirits made from corn and rye grown by early settlers in the Yadkin River bottomlands. Twenty miles from Mount Airy, on the Virginia side of the border, is a rural community called Mayberry that dates back to the early nineteenth century. According to Jewell Mitchell Kutzer, who grew up in Mount Airy in the 1930s and 1940s, Griffith's mother was born in Mayberry, Virginia. See *Memories of Mayberry: A Nostalgic Look at Andy Griffith's Hometown, Mount Airy, North Carolina* (St. Augustine, FL: Dynamic Living Press, 2001), 6.

7. Kirby, *Media-Made Dixie: The South in the American Imagination* (Athens: University of Georgia Press, 1986), 49.

8. Anderson, *Poor White* (New York: New Directions, 1993), 44–45.

9. Jones, *Honey I'm Home!*, 86.

10. Varenne, *Americans Together: Structured Diversity in a Midwestern Town* (New York: Columbia Teacher's College Press, 1977), 204.

11. "The Rest of the Story," http://www.youtube.com/watch?v=qL8bCha2MlQ (accessed July 23, 2012).

2. Against Change

1. In "The Horse Trader" (1.14), Opie looks straight into the camera and wonders why different rules apply to adults and children.

2. The mutilation of the episodes is not the only reason to avoid watching TAGS in syndication. Another is the intrusion of commercials so dissonant with the mood and message of TAGS that they spoil the viewing experience. The original broadcasts included commercials, of course, but they advertised cereal and pudding and other General Foods products, not computer dating services, ambulance-chasing attorneys, fast-food burritos, and other unsavory reminders of the way we live now. Worst of all are the previews of episodes of contemporary sitcoms inserted in the middle of an episode. A too-true-to-be-good example: the interruption of the rerun on a cable channel of "The Pickle Story" (2.11), about Aunt Bee's and Clara's entries in the pickle competition at the county fair, with a preview of a sitcom episode that seemed to revolve around the sexual use of cucumbers.

3. Jim Bawden, "The Comedians: Lucille Ball, Carol Burnett and Andy Griffith Talk about TV's Golden Years and Their Own Futures," *The Gazette* [Montreal], August 12, 1986.

4. Lytle, "The Hind Tit," in Twelve Southerners, *I'll Take My Stand: The South and the Agrarian Tradition* (1930; Baton Rouge: Louisiana University Press, 1977), 234.

5. Hal Himmelstein, *Television Myth and the American Mind*, 2nd ed. (Westport, CT: Praeger, 1994), 124.

6. Georgia Jones-Davis, "Keep on Running," *Los Angeles Times*, September 12, 1993.

7. George Eliot, *Silas Marner* (New York: Signet Classics, 1960), 5.

3. Stopping the Story

1. As quoted in Jim Bawden, "The Comedians: Lucille Ball, Carol Burnett and Andy Griffith Talk about TV's Golden Years and Their Own Futures," *The Gazette* [Montreal], August 12, 1986.

2. Sherwood Anderson, *Winesburg, Ohio* (New York: Penguin, 1976), 119.

3. "Prisoner of Love," #19-D (114), p. 6. The Andy Griffith Show Scripts, Box 8, 1963–1964. Nos. 16D III to 20D 115, in the Andy Griffith Papers #4697, Southern Historical Collection, The Wilson Library, University of North Carolina at Chapel Hill.

4. Ibid., p. 1.

5. Earle Hagen, interview by Jon Burlingame, November 17, 1997, Archive of American Television. http://www.emmytvlegends.org/interviews/people/earle-hagen (accessed July 24, 2012).

6. William K. Boyd, ed., *William Byrd's Histories of the Dividing Line Betwixt Virginia and North Carolina* (New York: Dover, 1967), 90, 92.

7. "I remember one Sunday we sat around for a full ten minutes after dinner before a word was spoken. My uncle finally said, 'Anybody want to go down to the gas station and get a bottle of pop?'" Don Knotts, *Barney Fife and Other Characters I Have Known* (Thorndike, ME: G. K. Hall, 1999), 22.

8. As quoted in Richard Kelly, *The Andy Griffith Show* (Winston-Salem, NC: John F. Blair, 1982), 9.

9. As quoted in Neal Brower, *Mayberry 101: Behind the Scenes of a TV Classic* (Winston-Salem, NC: John Blair, 1998), 95.

4. *Great Pages in History*

1. Richard Kelly, *The Andy Griffith Show* (Winston-Salem, NC: John F. Blair, 1981), 99–100.

2. Walter Benjamin, "The Storyteller," *Illuminations* (New York: Harcourt, Brace & World, 1968), 84–85.

3. "Archaism and Futurism in Toynbee and Hardy," *Still Rebels, Still Yankees* (Baton Rouge: Louisiana State University Press, 1972), 68.

4. Marc, *Comic Visions: Television Comedy and American Culture*, 2nd ed. (Boston: Unwin Hyman, 1997), 85. The quotation that follows appears on p. 86.

5. J. Fred MacDonald, *Blacks and White TV: African Americans in Television since 1948*, 2nd ed. (Chicago: Nelson Hall Publishers, 1992), 79–80. For more on *Riverboat*, see S. L. Kotar and J. E. Gessler, *Riverboat: The Evolution of a Television Series* (Albany, NY: Bear Manor Media, 2010).

6. Joseph A. St. Amant, "Mrs. Peterson Tells NAACP How the Poor Are Victimized," *Washington Post Times Herald*, July 8, 1966.

7. Walter Burrell, "Hollywood Happenings: Why Dark Faces Scarce on 'Andy Griffith Show,'" *New Journal and Guide*, March 11, 1967, 18.

8. I take these figures from the following sources: Social Explorer Tables (SE), Census 1940, 1950, 1960, 1970, 1980 (US, County & State), Social Explorer & U.S. Census Bureau, digitized by Inter-university Consortium for Political and Social Research, edited, verified by Michael Haines, compiled, edited, and verified by Social Explorer, http://www.socialexplorer.com/pub/reportdata (accessed November 8, 2011); Josef H. Perry, *Population and Economic Report, Mount Airy, North Carolina*, Department of Conservation and Development, Division of Community Planning, State of North Carolina, August 1962, pp. 28, 30; and the *Eighteenth Decennial Census of the United States, Census of Population: 1960*, vol. 1, *Characteristics of the Population, Part 35: North Carolina*, U.S. Department of Commerce, Bureau of the Census, prepared under the supervision of Howard G. Brunsman, 1961, table 21, p. 59. The percentage of African Americans in Mount Airy has remained unchanged since 1930. According to the 2010 census, 8.2 percent of Mount Airy's 10,000 residents are African American. In Surry County the figure is 3.7 percent. *Fifteenth Census of the United States: 1930, Population*, volume 3, part 2, U.S. Department of Commerce, Department of the Census, prepared under the supervision of Leon E. Truesdell, 1933, table 22, page 401. Social Explorer Tables (SE), Census 2010 (US, County & State), Social Explorer & U.S. Census Bureau, digitized by Inter-university Consortium for Political and Social Research, edited, verified by Michael Haines, compiled, edited, and verified by Social Explorer.

9. Bill Bryson, *Made in America: An Informal History of the English Language in the United States* (New York: Perennial, 1996), 152. On the issue of race in *TAGS*, see also Derek H. Alderman, Terri Moreau, and Stefanie Benjamin, "The Andy Griffith Show as Working-Class Utopia," in *Blue-Collar Pop Culture: From NASCAR to Jersey Shore*, ed. Keith Booker (Santa Barbara, CA: Praeger, 2012), 51–69. According to the authors, Mayberry is "a racialized place that works to normalize whiteness and creates a racially selective image of working people and small-town life" (61).

10. Jennifer Howard, "Doris Betts: Conventional 'Southern' Themes Do Not Interest This Southern Writer," *Publishers Weekly*, April 25, 1994, 42; Virginia A. Smith, "On Regionalism, Women's Writing, and Writing as a Woman: A Conversation with Lee Smith," in *Conversations with Lee Smith*, ed. Linda Tate (Jackson: University Press of Mississippi, 2001), 74–75.

11. As quoted in *Mayberry 101: Behind the Scenes of a TV Classic* (Winston-Salem, NC: John F. Blair, 1998), 181.

12. Owsley, "The Fundamental Cause of the Civil War: Egocentric Sectionalism" (1941), in *The Literature of the South*, ed. Richmond Croom Beatty et al. (Chicago: Scott, Foresman, 1952), 659–668.

13. On Confederate toy soldiers, see http://www.marxwildwest.com/civil%20war/civilwar4.html (accessed July 25, 2012).

14. Percy, *The Last Gentleman* (New York: Farrar, Straus and Giroux, 1966), 185.

15. C. Vann Woodward, "The Irony of Southern History," *Journal of Southern History* 19 (1953), 13.

5. From R.F.D. to R.I.P.

1. Arnheim, *Film as Art* (Berkeley: University of California Press, 1966), 66.

2. As late as the end of the seventh season, Mayberry's population was still 1,800 (7.23). The following season, when the Vincentis arrive in town, the sign at the train station gives the population as 5,360 (8.30).

3. As of 2012, *Mayberry R.F.D.* (henceforth: RFD) has not been released on DVD, but tapes of the episodes are available from vintage-TV collectors. David Fernandes and Dale Robinson give a detailed episode-by-episode summary of the series in *A Guide to Television's* Mayberry R.F.D. (Jefferson, NC: McFarland, 1998).

4. Although the scripts give this character's name as "Mr. Schwamp," I follow most guidebooks and websites about TAGS in spelling his name "Schwump."

5. The slogan with which CBS advertised the show. "The Look of a Winner: Monday Night on CBS," *New York Times*, September 30, 1968.

6. Tipsy from drinking Colonel Harvey's magic elixir, Aunt Bee says to Andy: "Look! It's Sheriff Matt Dillon! Where's Chester?" (3.24). There may be more to the parallel than drunken whimsy: Barney's frail physique is the equivalent of Chester's gimp; Andy is Mayberry's Matt Dillon, his chaste relations with Helen analogous to Matt's with Kitty. A *Gunsmoke* episode from the fourth season (1958–1959), "Marshall Proudfoot," deals with Chester's apprehension upon finding out that his big-shot uncle is planning to visit Dodge City. To make Chester look good, Kitty and Doc Adams stage a fake holdup; instead a real holdup occurs, which Chester bravely disrupts. The episode anticipates those in TAGS where Andy strokes Barney's ego by contriving situations in which Barney—another "Marshall Proudfoot"—will emerge as the hero, either because he rises to the occasion or because Andy convinces him that he did.

7. "Jack Dodson of *Mayberry* RFD: Mother's Boy Grows Up," *TV Guide* June 19, 1971, 38.

8. Canceled in 1971, *The Lawrence Welk Show* lived on in syndication for many years,

as did *Hee Haw* (with Goober as one of the regular characters). In "The Lawrence Welk–Hee Haw Counter Revolution Polka" (1972), country singer Roy Clark has the last word about the rural purge: "They still do the polka in Milwaukee. They still do the waltz in Tennessee. They're still picking bluegrass in Kentucky with old-fashioned country harmony." *Roy Clark: Greatest Hits*, Varèse Saraband Records, Studio City, CA, 1995.

9. Everett Greenbaum: "Every once in a while, Jim Fritzell and I would go on the set. We loved Sweeney, Don, and Andy, just about everyone there, but we never got along with Aunt Bee. . . . I'll tell you something she'd do to me. Whenever there was a party—a wrap party or something, she'd say to me: 'You know, there's only one thing wrong with this show.' I'd say, 'What is it, Frances?' 'The writing,' she'd say. 'The writing is vile.'" Everett Greenbaum, interviewed by Henry Colman, October 3, 1997, Archive of American Television, Academy of Television Arts and Sciences Foundation, http://emmytvlegends.org/interviews/people/everett-greenbaum (accessed July 31, 2012).

INTERLUDE: THE ROAD TO MAYBERRY

1. As quoted in M. S. Mason, "Forever Opie . . . and Lucy, Rhoda, Beaver, and the Fonz," *Christian Science Monitor*, July 9, 1999.

2. As quoted in William Pfaff, *The Wrath of Nations: Civilization and the Furies of Nationalism* (New York: Simon & Schuster, 1993), 174.

PART 2: THE PEOPLE

1. Sheriff without a Gun (Andy Taylor)

1. Elinor Donahue, interviewed by Jennifer Howard, April 25, 2006, Archive of American Television, http://www.emmytvlegends.org/interviews/people/elinor-donahue (accessed May 2, 2012). See also Elinor Donahue, *In the Kitchen with Elinor Donahue* (Nashville: Cumberland, 1998), 127.

2. Aaron Ruben remarked in a 1963 interview that Moore as Peggy McMillan "almost caught fire," but Andy objected by saying, "I don't want a show with fights in the kitchen" ("The Show That Has H.A.Q." *TV Guide*, May 11, 1963, 25). Although Moore appeared in many TV shows and several movies in the 1950s and 1960s, she is best remembered today as Tatum and Griffin O'Neal's mother.

3. As quoted in Kelly, *The Andy Griffith Show*, 54–55. Richard Linke, Griffith's manager and executive producer of the show, echoed Griffith's comments: "Andy, you have to realize, is not really a lady's man. He doesn't know how to go chasing the ladies. If you'll notice, he rarely kissed anybody in the series, and only rarely did he hold Helen Crump. He never did a real kiss. He is that way in real life." Ibid., 55.

4. "Remembering Andy Griffith," *eBullet*, official newsletter of the *TAGS* Rerun Watchers Club 12.3 (June–July 2012), http://TAGSrwc.com/the_ebullet/2012/07/the-ebullet-volume-12-special-edition-remembering-andy-griffith-july-2012/ (accessed July

23, 2012). According to Earle Hagen, Griffith thought that this episode was "duller than hell." Earle Hagen, *Memoirs of a Famous Composer Nobody Ever Heard Of* (Bloomington, IN: Xlibris, 2000), 181.

5. Kelly, *The Andy Griffith Show*, 55.

6. Leslie Raddatz, "Aneta Corsaut," *TV Guide*, May 20, 1967, 17.

7. The photograph appears in several episodes: "A Feud Is a Feud" (1.9), "Andy, the Marriage Counselor" (1.18), "Andy and Opie, Housekeepers" (1.23), "Aunt Bee's Brief Encounter" (2.9). See Dale Robinson and David Fernandes, *The Definitive Andy Griffith Show Reference* (Jefferson, NC: McFarland, 1996), 24.

8. Kelly, *The Andy Griffith Show*, 54.

3. Life Imitates Fife (Barney Fife)

1. Barney's show business ambitions may have reflected Don Knotts's. A few years after leaving *TAGS*, he hosted a weekly variety show, *The Don Knotts Show* (1970–1971), which flopped. According to Everett Greenbaum, Knotts "wanted to be Frank Sinatra." Everett Greenbaum, interviewed by Henry Colman, October 3, 1997, Archive of American Television, http://www.emmytvlegends.org/interviews/people/everett -greenbaum (accessed May 10, 2012).

5. Growing Up, Growing Old (Opie and Floyd)

1. *Variety Television Reviews* vol. 8, ed. Harold Prouty (New York: Garland Pub. Inc., 1989), October 2, 1963. This lesson of "Opie the Birdman" is not soon forgotten. Twenty-three years later, in *Return to Mayberry*, Opie doesn't know whether to take a bigger and better-paying job with the *Binghamton Post* or remain in his hometown. As little Opie used to do, he asks Andy — now Papa Taylor, grandfather to Opie's newborn — what he should do. Should he stay put or should he leave? Andy replies by recalling the incident with the birds.

2. *Leave It to Beaver*, "The Shave," broadcast on November 20, 1958; *I Love Lucy*, "Little Ricky Gets Stage Fright," broadcast on October 22, 1956; *The Donna Reed Show*, "Love Thy Neighbor," broadcast on February 18, 1959, and "The Grateful Patient," broadcast on April 29, 1959.

3. Hollywood columnist Hedda Hopper wrote about McNear: "He has a theory that such characterizations aren't copied from any one thing or combination of things that a comedian has seen or heard. 'I think they evolve from the person himself. I think perhaps it's my own mannerisms — exaggerated of course. I've often wondered if such portrayals aren't built up from the subconscious.'" ("McNear Hailed as Acting Specialist," *Los Angeles Times*, January 12, 1960).

4. As quoted in Dan Harrison and Bill Habeeb, *Inside Mayberry: "The Andy Griffith Show" Handbook* (New York: HarperCollins Publishers, 1994), 96.

7. Mayberry Maidens (Aunt Bee, Helen Crump, and Thelma Lou)

1. Interview with Stephen J. Spignesi, *Mayberry: My Hometown* (Ann Arbor MI: Pierian Press, 1991), 201.
2. Sherwood Anderson, *Winesburg, Ohio* (New York: Penguin, 1976), 224.
3. As quoted in Neal Brower, *Mayberry 101* (Winston Salem, NC: John F. Blair Publisher, 1998), 464.

8. Beasts of the Southern Wild (Ernest T. Bass and the Darlings)

1. Howard Morris, interviewed by Jennifer Howard, Archive of American Television, February 27, 2004, http://www.emmytvlegends.org/interviews/people/howard-morris (accessed May 16, 2012). In the scripts in which Ernest T. appears, the scene headings do not even attempt to describe his character.
2. Richard Bernheimer, *Wild Men in the Middle Ages* (Cambridge: Harvard University Press, 1952), 1.
3. Morris interview.

10. Love in the Country (Gomer Pyle, Goober Pyle, and Howard Sprague)

1. "A Date for Gomer," #9-D (118), The Andy Griffith Show Scripts, 1963–1964, nos. 1D III to 10D 119, in the Andy Griffith Papers #4697, Southern Historical Collection, the Wilson Library, University of North Carolina at Chapel Hill.
2. As quoted in Dan Harrison and Bill Habeeb, *Inside Mayberry: "The Andy Griffith Show" Handbook* (New York: HarperCollins Publishers, 1994), 85.

11. Trashy Women (Daphne and Skippy)

1. Lee Pfeiffer, *The Official Andy Griffith Show Scrapbook* (New York: Citadel Press, 1994), 90.

CONCLUSION: OLD SAM

1. Brower, *Mayberry 101*, 484.

EPILOGUE: A CUBAN IN MAYBERRY

1. "Andy's English Valet," #26-C (89), The Andy Griffith Show Scripts, Box 5, 1962–1963, nos. 21C 84 to 26C 89, in the Andy Griffith Papers #4697, Southern Historical Collection, the Wilson Library, University of North Carolina at Chapel Hill.

Index

The abbreviation *TAGS* refers to *The Andy Griffith Show*. The abbreviation *RFD* refers to *Mayberry R.F.D.*